The Social Scientist's Grant Guide

The Social Scientist's Grant Guide

Funding Your Future in Research

Keri K. Stephens
The University of Texas at Austin, USA

Kerk F. Kee
Texas Tech University, USA

BLOOMSBURY ACADEMIC
NEW YORK • LONDON • OXFORD • NEW DELHI • SYDNEY

BLOOMSBURY ACADEMIC
Bloomsbury Publishing Inc, 1359 Broadway, New York, NY 10018, USA
Bloomsbury Publishing Plc, 50 Bedford Square, London, WC1B 3DP, UK
Bloomsbury Publishing Ireland, 29 Earlsfort Terrace, Dublin 2, D02 AY28, Ireland

First published in the United States of America 2026

Cover design: Chloe Batch
Cover images © iStock.com

A catalog record for this book is available from the Library of Congress.

ISBN: HB: 979-8-8818-0186-1
PB: 979-8-8818-0187-8
ePDF: 979-8-8818-5861-2
eBook: 979-8-8818-0188-5

Typeset by Integra Software Services Pvt. Ltd.
Printed and bound in the United States of America

For product safety-related questions, contact productsafety@bloomsbury.com.

To find out more about our authors and books visit www.bloomsbury.com and sign up for our newsletters.

Contents

Boxes

Notes on Contributors

This book uses pseudonyms in many places to share experiences without identifying specific individuals or institutions. We would like to thank all our colleagues and friends who have had conversations with us about this book. We would especially like to thank our students, whose experiences inside our grant writing courses and while collaborating on writing and executing externally funded research have contributed greatly to this book.

We also want to thank some very important key contributors whose names are mentioned in this book. The research administrators and directors of research who have contributed greatly to this book include Julie Campos, Tyler Myatt, Cory Blackwell, and Elizabeth Carroll.

We would also like to thank a group of international scholars who participated with us as part of an International Communication Association conference in Toronto, Canada; those conversations shaped several sections of this book. Those scholars include Shiv Ganesh, Christian Burgers, Vivian Chen, Kirstie McCallum, Amanda Porter, Jack Linchuan Qiu, and Tien Ee Dominic Yeo.

Finally, we would like to thank Kasey Faust in civil engineering and construction management, whose close collaboration with Keri has taught her the difference between how engineers view action-oriented research versus the use of theory. We thank her for allowing us to use her direct examples in this book because many other researchers can now benefit from her expertise.

Acknowledgments

One of the core values that Keri and Kerk both share is the need to pay forward what people have provided to us in the past. This book, in many ways, provides a great opportunity for us to honor all the training, all the help we have received along our paths, and all the people who have been patient with us as we have asked what probably on the surface appeared like really stupid questions or very ignorant questions, but who have coached us, mentored us, and helped us along the way.

We both want to thank Larry Browning for his mentorship. He advised both of us and introduced us to the world of corporate funding and the idea that research can be theoretically rich, empirically rich, as well as fundable. Larry had the foresight early in Kerk's dissertation journey to recognize the fundability of cyberinfrastructure research and simply said, "It's fundable, run with it." We also want to thank Vernon Miller, Noshir Contractor, Janet Fulk, Peter Monge, and M. Scott Poole for organizing and leading the grant funding workshop in 2008–2009 that provided critical early exposure to the world of external funding for both of us. We would also like to thank our graduate students, postdoctoral scholars, and collaborators who have encouraged us to write down our experiences and share them with others.

Kerk would like to thank the many mentors and colleagues who shaped his understanding of grant funding and academic research throughout his career. Bill Eadie, his faculty mentor at San Diego State University, who spearheaded efforts to bring a group of communication faculty to meet with the NSF to redefine communication as a science while Bill was the Associate Director of the National Communication Association. This planted an important seed early about one of the battles of defining our field as a science rather than solely as a professional study. Jim Dearing mentored him into his very first exposure to the grant funding world. Dawna Ballard planted an early seed for pursuing an NSF CAREER grant. At Chapman University, he benefited from the guidance of Yolanda Uzzell and Michelle Miller Day, and Gary Kreps from George Mason University when Gary visited Chapman. He is grateful to Michelle Shumate, Paul

Leonardi, Charlotte Lee, David Ribes, Steve Jackson, Chris Kim, and Jennifer Funk, who shared their NSF CAREER proposals. He thanks his collaborators Amy Koerber, Glenn Cummins, Lyombe Eko, Jesse Starkey, Trent Seltzer, David Perlmutter, Don Shin, Shan Xu, Ioana Coman, Harrison Gong, Patrice Buzzanell, Stacey Connaughton, Seungyoon Lee, Sorin Matei, Prasad Calyam, Ewa Deelman, Changwon Son, Angela Murrillo, Anirban Mandal, Jaroslaw Nabrzyski, Valerio Pascucci, Tyree Mitchell, Marshall Watson, Rion Dooley, Steve Brandt, Sandra Gesing, Richard Knepper, Winona Snapp-Childs, Harmony Jankowski, Craig Stewart, Satish Nair, Praveen Rao, Wenxuan Guo, Chenggang Wang, Saurav Kumar, Ebrahim Ahmadisharaf, Brian Spitzberg, Christian Burgers, and Roselyn Du for their partnership on various projects and proposals. He also thanks administrators such as Coy Callison, Sherice Gearhart, Asheley Landrum, Justin Keene, Elizabeth Carroll, Cory Blackwell, Tyler Myatt, and Tiara Wilhelm. And finally, he thanks Keri, whose strategic activities really inspired him and served as a role model for navigating the academy and this terrain.

Keri would like to thank the many individuals and organizations who have supported and shaped her funding journey. Matthew Weber shared the resources he provided to his graduate students with her, which she has continued to share with her own students. Her interdisciplinary collaborators Kasey Faust and Suzanne Pierce taught her a great deal about the meaningful work possible with external funding through their successful collaborative work. She is deeply grateful to the Office of the Vice President of Research at the University of Texas, particularly Allison Preston, Jennifer Lyon Gardner, Melanie Morgan Gomez, Heidi Schmalbach, Stacy Ingram, Kayla Dryden, Kimberly Jennings, and Scott Ridings. She thanks her colleagues at other institutions with whom she has collaborated on funding proposals and bringing meaningful projects to life. Those include Sam Brody, Esha Clearfield, Nick Diaz, Wes Heighfield, Andrew Juan, and Katherine Teleki at IDRT. She also thanks Amanda Hughes, Hemant Purohit, Steve Rains, Brett Robertson, Adriana de Souza e Silva, and Zhe Zhang. Her community collaborators have been instrumental in grounding her work in real-world applications, including Francisco Guajardo, Joanna MacKenzie, Steve Peterson, Cody Powell, and many others. At the University of Texas, she has been fortunate to be supported by deans and administrators including Jay Bernhardt, Julie Campos, Maya Henry, Brianna Jackson, Vanessa Lopez, Craig Scott, and Anita Vangelisti. She has also collaborated with supportive colleagues across disciplines, including Sam Baker, Dawna Ballard, Joydeep Biswas, Justin Hart, Elliott Hauser, Junfeng Jiao, Katherine Lieberknecht, Matthew McGlone, Roselia Mendez Murillo, Paolo Passalacqua, Luis Sentis, Peter Stone, Talia Stroud, Sharon Strover, and Sean Upshaw. She is grateful to the Texas Water Development Board and the Texas General Land Office, which have funded her work for the state of Texas and allowed her to lean into the important role that communication and organizing play in flood communication, as well as the National Science Foundation and Merck Investigator Studies Program, along with her program officers at these various organizations who have provided invaluable guidance and support. And finally, she thanks her husband, Tab, and her kids, Sarah Kay and Kyle. Their support, encouragement, and willingness to call out her overwork behavior has helped her learn to advocate for herself and set boundaries. Now she can better pursue the types of meaningful work that make a difference.

Introduction: Why Social Scientists Need This Book Now

When Dr. Sarah Martinez signed her faculty contract at a regional university in 2025, she was thrilled to land a tenure-track position. While her interview process had mentioned that she would be expected to apply for $75,000 in external funding by her third year—part of the institution's effort to make social science faculty as "grant savvy" as their STEM colleagues—she hadn't thought much about it until she saw her contract. Then reality hit. Her graduate program had never offered grant-writing training. When she arrived and asked her new colleagues for guidance, they literally shrugged. It wasn't something they had been expected to do either. Sarah's situation isn't unique—it's becoming the new normal.

Across the country, similar scenarios are playing out in departments of communication, sociology, political science, psychology, urban planning, architecture, and other social and behavioral science fields. Assistant professors discover funding requirements buried in their contracts. Associate professors learn that external grants have become essential for promotion to full professor. Senior scholars find themselves leading research centers with mandates to bring in funding, despite never having written a grant proposal themselves.

"I keep getting mixed messages about whether I actually need to receive funding or not," one early-career colleague told us, "but I feel this increasing sense of pressure to seek funding. Yet I still have not had experience in knowing how to do this." Meanwhile, a mid-career scholar pursuing promotion to full professor told us explicitly: "I'm applying for grants because I want to get full." He believed—correctly or not—that without external funding, he could not qualify for promotion.

The pressure is real and the stakes are high. At some institutions, failing to meet funding requirements by the third-year review can lead to contract termination. At others, the expectation becomes clear only at promotion time, when external funding suddenly becomes a criterion for advancement. We've seen colleagues attempt grant after grant to meet dollar amounts, knowing they're unlikely to succeed but required to try anyway. The result? Talented scholars spending precious time on applications that don't align with their research strengths, often feeling like they're "wasting time to fulfill contractual requirements" and/or new institutional expectations rather than pursuing meaningful research opportunities.

Why This Book Matters Now

External funding isn't primarily about meeting institutional requirements; it's about amplifying your ability to address complex interdisciplinary social problems. Agencies and organizations fund grants because these partnerships enable them to carry out their missions in ways they couldn't achieve alone. When you secure external funding, you're gaining resources to tackle research questions that matter, building collaborations that expand your impact, and contributing solutions to real-world challenges. This is the positive opportunity that funding represents.

That said, three major shifts in academia mean that social scientists can no longer afford to ignore the world of external funding:

First, institutions are increasingly treating social scientists like STEM researchers. Universities are writing funding requirements into faculty contracts, regardless of whether those faculty received any training in grant writing. These expectations exist whether you're hired as an assistant, associate, or full professor—only the dollar amounts change. What's more, chairs and deans leave institutions, and new leadership can completely upend expectations overnight.

Second, funding priorities of agencies and institutions are constantly shifting. While funding landscapes have always evolved with different political administrations and institutional pressures—from enrollment cliffs (Campion, 2020, 2022) to budget cuts (Moody, 2025)—these changes are more visible than ever. The funding that supported your colleague's career might not be available when you need it. This is why diversifying your funding portfolio and staying adaptable matters more than ever.

Third, doors are opening wider for social scientists in interdisciplinary collaborations. Funding agencies increasingly emphasize interdisciplinary research (Buyalskaya et al., 2021; Van Noorden, 2015) that includes social science perspectives. This creates unprecedented opportunities—but only for those ready to seize them.

The second half of the 2020s has proven particularly disruptive to the federal funding landscape. During this period, certain research terms and topics became less palatable to federal funders, requiring researchers to adapt their framing strategies. For instance, researchers studying climate-related phenomena found success by reframing their work around "extreme weather events" or "environmental changes" rather than using politically charged terminology. This example illustrates a broader truth: funding landscapes will continue to shift with each administration, and the specific sensitivities of one period may differ dramatically from another.

This reality demands strategic flexibility. When you're working on research that is deeply integrated with your identity—topics so central to who you are that the specific terminology truly matters—don't compromise. Instead, seek funding sources that align with the language and values you want to maintain. Private foundations, international funders, or specific programs within federal agencies may better align with your mission. However, if your research can be authentically described in different ways without compromising your core work, consider how alternative framing might open doors to funding opportunities. ***Remember: not all funded research is good research, and not all good research gets funded.*** The goal is to find the path that serves both your research integrity and your career sustainability.

To navigate these ongoing shifts effectively, develop these habits:

- Regularly check funding opportunity announcements directly on agency websites rather than relying on downloaded versions, as requirements and priorities can change between the time an announcement is first posted and when you submit
- Sign up for agency listservs and institutional research e-lists (if available at your institution) to receive updates about policy changes and funding priorities in real-time

- Build relationships with your research support staff and research administrators early; they monitor regulatory changes and can alert you to potential issues before you invest significant time in a proposal that might face new restrictions
- Maintain a diverse funding portfolio across federal, state, private, and institutional sources to reduce vulnerability to any single agency's shifting priorities

The strategies in this book focus not on navigating any specific political moment, but on building the adaptive capacity to thrive regardless of which way the political winds are blowing.

Why Generic Grant Guides Fail Social Scientists

If you have attended grant writing workshops or read existing grant guides, you've probably noticed a problem: most focus on STEM or health-related fields. You sit through sessions about equipment budgets and lab management that have nothing to do with your work. The examples do not resonate, and the funding-specific jargon is overwhelming. The strategies assume you're already embedded in a "grant-getting culture"—but as social scientists and humanities scholars, many of us are not.

More importantly, these resources typically focus on writing mechanics. You already know how to write for an audience. You're English scholars, anthropologists, communication scientists, sociologists, political scientists—you know how to communicate. What's missing is the logic, the rationale, the strategy behind grant seeking and setting up a grant infrastructure. What's missing is understanding how to navigate the politics and social dynamics of the funding world. What's missing is someone helping you understand why you're doing all these things in the first place.

Here's an important caveat: while STEM fields may have more of a grant-seeking culture overall, many STEM researchers also lack formal grant-writing training before their first faculty position. Social scientists aren't alone in feeling underprepared; the difference is that STEM faculty often have colleagues, lab groups, or mentors who can provide informal socialization into grant culture, advantages that many social scientists and humanities scholars don't have. This book aims to provide the socialization and strategic foundation you need, regardless of your field's prevailing culture.

Our book doesn't teach you how to write a National Science Foundation (NSF) proposal or craft a budget for a foundation award. Instead, we socialize you into grant-getting culture when you haven't grown up in one. Once you understand the broader landscape and strategic thinking we present here, you can attend those writing workshops and buy those how-to guides with confidence. But first, you need the foundation this book provides.

Unlike those mechanical writing guides, we focus on the strategic thinking and cultural knowledge that determine success. We help you understand how to identify funding opportunities that genuinely align with your research strengths. We show you how to position your work for maximum impact across multiple funding contexts. We demystify the unwritten rules and social dynamics that shape reviewer decisions. Most importantly, we help you develop the adaptive mindset needed to thrive as funding landscapes inevitably shift.

Your Social Science Training Is Actually an Asset

Here's what those other guides won't tell you: your social science training gives you significant advantages. You're already skilled at adapting to different audiences—a crucial grant writing skill. You understand the politics and social dynamics of organizational systems, which is exactly what navigating funding agencies requires. You have rigorous research methods that can address real-world problems that funders care about.

You're trained to think about broader impacts and societal implications of research—elements that are increasingly central to funding decisions. Your expertise in human behavior, social systems, and communication makes you invaluable for interdisciplinary teams. You understand how to translate complex ideas for different stakeholders, a skill that serves you well when writing for diverse review panels.

Most importantly, you're naturally attuned to interdisciplinary collaboration in ways that many STEM researchers aren't. As funding agencies increasingly emphasize team science and societal benefits of research, your collaborative mindset and ability to work across disciplinary boundaries become a significant competitive advantage. The door is opening wider for social scientists, and we need to be ready to walk through it.

Quick Diagnostic: Where Are You?

Before diving into the book, ask yourself:

- Do I need to get funding right now due to contract requirements or tenure expectations?
- Will I need to get funding in the future as my career progresses?
- Am I simply curious and want to be prepared for future opportunities?

Your answer will help you navigate this book, though we've designed all chapters to provide value regardless of your timeline.

How to Use This Book

This book functions like a transit map for your funding journey. Depending on where you're starting, you'll need different routes to reach your destination. Graduate students might need to travel through more stations to reach funding success, while mid-career scholars may have shorter distances to cover because they already know how to publish and manage research agendas.

- **If you're a graduate student**, Chapter 11 on graduate funding opportunities will be especially relevant as you think about your career trajectory.
- **If you're early career**, Chapter 9 on managing early career pressures will resonate with the feelings you're experiencing and provide concrete action plans.
- **If you're mid-career or later**, Chapter 10 addresses the specific challenges of learning grant writing when you're already established in your career.

- **If you're a research administrator**, this book will help you understand the pressures faculty face and how to better support them, particularly through the early career and graduate student chapters.
- **If you're a department chair, dean, or Associate Dean for Research,** this book will help you support your researchers as they seek external funding. Chapter 22 is especially important for you because it provides ways to advocate for resources that can grow your research enterprise.

Remember: this book is designed so you can jump between chapters as needed. Some sections will be more immediately relevant than others, but all contribute to developing your strategic funding mindset.

What You'll Gain

By the end of this book, you will have:

- **A personalized funding action plan** that aligns with your research interests and career stage, including concrete next steps you can take regardless of your timeline.
- **The ability to translate your research** for different funding audiences and goals, turning your expertise into compelling narratives that resonate with diverse reviewers.
- **A clear understanding of institutional support systems**—both at your current institution and any future positions you might consider, including questions to ask when interviewing for jobs and during job negotiations.
- **The mindset and tools to adapt** when funding priorities shift or career circumstances change, helping you remain resilient through inevitable setbacks and changes.
- **Confidence to navigate** the politics and social dynamics of the funding world, from building relationships with program officers to managing interdisciplinary collaborations.
- **Strategies for building and sustaining** a funding portfolio that supports your long-term research goals while meeting institutional expectations.

Meet Your Guides

We, Keri Stephens and Kerk Kee, have walked this path ourselves—and made plenty of mistakes along the way. When we first ventured into external funding, we were winging it despite our academic training at top-tier research institutions. We learned the hard way that success in external funding requires different skills than those developed in graduate seminars or journal publishing.

Our approach is grounded in our own experiences as grant writers, mentors, and institutional change agents. Keri is the George Christian Centennial Professor, a professor of organizational communication and technology, codirector of the Technology and Information Policy Institute at the University of Texas at Austin, and a fellow in the International Communication Association. Kerk is the Virginia and Choc Hutcheson Professor in Mass Communication in the College of Media and Communication at Texas Tech University. We both hold doctoral degrees in communication, but our intellectual backgrounds are diverse, spanning engineering, natural sciences, social sciences, and liberal arts.

Over the course of our careers, we have served as principal investigators, co-principal investigators, senior personnel, and consultants on grants from a wide range of sponsors, including the National Science Foundation, the National Institutes of Health, National Academy of Sciences, the Department of Defense, State of Texas government agencies, the Gates Foundation, Merck Research, Facebook, and the Robert Wood Johnson Foundation, among others. Importantly, we've served as reviewers and panelists for numerous funding agencies in the United States, Europe, Canada, Japan, and Latin America giving us insider knowledge of how decisions really get made. We've reviewed hundreds of proposals and participated in panel discussions that determine which projects receive funding. This experience has taught us what separates successful proposals from those that fall short. These are the insights we share throughout this book.

We've also mentored countless students and colleagues through this process, teaching graduate-level grant writing courses and serving as advisors on over one hundred successful proposals. Our advisees have won dissertation awards, NSF CAREER grants, and major early career recognitions. We've given over thirty keynote talks on research funding and have received awards for our community-engaged work from national and state associations.

We bring diverse perspectives to this challenge. Keri pursued her research agenda exclusively until she was close to receiving tenure, then strategically adapted her work to attract funding opportunities in crisis and disaster contexts. This approach allowed her to translate her organizational communication expertise into new domains while maintaining theoretical rigor. Kerk's research direction was shaped by funding opportunities from his graduate student days, when his advisor said of cyberinfrastructure research: "It's fundable, run with it." This early alignment between research interests and funding priorities set the foundation for his sustained success.

These different approaches both led to success, demonstrating that there is no single path to funding achievement. Whether you prefer to establish your research identity first or allow funding opportunities to shape your scholarly development, both strategies can work—if you understand the landscape and make informed choices.

Our Commitment to You

We take a candid, practical approach. We won't sugarcoat the challenges or offer empty platitudes. Instead, we'll equip you with clear-eyed understanding of the funding landscape and the strategic tools to navigate it effectively. We'll share real examples, honest mistakes, and practical strategies. We'll help you understand not just what to do, but why—and how to adapt when circumstances change. Because they will change. Funding priorities shift, leadership changes, and new opportunities emerge. Your ability to stay flexible while remaining true to your research vision will determine your long-term success. We will reveal much complexity in this book, but it shouldn't discourage you from pursuing external funding; it should prepare you to approach external funding thoughtfully and strategically.

Throughout this book, we illustrate key concepts with real-world examples and case studies drawn from a range of social and behavioral sciences and humanities disciplines as well as funding contexts. We offer practical tools and resources, including self-assessments, submission timelines, budget templates, and checklists for key milestones in the grant-writing process. You'll find institutional assessment worksheets to help you understand your local support systems, templates for building collaborations, and strategies for managing the inevitable rejections and setbacks.

We also recognize that seeking external funding is not a one-size-fits-all pursuit. The funding landscape is constantly evolving, and what works for one scholar or institution may not work for another. Therefore, we approach each chapter by presenting options and strategies you can adapt to your own situation. We encourage you to ground your funding seeking in your own research agenda while remaining open to diversifying your funding portfolio over time.

The Road Ahead

Getting external funding isn't just about money, though the financial support certainly matters. It's about amplifying your research impact, building collaborations that would not otherwise exist, and contributing to knowledge in ways that can shape policy and practice. External funding can provide resources to support community partners, fund graduate student training, and create opportunities for extensive collaboration. It can also enhance your visibility and credibility within your field and beyond.

The funding landscape will continue evolving. New administrations will shift federal priorities. Institutions will change their expectations. Technology will create new opportunities and challenges. Global crises will reshape research priorities. By developing the strategic mindset and practical skills this book provides, you'll be prepared to navigate whatever changes come next.

Consider this book as building your funding Global Positioning System (GPS), an electronic navigator. Just as GPS helps you navigate road closures and traffic jams by recalculating routes, the strategic framework we provide will help you adapt when your original funding plans need to change. You'll learn to pack the right tools in your grant-seeking suitcase, understand when to take detours, and maintain momentum toward your research destinations even when the paths shift.

More than anything, we hope this book catalyzes honest conversation about external funding in the social sciences. For too long, getting external funding has been shrouded in mystery, with successful scholars keeping their strategies close to the vest. If you decide not to pursue external funding at the end of reading this book, we thank you for taking the time to consider what we shared in this book. But if you decide to join us on the funding journey, we believe that by building a community of scholars who support and learn from one another, we can collectively navigate this landscape more effectively. We encourage you to share what you learn, mentor others along the way, and contribute to a more transparent and supportive funding culture in the social sciences.

Whether you're staring down a funding deadline, exploring new research directions, or preparing for future opportunities, we welcome you to this journey. With the right mindset, strategic approach, and adaptive tools, you can find your path to funding success.

Let's get started.

1

Grant Readiness: Building Your Foundation

The Grant Culture Shift: Why Preparedness Matters Now

Keri was excited to write her first large National Science Foundation (NSF) grant. She worked very hard for six months ahead of time, collaborating with her institutional research administrators to get everything prepared and ready. At that time, around 2010, her institution didn't have extensive support in her college, so she was trying to find people to assist her along the way.

The research administrator submitted her proposal, they celebrated the massive accomplishment, and they waited. The next day, they received notification that the funding call had actually ended six months before the date they submitted the proposal, and that NSF would not be accepting proposals on that topic moving forward. Keri was embarrassed because she had misread the date on the call and submitted it after the deadline.

After a week or two of feeling mortified, Keri approached the research administrator who had helped her put the proposal together. The staff member said, "Oh, I didn't check the dates. I assumed that you knew when this needed to be submitted." Looking back at the funding solicitation together, they discovered that Keri simply didn't know how to read a funding announcement. The solicitation stated that proposals would start being accepted on May 1, 2007, but in subsequent years all proposals would be due on January 15 and that the funding call was only valid for three years. Keri had read that statement and understood that the due date was May 1. She had completely misunderstood how to read the funding announcement's due date structure. All that work on the grant application couldn't be submitted to the intended call because it was the final year of that program, and it was over. Keri didn't have anywhere close to the background training she needed to pull off that kind of grant.

Kerk also found reading funding calls difficult, although he never missed a deadline. He found the way they were written confusing because grant submission due dates aren't structured like anything he saw in his field. In journals, submission dates are not formatted that way. Only after working with experienced research administration staff did he learn to navigate these complex documents.

These stories illustrate a fundamental challenge facing social and behavioral scientists today: **grant readiness has become the new literacy for academics**. The landscape has shifted dramatically. Funding is increasingly required, not optional. Even at relatively small liberal arts institutions, faculty moving from associate to full professor are feeling pressure to have secured external funding to strengthen their cases. Institutional expectations can change suddenly—what wasn't required when you were hired can become essential for promotion.

The preparedness gap is real. Unlike our STEM colleagues, who are often trained in grant culture from graduate school, social scientists and humanities scholars can find themselves caught off-guard by suddenly shifting institutional expectations. A new dean implements new requirements. Budget pressures lead to increased emphasis on external funding. What seemed like a stable career trajectory suddenly requires new skills and strategies. This chapter focuses on concrete preparation—the practical steps you can take to ensure you're never caught as unprepared as Keri was with that NSF submission.

The Three Levels of Grant Engagement

Think of grant engagement like planning travel to Norway. At the **exposure level**, you've heard Norway is beautiful and might be worth visiting someday. At the **knowledge level**, you're actively researching Norway—watching documentaries, reading travel guides, understanding costs and logistics. At the **action plan level**, you're booking the trip—purchasing tickets, making reservations, and packing your bags. This analogy provides a strong basis for understanding how we all experience external funding options. Take a look at Figure 1.1.

Exposure Level: Understanding Without Participating

At this foundational level, you're developing grant literacy—the ability to understand and discuss the grant world without personal involvement. This creates valuable empathy for grant-active colleagues and informed decision-making about your own career trajectory. Key activities include attending institutional grant seminars, reading about colleagues' funding successes and challenges, observing how grants are discussed in job talks and faculty meetings, and learning basic grant terminology and processes.

Success means you can participate intelligently in grant-related conversations, understand why grant-active colleagues have different workloads and pressures, ask informed questions during job interviews about institutional support, and make educated decisions about whether grant seeking aligns with your career goals.

Knowledge Level: Knowing What Would Be Required

At this developmental level, you're building comprehensive understanding of grant requirements without yet committing to active pursuit. You're answering the question: "What would I need to do if I decided to pursue grants?"

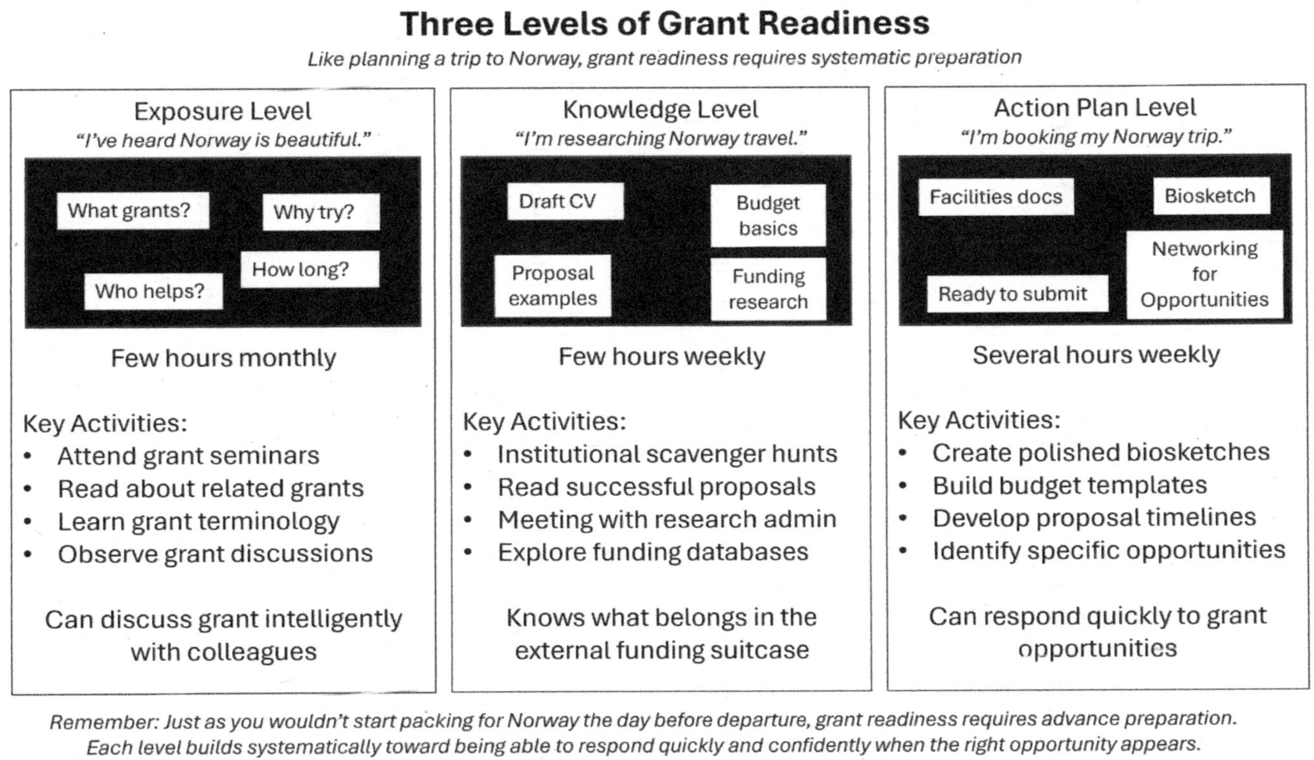

Figure 1.1 Project visualization useful in proposal and for websites explaining project.

Box 1.1 Definitions of Key Terms

Please remember there is a helpful appendix that lists all the grant terms and jargon used throughout the book. Detailed explanations of some terms are covered later in the book.

We recommend systematic institutional exploration at this level—what we call "scavenger hunts." Visit your sponsored programs office to understand pre-award and post-award support structures. Meet with research development staff to learn about funding databases and proposal assistance. Connect with successful grant recipients in your field to understand their experiences and timeline. Review successful proposals in your discipline to understand structure and expectations. This book gives you many ideas for creating your own scavenger hunt.

Success means knowing what belongs in your metaphorical grant readiness suitcase, even if you haven't packed it yet. You need to understand the landscape, requirements, and commitments involved.

Action Plan Level: Actively Preparing to Pursue Funding

At this implementation level, you're systematically preparing for active grant pursuit. You've moved from understanding requirements to creating the tools and systems needed for success. This involves creating essential documents, such as Curriculum Vitae (CVs)—often called biosketches—in multiple formats, providing current and pending support forms (reports of existing funding so funders can verify this project is not funded by other sources), developing budgeting capabilities and templates, building active relationships with institutional research staff, establishing efficient systems for managing proposal development, and identifying specific funding opportunities with concrete timelines.

Success means having everything prepared so that when opportunities arise, you can respond quickly and confidently rather than scrambling to create basic materials under pressure.

Chapter 2 will explore the crucial mindset shift that often needs to occur between the knowledge and action plan levels—the psychological and philosophical preparation that enables effective grant seeking.

The Grant-Ready Toolkit: Your Preparedness Suitcase

Just as experienced travelers maintain a partially packed suitcase with essentials, grant-ready scholars keep core documents updated and accessible. When a frequent business traveler receives a last-minute opportunity, they don't start from scratch—they grab their prepared suitcase and add trip-specific items.

This same principle applies to grant readiness. A prepared scholar maintains:

- Updated CVs or biosketches in various formats (NIH, NSF, foundation-specific)
- Current and pending support documentation of funding they have and are seeking
- Conflict-of-interest forms, used to determine who might be conflicted with your proposal and should not review your work
- Budget templates with current rates (note, salaries, fringe benefits, tuition rates, and related items on a budget can change yearly)
- Standard research statements that can be customized

The power becomes evident when opportunities arise with tight deadlines. Rather than scrambling to create basic documents, you focus on crafting the most compelling case for your specific research.

Box 1.2 Essential Suitcase Contents

Your grant readiness toolkit should include:

Core Documents:

- Professional biosketches formatted for different agencies
- Current CV with grant-relevant formatting

- Current and pending support documentation
- Institutional facilities and resources descriptions

Budget Components:

- Template budgets with current salary rates
- Fringe benefit percentages for your institution
- Indirect cost rates, extra costs that your institution will require to pay for facilities and administrative (F&A) costs. This is also called overhead.
- Standard cost estimates for common expenses

Research Materials:

- Boilerplate descriptions of your research program
- Data management plan templates, required to demonstrate you will handle data privacy and confidentiality in a responsible manner
- Standard broader impacts language, details around how your research will impact society
- Graduate student and postdoctoral scholar mentoring plan
- Letters of support templates, often needed for grant partners to complete to explain how they will collaborate with your team or that they will provide resources for your team

Administrative Tools:

- Contact information for key institutional staff
- Submission checklists for major agencies
- Timeline templates for proposal development

From Reactive to Systematic Preparation

Many scholars enter grant seeking reactively—receiving last-minute invitations to join proposals or discovering perfect opportunities just before deadlines (see Chapter 5 for the pros and cons of these requests).

While systematic preparation is ideal, even partial readiness can make the difference between participating and declining opportunities. Each grant experience should contribute to building your suitcase. After each submission, update documents, refine templates, and identify preparation gaps. The goal is to move from frantic reaction to confident readiness.

Self-Assessment: Where Are You Now?

Before developing your action plan, assess your current readiness level. For each statement, rate your agreement on a scale from 1 (strongly disagree) to 5 (strongly agree):

Strongly Disagree Strongly Agree
Please circle the number

Grant Landscape Knowledge:

1 I understand the major sources of funding for my work
1 2 3 4 5

2 I am aware of the funding support resources at my institution
1 2 3 4 5

3 I know how to read and interpret funding solicitations
1 2 3 4 5

Collaborations and Networks:

4 I have strong funding mentors and collaborator networks
1 2 3 4 5

5 I'm knowledgeable of external funding peer review processes
1 2 3 4 5

Audience Communication:

6 I am willing and able to align my research with agency priorities
1 2 3 4 5

7 I can articulate the impacts of my work for nonspecialists
1 2 3 4 5

8 I can craft compelling brief and extended project summaries
1 2 3 4 5

Project Management:

9 I understand the project management requirement for grants
1 2 3 4 5

10 I can develop detailed, appropriate budgets for research
1 2 3 4 5

11 I can balance external funding work with other responsibilities
1 2 3 4 5

Scoring

- **45–55**: Strong foundation for grant seeking
- **35–45**: Good strengths with some development areas
- **23–35**: Significant capacity building needed
- **Below 22**: Focus on foundational skills first

Regardless of where you score, responding to these questions likely forced you to think about your current knowledge and your current support networks. Is there one of the four areas (Grant Landscape, Collaborations and Network, Audience Communication, and Project Management) where you feel especially strong? What about your weaker areas? Use these results to identify specific areas for development as you work your way through this book. The next section discusses three levels of grant exposure scholars often experience. Use your self-assessment to determine which level of grant engagement best describes your current position.

Building Your Grant-Seeking Capacity

Earlier in this chapter, you learned about the three levels of grant capacity. At the exposure level, you've heard about grants and might be interested in pursuing them, but you don't have any experience yet. If you have a low self-assessment score, you are likely at the exposure level.

Here are some tips for scholars at this particular level:

- Attend grant-related seminars and workshops
- Read successful proposals in your field
- Interview grant-active colleagues about their experiences
- Observe the grant components of job talks and faculty presentations

At the knowledge level of grant seeking, you're typically actively researching grants and trying to decide if this is what you need or want to pursue. Your self-assessment score probably fell in the low to middle of the range if you are at this level. Here are some tips for scholars at this knowledge level:

- Complete institutional grant-writing workshops.
- Volunteer for grant review panels when eligible.
- Develop relationships with research development staff.
- Create your first biosketches and budget templates.

At the action level of grant seeking, you're creating items to put into the grant suitcase so you are ready to apply when needed. You likely scored in the middle to higher range of the self-assessment. Here are some tips for scholars at this knowledge level:

- Identify two or three specific funding opportunities for the coming year.
- Develop comprehensive proposal timelines.
- Build collaborative relationships for future proposals.
- Create systematic tracking systems for opportunities and deadlines.

Your Personalized Action Plan

Based on your assessment results and engagement level, the next step is for you to develop your specific plan. Here is a timeline and list of actions for you to follow:

- **Immediate Actions (Next 3 Months):**
  - Which documents do you need to create or update?
  - What institutional resources should you explore?
  - Who are key people to connect with?
- **Medium-Term Goals (3–12 Months):**
  - What skills need development?
  - Which workshops or training should you attend?
  - What collaborative relationships should you build?
- **Long-Term Vision (1–3 Years):**
  - What specific funding opportunities align with your research?
  - How does grant seeking fit your overall career strategy?
  - What mentoring or support structures do you need?

Chapter Wrap-Up

Grant readiness represents a fundamental shift in how social scientists approach their careers. By understanding the three levels of engagement, building your preparedness toolkit, and developing systematic approaches to capacity building, you position yourself to respond effectively when opportunities arise.

The goal isn't to change who you are as a scholar, but to develop the practical skills needed to communicate your work's value to funding agencies. Whether you're at the exposure level building understanding, the knowledge level developing capabilities, or the action plan level preparing for active pursuit, systematic preparation beats last-minute scrambling.

In Chapter 2, we'll explore the mindset shifts that often need to occur as you move between these levels—particularly the transition from knowledge to action that requires developing what we call the "multilingual scholar" identity. This psychological and philosophical preparation is just as important as the practical tools we've covered here.

Remember: every successful grant seeker started somewhere. The stories that opened this chapter—of misreading deadlines and not knowing how to navigate new systems—are nearly universal experiences. The difference is learning from these experiences and building the systematic preparation that prevents repeating them. Your grant readiness journey begins with a single step: choosing your level of engagement and taking the first concrete action toward building your capabilities. With systematic preparation and the right mindset, you can transform from unprepared to grant-ready.

2

The Multilingual Scholar: Mindset for Grant Success

Learning to Speak Each Other's Academic Languages

Keri now works extensively with civil engineer Kasey Faust, and together they've learned a tremendous amount about the different languages they speak, the different academic cultures they come from, and the different training they've received around external funding. Today, they work together like an integrated team—they have even coedited an interdisciplinary *Handbook of Infrastructure Communication* together, but when they started, they had to navigate some fundamental differences in how they approached research.

Early in their collaboration, Kasey asked Keri why she measured everything on a scale. "Why does variance matter to you? I just want to know if people did the action or not. Did the action work, or did it not work? I don't care that it worked at a 5 out of 7 level." Kasey would recommend switching Keri's variable measures to dichotomous measures, and Keri would jump up and down saying, "No, no, no, I need the variance!" Kasey would respond, "Why?" And Keri would explain, "Because I want to understand the level to which they vary." Kasey's response: "OK, but in my field, I want to know—did they do it, or did they not?"

Another ongoing discussion centered on theory. Keri would always lead with theory in journal articles, and Kasey would come back and say,

"Keri, a little bit of theory is OK, but you've got to make sure to make this practical. I don't understand why we're talking about these theories." Kasey comes from a field that's more practice-driven than theory-driven.

They talked very openly and bluntly about the different cultures of engineering and social science, learning how to take the best of each and merge them together to create incredible proposals. Together, they have now secured five funded proposals. They've developed a formula that works, and at its heart is their ability to speak each other's academic languages. This story illustrates the essence of what we call developing a "multilingual scholar" identity—the mindset shift necessary for successful grant seeking as a social scientist.

In Chapter 1, we discussed the three levels of grant engagement: exposure, knowledge, and action planning. The transition from knowledge to action often requires more than just practical preparation—it demands a fundamental mindset shift. This is where many social scientists get stuck, not because they lack the technical skills, but because they struggle with the psychological and philosophical aspects of grant seeking.

The multilingual scholar mindset provides the bridge between understanding what grants require and actually pursuing them successfully. It addresses common concerns about "selling out," helps maintain scholarly authenticity while adapting to funder expectations, and provides a framework for navigating the complex discourse communities of the funding world.

Debunking the "Selling Out" Myth

Many social scientists and humanities scholars worry that adapting their work for funders means compromising their intellectual integrity or "selling out." This concern reflects a deep-seated myth in our fields—the belief that being a social scientist means being poor and not accepting money for your work. There's a sense that the kind of research you publish is somehow not worthy if you make money from it. We're expected to give all this time and service for no compensation, which is fairly common in the social sciences and humanities. Many assume that getting funding for your work will somehow "pad your pocket," but this is typically not what happens with external funding.

Kerk reflects on this myth through a conversation with his father:

> I explained to my dad about why I publish and then don't expect to get paid. I told him that if I get paid for each publication, how can you trust that I'm telling you the truth and not being motivated by the money I'll be getting based on what I say? That's why when I publish academic work, it's supposed to be free. I'm not getting paid to publish, so that limits bias. It shows how I'm willing to contribute to public knowledge and the betterment of the world. It's more selfless, not selfish, because when selfishness is there, you question the motivation and intention.

This perspective is also common among critical cultural scholars who often believe that research needs to resist commercialization and power structures. While these perspectives bring important voices to the academic community, some critical cultural scholars have found very fruitful ways to get external funding while truly advancing their research agendas. Environmental justice researchers, for example, have conducted amazing community-engaged work that they could never have pursued without external funding to support meaningful partnerships with communities.

The reality is that external funding often holds researchers to higher standards of rigor and accountability, not lower ones. When you accept funding from foundations or federal agencies, you become responsible to taxpayers or foundation missions. The rigor we maintain in academic institutions to ensure we don't have conflicts of interest is actually higher when our research is funded because we're forced to report our results and are scrutinized more carefully. We are held to a higher standard regarding bias precisely because we're using dollars that have been entrusted to us.

Moreover, the assumption that grant recipients are somehow profiting personally from their funding reveals a fundamental misunderstanding of how academic grants work. As Kerk explains to his graduate students: "If there is anything left over after funding graduate students, covering participant compensation for research participants and community stakeholders, funding travels to conferences for research dissemination, paying institution overhead, and the direct costs of the research, principal investigators might get paid for some of their summer." Since many academic positions are nine-month positions, they work on grant-funded projects without additional compensation during the nine months of fall and spring. Because they are not paid by their universities for the three summer months, they may request to have some of the summer months be paid by the grants when they work on these projects during the summer. It is rare that they get enough of the right types of funding to compensate them for the full remaining three months of a year.

The irony is that grant-active scholars are actually funding more graduate students in their disciplines, creating more opportunities for the next generation of researchers. Kerk notes that at some institutions, research administrators appreciate social scientists who get funding because they are financially supporting graduate students. One year, he supported eight research assistants and that allowed his college to admit more students into the PhD program.

Furthermore, external funding enables more ethical and equitable research practices. Keri has a principle now where she will not do community-engaged work unless she can compensate community members for their time when they participate in her studies. Why should we assume they volunteer their time? She works a lot with people who have lower incomes. They are giving their time to participate in research and we must compensate them for it. It is an equity issue, and it's incredibly important to fairly distribute representation and make sure we are getting input from the right types of people to address our research questions.

This principle challenges another false assumption in our fields: that just because the majority of people in our field do research without paying participants doesn't mean paying participants is wrong. Similarly, just because the majority of our colleagues don't get grants doesn't mean getting grants is wrong. The idea of what is "normal" is shifting as the funding landscape changes and institutional expectations evolve.

It is also crucial to recognize that having more diverse perspectives among grant-funded social scientists and humanities scholars enhances the overall quality of research. We need people with different viewpoints—including critical and cultural foci—bringing important new ideas to bear on crucial societal challenges. When critical cultural scholars get funded in a collaborative grant, they get a seat at the table to influence the direction of the project for social justice. For example, increasingly there are concerns around ethics of new technologies, like artificial intelligence or medical research. It's important that scholars who have traditionally not thought about themselves as the type who would get external funding consider how they could do even more meaningful work through strategic resource acquisition.

Maintaining Scholarly Identity Through Strategic Authenticity

The most crucial aspect of developing multilingual capacity is maintaining your core intellectual identity while adapting your presentation for different contexts. For many social scientists, certain elements remain nonnegotiable: your theoretical commitments, your methodological standards, your ethical principles, and your intellectual integrity. However, other elements can be flexibly adapted depending on audience and context: how you frame significance, which aspects you emphasize, the vocabulary you use, and the examples you provide.

Box 2.1 "Strategic authenticity"

The ability to present your work genuinely while making strategic choices about which aspects to emphasize for particular audiences.

The translation process often involves emphasizing different aspects of your research program rather than fundamentally changing your agenda. You maintain intellectual consistency while adapting communication strategies. This approach requires developing what we call "strategic authenticity"—the ability to present your work genuinely while making strategic choices about which aspects to emphasize for particular audiences.

Rather than viewing this as compromise, consider these reframes: Instead of "I'm selling out by emphasizing practical applications," think "I'm expanding my impact by connecting theory to practice." Instead of "Funders don't value rigorous social science," consider "Funders may be unfamiliar with social science methods and we have the opportunity to help them understand how our methods could advance their funding priorities." Instead of "I have to change my research to get funding," recognize "I'm learning to articulate why my research matters to broader audiences."

Early in your career, this translation process may feel challenging or uncomfortable. It may seem like you're compromising your intellectual integrity or abandoning your disciplinary training. However, with practice, most scholars find that this multilingual approach actually enriches their understanding of their own work by forcing them to articulate its significance in multiple ways and consider its implications for diverse audiences.

Understanding Academic Code-Switching

Successfully navigating grants as a social scientist requires developing what we call "academic code-switching"—the ability to translate your work for different audiences while maintaining your intellectual integrity. Just as multilingual individuals adjust their language depending on context, grant-savvy researchers learn to frame their work in ways that resonate with different funding agencies and review panels. This doesn't mean abandoning your disciplinary commitments or changing your research agenda. Rather, it involves strategic emphasis—highlighting different aspects of the same work for different audiences while maintaining consistency in your core intellectual commitments.

The Challenge of Different Academic Cultures

The academic culture that shaped your graduate training likely emphasized:

- Theoretical sophistication and innovation
- Methodological rigor within established paradigms
- Contributions to ongoing scholarly conversations
- Peer recognition within your discipline

Grant culture, by contrast, often values:

- Practical applications and measurable outcomes
- Innovation and novel intellectual contributions across disciplinary boundaries
- Alignment with agency missions and priorities
- Broader societal impact and engagement

These value systems aren't incompatible, but they require different presentation strategies. The multilingual scholar learns to navigate between these cultures without compromising their intellectual integrity.

Box 2.2 Practical Examples of Academic Translation

Consider how the same research project studying workplace communication might be framed for different audiences:

- **For Disciplinary Journals:** Emphasize theoretical contributions to organizational communication theory, methodological innovations in ethnographic research, and implications for ongoing scholarly debates within communication studies.
- **For NSF Proposals:** Frame as advancing understanding of team dynamics in STEM workplaces, emphasizing broader impacts for scientific productivity and workforce development while maintaining theoretical sophistication.
- **For NIH Proposals:** Focus on communication patterns affecting health care delivery, highlighting potential improvements in patient care or reductions in medical errors while using the same underlying research methods.
- **For Private Foundations:** Emphasize evidence-based practices for creating more inclusive and effective work environments, focusing on practical interventions and social change.

The underlying research remains consistent; what changes is which aspects you emphasize and how you articulate significance.

Learning Multiple Academic Languages

Developing multilingual capacity requires understanding that different funding agencies operate within distinct discourse communities, each with its own vocabulary, priorities, and evaluation criteria. When you write grants, you're entering these communities and must communicate effectively within their frameworks.

If you examine the websites of funding agencies, you will see they often clearly articulate their funding priorities. NSF emphasizes intellectual merit, broader impacts, advancing scientific knowledge, education and outreach, and innovation across disciplines. NIH focuses on health outcomes, clinical relevance, translational potential, reducing disease burden, and improving quality of life. Federal education initiatives prioritize educational improvement, evidence-based practices, student outcomes, policy implications, and scalability. Private foundations often value social change, equity, practical interventions, organizational mission alignment, and measurable community impact. Corporate foundations typically emphasize innovation, economic development, workforce preparation, industry relevance, and return on investment.

These different priorities can change over time, so it is important to revisit their goals and objectives before beginning to write a proposal. Just like academic journals with special-issue calls specify the topics they will consider, so do different funding sources. It would not make sense to submit research on human-artificial intelligence teaming with flood models to a special issue call on mental health innovations when working with young mothers. Thus, think about submitting proposals as a process of finding the special-issue call that matches the research you want to do.

Building Translation Skills

Developing multilingual capacity requires deliberate practice: studying successful proposals from multiple disciplines and agencies, noting how researchers frame significance and impact; reading agency strategic plans to understand priorities and preferred vocabulary; attending interdisciplinary conferences to observe how different fields present their work; collaborating across disciplines to practice explaining your work to nonspecialists; and engaging with practitioners to understand how your research might apply in real-world contexts.

Personal Stories of Strategic Mindset Development

Keri's Intentional Approach to Tenure

> I made a very intentional decision to very selectively pursue external funding while working toward tenure. My tenure requirements were substantial, and I was at an institution that required theoretical advancements and did not place emphasis on practical applications at that time. I carefully assessed what my institution valued and made a conscious choice to focus my limited time and energy accordingly. I did attempt NSF CAREER grants twice and was not successful, but looking back, I wasn't successful because I didn't have my suitcase packed. I didn't know what I was doing or what the requirements were. I wasn't remotely ready to write a CAREER grant when I attempted it. It was essentially a waste of time because I hadn't done any of the groundwork we discuss in this book. My senior faculty were very honest about what counted for tenure—funding wasn't part of my requirements at all. I knew that if I spent time on grants, it wouldn't even be counted toward my tenure case, so I focused strategically on what they told me: publish in top-tier journals and ensure excellent teaching. Once I got tenure, then I spent focused time learning how to incorporate applied research and get that work funded.

This underscores how important it is to understand your institutional context and be willing to adjust your strategy based on where you are and what stage of your career you're in. Being strategic means making informed choices about where to invest your energy based on clear understanding of expectations and rewards.

Kerk's Perspective: Institutional Context Matters

> I started my career at a liberal arts university, whose publishing requirements at that time were more flexible than what is often found at an R1 (high research-active institutions). This allowed me to experiment with grant seeking without the pressure of publishing in a narrow list of top-tier journals. But I want to be clear—what I did by focusing on

grant-seeking during my tenure track time probably took time away from my publishing.

The key insight is that institutional context matters enormously. Some people may be at institutions where they can afford to delay grant seeking while building other credentials. Others face immediate pressure and need to develop grant skills quickly. The multilingual scholar mindset helps in both situations—it just operates at different timelines and intensities.

Developing multilingual scholarly capacity provides several strategic advantages. Rather than being limited to narrow disciplinary funding, you can compete for interdisciplinary programs and mission-driven initiatives. You become a valuable team member for interdisciplinary projects because you can translate between different field perspectives. You can communicate your work's significance to administrators, policymakers, and practitioners who influence funding decisions. The translation process often leads to new insights about your work's implications and applications, fostering intellectual growth.

Building Resilience for Grant Seeking

Grant seeking requires significant psychological resilience. Even successful researchers face multiple rejections. Success rates can be less than 5 percent; most people are not funded on their first submission, and many agencies and organizations do not allow resubmissions. Keri submitted over twelve federal grant applications before she had her first success. Building mental frameworks for handling this reality can help, especially when there are community partners involved in supporting your grant-seeking efforts. Cultivating a growth mindset means viewing rejections as learning opportunities, seeing feedback as valuable input for improvement, understanding that success builds over time, and recognizing that persistence often matters more than perfection. Developing portfolio thinking involves pursuing multiple opportunities simultaneously, balancing high-risk, high-reward applications with safer bets, building incrementally from smaller to larger grants, and celebrating incremental progress and small wins. Building support networks means connecting with other grant-seeking scholars, finding mentors who can provide perspective during setbacks, participating in writing groups or accountability partnerships, and maintaining relationships that extend beyond grant-specific interactions.

Box 2.3 Types of Research Support at Universities

Understanding who does what at your institution is crucial for getting the right help at the right time. Here are the key players and their typical roles (note that smaller institutions may combine these functions, while larger universities may have highly specialized teams):

Research Administration Handles institutional pre-award and post-award compliance, including proposal submission procedures, budget development and monitoring, compliance with sponsor terms and conditions, and award setup and closeout. These professionals ensure your proposal and project meet all institutional and sponsor requirements.

Research Development A relatively newer field in academia that focuses more comprehensively on helping researchers develop fundable concepts from initial idea through proposal development. Research developers often have doctoral training and deep understanding of research processes. They may help with literature reviews, study design, identifying team members, and strategic positioning of proposals. Not all institutions have dedicated research development staff.

Institutional Review Board (IRB) Reviews research involving human subjects to ensure ethical treatment and regulatory compliance. You'll work with IRB to obtain approval before beginning human subjects research and to maintain ongoing compliance during your project.

Institutional Animal Care and Use Committee (IACUC) Oversees research involving animals to ensure humane treatment and regulatory compliance. Required for any research involving vertebrate animals.

Authorized Representative/Signing Official The institutional official with authority to legally commit the institution to the terms and conditions of a grant or contract. This person (often someone in research administration) must sign all proposals before submission.

Foundation Relations/Development Manages relationships with private foundations and philanthropic organizations. These staff members may have inside knowledge about foundation priorities, processes, and program officers that can be invaluable when pursuing private funding.

Action Step: Find out which of these support structures exist at your institution, who the key contacts are, and what services they offer. Create a contact sheet for your files so you know who to reach out to for different needs.

Understanding Institutional Contexts

One crucial aspect of developing the multilingual scholar mindset is recognizing that institutions vary dramatically in their approach to external funding. Many R1 research universities expect significant external funding for promotion and tenure, provide extensive support infrastructure, but also create intense competition. In 2025, Duke Medical School announced that all its researchers would be expected to achieve minimum amounts of external funding or risk having their salary substantially reduced (Lin, 2025). But keep in mind that department cultures vary; Keri's department, a top program at a highly rated R1 institution, did not require external funding for tenure and promotion as she was navigating that system. Liberal arts colleges may value grants for professional development but not require them for advancement; often they have limited support staff but provide more flexibility in timeline and approach. Emerging research universities are often in transition, with changing expectations and developing support systems, requiring careful attention to institutional trajectory. Community colleges and teaching-focused institutions may offer opportunities for education-focused grants and often emphasize practical applications and student impact. Understanding your institutional context helps you calibrate your grant-seeking strategy and set realistic expectations for yourself and your career trajectory.

Practical Exercises for Developing Multilingual Capacity

Exercise 1: Translation Practice

Take one of your recent papers or research projects and write three different one-paragraph descriptions:

1. For your disciplinary colleagues
2. For a government funding agency
3. For a private foundation

Notice what changes and what stays the same. For your discipline, you likely mention the contribution of work to your field. For the government funding agency, you likely stress the impact and novelty of the work. For the foundation, the focus is more on societal impact. If you found this exercise difficult, please return to this exercise after you finish reading this book. Having this ability to translate your work is crucial to developing a flexible funding agenda.

Exercise 2: Mission Alignment Analysis

Choose three funding agencies relevant to your work (for ideas see Chapter 3 in this book). Read their mission statements and strategic plans. Identify:

- Key vocabulary and concepts they emphasize
- Types of outcomes they value
- How your research might align with their priorities

Exercise 3: Interdisciplinary Conversation

Find a colleague from a different discipline and practice explaining your research to them. Ask them to identify:

- What aspects seem most relevant to their field
- What vocabulary or concepts need clarification
- How your work might contribute to interdisciplinary projects

Regardless of whether you plan to pursue interdisciplinary research or find funding more focused in your field, having these conversations helps you better understand how different audiences comprehend the value of your research.

Chapter Wrap-Up

The multilingual scholar mindset represents more than just practical skill development—it's a fundamental reorientation toward how you understand and present your scholarly identity. By learning to code-switch between academic cultures while maintaining your intellectual integrity, you open new possibilities for impact and collaboration. This mindset shift often represents the crucial bridge between having grant knowledge and taking grant action. It addresses the psychological and philosophical barriers that keep many capable scholars from pursuing external funding, providing frameworks for navigating these challenges while staying true to your scholarly commitments.

The examples of Keri and Kasey's collaboration, along with the personal stories of mindset development, illustrate that becoming a multilingual scholar is an ongoing process of learning and adaptation. It requires patience with yourself, willingness to experiment with new ways of presenting your work, and confidence that you can maintain your scholarly identity while expanding your impact. As you continue developing this mindset, remember that the goal isn't to become someone different, but to become more skillful at communicating who you already are to diverse audiences. Your disciplinary training remains valuable; you're simply adding new capabilities for translation and adaptation.

In the next section of the book, we'll explore how to apply this multilingual scholar mindset to the practical work of identifying funding opportunities and building collaborative relationships. The foundation you've built through grant readiness preparation and multilingual mindset development will serve you well as we move into the active phases of grant seeking.

3

Finding a Funding Match for Your Research

Almost every scholar beginning this funding journey questions if the research they do is fundable. Our view is that most research is fundable, the key is finding the right funding opportunity where your research fits. Furthermore, sometimes the key to getting funding is to place theoretical work into a fundable context. Kerk has been very successful in transitioning his theoretical work on cyberinfrastructure into fundable research. See Chapter 4 for details about his journey. Keri also took her research on mobile communication and organizing and placed it into a disaster context, something that also resonated with her life experiences and true desire to make the world a safer place to live. Let's take a look at how that happened for her.

Keri was applying for an NSF RAPID grant (a funding mechanism where you get an award quickly because it only undergoes internal agency review, and it is designed to capture important research data that will disappear if not collected immediately). The program officer looked over her one-page summary and asked her to give him a call at 5 p.m. on a Friday afternoon. She got her verbal pitch ready, called, and started the conversation. In the background, she heard a sizzling noise but continued talking. After several questions, the program officer told her he needed to flip the fish on the grill, so he had to set the phone down for a minute. When he returned, he asked her to send over a five-page proposal by Monday morning. The sizzle was not only the fish frying, but also the speed at which Keri had to turn around the first NSF RAPID proposal she was awarded the following week.

This type of funding mechanism is very specific, and not many operate this way. However, because funding sources vary tremendously, being aware of a range of funding options and knowing how to find those that connect to your research interests are key. Some funders value theory, almost all value contributions to knowledge, and some want the focus on research outcomes. In Chapter 2, you learned the importance of having the right mindset, and this chapter helps you use that mindset to identify opportunities you want to pursue.

The best way to understand finding external funding is to recognize it's a lot like finding the right journal for your research. When you have a manuscript ready for submission, you don't randomly send it to the first journal you find. You investigate which journals publish work like yours, study their aims and scope, read recent issues to understand their preferences, and often choose your target journal before you even begin writing. You sign up for table of contents alerts, follow editorial board changes, and ask colleagues about their experiences with different editors.

Finding funding follows the same systematic process, yet many social scientists don't make this connection. They approach funding searches haphazardly, growing frustrated when they can't find obvious matches for their work. Once you recognize that finding funding is just like finding journals—a process you've already mastered—the mystery disappears and strategic thinking takes over.

This chapter provides a comprehensive framework for identifying funding opportunities that genuinely align with your research. We'll explore how different types of funders operate, examine search strategies that evolve across career stages, and provide practical tools for evaluating potential matches. Most importantly, we'll help you develop the judgment to distinguish genuine opportunities from time-wasting poor fits.

The Journal Special-Issue Mindset

Many social scientists make a fundamental error when approaching funding agencies. They assume that broad agencies like NIH or the National Endowment for the Humanities (NEH) should fund any good research in their domain, like how flagship journals in their field might consider any strong manuscript. This assumption leads to frustration and rejection.

The reality is that funding agencies operate more like collections of special issues than general journals. NSF doesn't have a general "fund any good social science" program. Instead, it has specific sections (previously called directorates), each with particular programs, each of those with distinct priorities and preferred approaches. Even within a single program, the priorities and approaches may shift depending on who the program directors are and/or how the program responds to agency-wide priority changes. The Directorate of Social, Behavioral and Economic Sciences values different things than the Education Directorate and the Human Resources Directorate, even within the same agency. Please note that as of January 2026, some of the names of these programs are in flux.

This explains why colleagues complain, "I can't find anything on NEH's website that fits my work," or "They keep rejecting my proposals as if my research isn't interesting." They're looking for a general issue that doesn't exist because the National Endowment for the Humanities funds a particular type of research. Success requires finding the specific "special issue"—the particular program or call—that aligns with your research. Understanding this fundamental difference transforms how you approach funding searches. Instead of trying to convince agencies they should fund your work, you're looking for places where your work already fits their priorities. It's not about making a better argument; it's about finding the right match.

Your approach to finding funding should evolve throughout your career, just as your publication strategies mature from graduate student to senior scholar. What works at one stage may be inefficient or inappropriate at another. Early in your career, or early in your funding journey, you may lack the networks and experience that senior scholars take for granted. Technology tools become essential teachers. Databases like Pivot, Grants.gov, and Foundation Directory Online serve as training grounds, introducing you to the funding landscape. You may have access to institutional grant-writing workshops, and if you do not, seek regional or online events from funding agencies and organizations like the American Association for the Advancement of Science (AAAS). At this stage, cast a wide net. Sign up for multiple funding databases, even if many suggestions seem tangential. Each poorly matched notification teaches you something about how funders categorize research. Set up Google Scholar alerts for funded researchers in your area. Attend every grant writing workshop your institution offers, even those seemingly outside your field.

Most importantly, mine your colleagues' networks. Ask directly: "Who funds work like mine? Can you introduce me to colleagues who've been successful with grants?" Many senior scholars are happy to make introductions but won't think to offer unless asked.

As you establish your research agenda and publication record, your funding search strategies should become more targeted. Technology tools become less central as you develop direct relationships with program officers and understand the funding landscape related to your specific research. This is when conference attendance becomes strategic rather than exploratory. Kerk deliberately presents at computer science conferences, despite being a communication scholar, because that's where potential collaborators from other disciplines and program officers are more likely to show up.

Mid-career and senior scholars have new challenges and opportunities. They may be asked to lead a larger center-scale project which takes a very different skill set (see Chapter 10 for a full discussion of these issues). These more advanced scholars should also begin serving on review panels when invited. This inside view of the review process proves invaluable for understanding what makes proposals competitive. You will see common mistakes, recognize what excites reviewers, and build relationships with program officers who need reliable reviewers. Senior scholars often find funding through established relationships and reputation. Program officers may reach out directly about new opportunities. Colleagues may invite collaboration on large grants. The challenge becomes being selective rather than finding opportunities. At this stage, your role expands to include mentoring junior scholars in finding funding. Share your networks generously. Include junior colleagues on grants to help them build track records. Most importantly, demystify the process by sharing both successes and failures.

Box 3.1 Exercise: Map Your Funding Potential Using Published Research

This systematic exercise (originally developed for Keri's Graduate Students Grant Writing course) helps you identify potential funding sources by learning from successful researchers in your field. Plan to spend four to six hours across several sessions on this investigation.

1. **Building Your Sample:** Select five to seven recently published articles (within three years) that closely relate to your research interests and have received external funding. Ensure they come from respected journals in your field and include both single-author and collaborative pieces. This diversity helps you see different funding patterns.
2. **Mining the Acknowledgments:** For each article, carefully read the acknowledgments section and document all funding sources mentioned, including agency names and grant numbers. Note when multiple funders support the same work—this signals funders who might work together.
3. **Deep Investigation:** Take each grant number and search for it online along with the agency name. This often reveals the original grant abstract, showing how the research was pitched to funders. Download or screenshot these abstracts. Note the funding amount, project duration, and all investigators listed. This shows you not just what got funded but how it was framed for the funder.
4. **Team Analysis:** Visit the principal investigator's website or CV. Count how many publications emerged from this grant. Note whether they hired postdocs, graduate students, or staff. Look at author orders on resulting publications to understand team composition. This reveals what different funding levels actually support in terms of personnel.
5. **Pattern Recognition:** For each funding agency you've identified, visit their website and find lists of recently funded projects. Look for patterns in project sizes, durations, topics, and methodological approaches. Sign up for their newsletters or funding alerts. Create a spreadsheet tracking which agencies fund what types of work.
6. **Network Mapping:** Notice which scholars appear as coinvestigators across multiple grants. These are potential collaborators who understand the funding

landscape. Consider reaching out to researchers whose funding portfolios you admire.

7. **Synthesis and Action:** Create a summary document listing agencies that fund work like yours, typical award amounts, common team structures, and key terms that appear repeatedly in funded abstracts. Identify three to five agencies to explore further and note any gaps where your work might not currently fit. Set up calendar reminders for relevant deadline cycles.

Key Questions for Reflection: What surprised you about the funding landscape in your area? Which funders support theoretical versus applied work? How do successful researchers in your field build their funding portfolios over time? Where might your work fit that you hadn't previously considered?

Becoming a Funding Detective

One powerful strategy works across all career stages: becoming a detective who investigates how successful researchers in your area secure funding. This approach starts with published papers but extends far beyond. When reading academic research, pay careful attention to the acknowledgments sections. Authors must acknowledge external funding, usually including the agency name and award number. This information is gold for your detective work.

Take it further than just noting who funded the work. Put award numbers into Google searches along with the agency name. This often reveals the original grant abstract, showing how the research was initially framed for funders. You're seeing not just what got published but how it was pitched. For example, a paper on social network analysis might acknowledge the Knight Foundation grant #1234567. Searching for this reveals the original abstract emphasizing theoretical advances in social capital theory—information that doesn't appear in the published paper focused on practical applications. This intelligence shows how the researchers balanced funder expectations with scholarly goals.

Continue your detective work by examining who was involved in funded projects. Look at author orders on publications, visit PI websites, and piece together team composition. Did they hire postdocs? How many graduate students? What disciplines were represented? This investigation reveals patterns. Perhaps successful grants in your area typically include a methodologist, a subject expert, and a community partner. Maybe they're usually $300,000–$500,000 in funding spread over three years. These patterns help you understand what funders expect and how to position your own proposals.

Once you've identified relevant funding agencies, study their recent awards systematically. Most agencies publish lists of funded projects with abstracts, amounts, and investigator information. Look for patterns in what methodological approaches they favor, typical project duration and budget, whether they fund single investigators or require teams, what keywords appear repeatedly in funded abstracts, and how successful projects frame their significance. This pattern recognition helps you understand not just what agencies say they fund but what they actually fund—sometimes these differ significantly.

Successful researchers don't wait for formal funding announcements. They position themselves to learn about opportunities before they're officially released, giving them crucial extra preparation time. NSF issues "Dear Colleague Letters" signaling upcoming opportunities or new priority areas. These aren't funding announcements themselves but rather indicators of where the agency is heading. A Dear Colleague Letter about "Human-Centered AI" suggests upcoming funding opportunities in that area, giving savvy researchers time to form teams and develop ideas before formal calls appear.

Other agencies have similar mechanisms with different names. NIH issues "Notices of Special Interest." Private foundations publish strategic planning documents indicating future directions. Learning to interpret these signals provides competitive advantages. Program officers often know about upcoming opportunities months before they're announced. Building relationships with them provides invaluable early intelligence. One researcher learned about a new NSF program six months before its announcement through a casual conference conversation with a program officer. This head start allowed assembling an ideal team and developing preliminary data, contributing to their successful proposal.

Direct Engagement Strategies

While websites and databases provide useful information, the most valuable intelligence often comes through direct human contact. Yet many researchers hesitate to reach out, fearing they'll annoy busy program officers or appear naive. This hesitation misunderstands program officers' roles and motivations. They want to fund excellent research. They prefer guiding potential applicants toward competitive proposals to reviewing doomed applications. A program officer who discourages your application is doing you a favor, saving months of wasted effort.

Some agencies, particularly NSF, employ rotating program officers—faculty members serving one- to three-year terms. These aren't distant bureaucrats but colleagues who understand your situation intimately. They know the tenure pressure you face, the challenge of balancing teaching and research, and the difficulty of finding collaborators. They're looking for the best ideas to fund, not reasons to reject your work.

Some of the most valuable funding intelligence comes through unexpected conference encounters. One social psychology program officer from NIH attends seven different academic conferences annually—not to promote funding opportunities but to stay current with the science. As he explained at a reception, "I have to keep up on the science because I'm making decisions about what to fund." These encounters can redirect entire research trajectories. A health communication researcher discovered their work aligned with an NIH division they'd never considered after a program officer attended their conference presentation. The resulting conversation revealed funding opportunities that no amount of website searching would have uncovered.

Box 3.2 Mastering the Art of Pitching Your Research

Presenting/pitching research to program officers requires different skills than academic presentations. You're demonstrating alignment with funding priorities while maintaining your research integrity. Success requires preparation, clarity, and strategic thinking.

The Foundation: Your One-Pager

Never approach a program officer without a carefully crafted one-page summary (often called your one-pager). This is not a rough draft but a distillation of a fully developed project. Before writing your one-pager, outline your entire project in detail and draft at least five pages of narrative. Only then can you effectively condense to one powerful page.

Essential elements your one-pager must include:

- *Problem Statement (two to three sentences):* What specific challenge does your research address? Why does this matter now? Use concrete examples rather than abstract concepts.
- *Project Overview (one paragraph):* What will you actually do? Be specific about methods, timeline, and scope. Avoid jargon that might confuse reviewers outside your specialty.
- *Funder Alignment (two to three sentences):* How does this advance the funder's mission? Use their language from recent program announcements. Show you understand their priorities.
- *Innovation (two to three sentences):* What's genuinely new here? Why hasn't this been done before? What makes your approach unique?
- *Your Qualifications (two to three sentences):* Why are you the right person? Highlight relevant experience, preliminary work, or unique access to populations or data.
- *Expected Outcomes (three or four bullets):* What specific deliverables will result? Include both scholarly products and practical applications relevant to the funder.

Preparing for Verbal Pitches

After sending your one-pager, be ready for "the call." Practice these different versions:

- The thirty-second elevator pitch: "I study X to understand Y, which matters because Z." This should roll off your tongue naturally.

- The two-minute expansion: Add your methodological approach, rough timeline, team composition, and why this funder is the right match.
- The five-minute discussion: Include preliminary data, potential challenges and solutions, budget scope, and specific questions about program fit.

During the Conversation

Listen more than you talk. Program officers often guide you toward what would make your project fundable. Take detailed notes on their suggestions—these are golden insights into review criteria. Be honest about limitations or challenges. Program officers appreciate researchers who acknowledge difficulties upfront. Show enthusiasm for your work while remaining professional. Ask specific questions like "What aspects of this work best align with your current priorities?" or "Are there other programs I should consider?"

Critical Mistakes to Avoid

Don't argue if they say your work isn't a fit—thank them and ask about other programs. Don't promise deliverables you can't achieve. Overpromising destroys credibility. Don't use your entire time talking. Silence gives program officers space to offer guidance. Don't take rejection personally. A "no" from one program often leads to a better fit elsewhere.

Follow-Up Excellence

Send a thank-you email within twenty-four hours, summarizing key points from your conversation. If encouraged to submit, reference specific suggestions in your proposal. If discouraged, ask permission to contact them about future work. Keep them informed of related publications or preliminary findings that demonstrate progress.

Remember: Program officers manage portfolios. If your work doesn't fit one program, they often know others where it might. Building these relationships takes time but pays enormous dividends throughout your career.

Internal Funding: Your Institutional Starting Point

Internal funding represents one of the most accessible entry points for researchers new to grant seeking. These opportunities vary tremendously between institutions, but almost all universities offer some mechanism for faculty to secure small pockets of money—typically ranging from a few thousand to $50,000—for research projects.

Understanding what internal funding opportunities exist at your institution should be one of your first priorities as a new faculty member. These funds serve multiple purposes beyond just supporting research. They help you generate preliminary data that strengthens external proposals, demonstrate to your institution that you're serious about research, and provide low-stakes practice for grant writing.

The review process for internal funding offers unique insights into the grant landscape. Unlike external competitions where reviewers share your disciplinary background, internal review panels often include faculty from vastly different fields. You might find yourself on a panel reviewing anthropology projects in remote countries alongside physics and astronomy proposals about which you know nothing. This interdisciplinary review process mirrors what happens with many external grants, making internal competitions excellent training grounds.

The Gig Economy vs. Record Deal Perspective

It is crucial to understand that seed or pilot grants operate fundamentally differently from major external funding. As we like to explain, a seed grant functions much like a musician performing a gig at a local venue. The scholar arrives, conducts a discrete research project—perhaps collecting survey data through an online panel or conducting a small set of interviews—and produces results rather quickly. The entire endeavor remains manageable, focused, and relatively straightforward. For many social scientists, particularly in humanities-oriented fields, these modest funding sources provide all they need to conduct meaningful research and produce publications efficiently.

In contrast, securing major external funding resembles signing a record deal in the music industry. You're no longer simply performing at individual venues; you've launched an enterprise that requires complex management structures and dramatically different expectations. The first year of a major grant often involves primarily administrative setup: establishing protocols, hiring personnel, navigating institutional processes, and managing relationships with funders. This extensive groundwork means that tangible research outputs typically cannot emerge for a significant period.

Just as musicians who sign record deals must suddenly concern themselves with marketing, social media presence, tour scheduling, and business operations, academics with major grants find themselves managing teams, coordinating with multiple institutional partners, navigating complex reporting requirements, and dealing with heightened scrutiny from both their institutions and their funders.

Internal funding success rates vary dramatically by institutional context. At small institutions with limited research activity, strong researchers often face little competition and enjoy high success rates. At major research universities, competition can be fierce, with many faculty members whose primary job is research vying for the same funds. However, larger institutions typically offer more opportunities and higher award amounts, recognizing the greater demand.

One of the most valuable uses of internal funding is generating pilot data for larger external proposals. Federal agencies and foundations find proposals more compelling when you can demonstrate feasibility through preliminary findings. A $10,000 internal grant that produces pilot data can be leveraged into a $500,000 external award. This multiplier effect makes internal funding particularly strategic for early-career researchers.

Beyond individual research projects, internal funding often supports other scholarly activities. You might secure funds to host a conference at your institution, bringing together potential collaborators to develop larger grant proposals. Speaker series funding can help you build relationships with scholars whose work complements yours. Some institutions even provide internal funds to host program officers from federal agencies, creating opportunities for multiple faculty members to learn about funding priorities.

The key to internal funding success lies in understanding your audience. Since reviewers come from diverse fields, avoid disciplinary jargon and clearly explain your project's significance in terms any academic can understand. Emphasize feasibility—internal funders want to see concrete outcomes from their limited resources. Most importantly, articulate how this seed funding will lead to larger external grants, demonstrating that you're a good investment for the institution.

Federal Agencies: Serving National Priorities

Federal agencies represent the largest and most structured funding source for social science research. Each agency operates under congressional mandates to advance specific national priorities, creating distinct cultures and expectations that researchers must understand and navigate.

The National Science Foundation stands as the primary federal funder of basic social science research. Within NSF, different directorates maintain distinct priorities and review cultures. The Directorate for Social, Behavioral and Economic Sciences values theoretical innovation, methodological rigor, and contributions to fundamental knowledge. They fund research because it advances science, not necessarily because it solves immediate problems. In contrast, NSF's Education and Human Resources directorate emphasizes practical applications, educational outcomes, and broader impacts on teaching and learning.

The National Institutes of Health, despite its health focus, increasingly funds social science research that addresses health disparities, behavioral interventions, and social determinants of health. NIH's culture differs markedly from NSF's. Where some NSF directorates value theory-driven research, some NIH programs demand clear pathways to improving health outcomes. A computational social scientist studying social media might frame the same project as advancing network theory for NSF or identifying effective health interventions for NIH.

As you will learn in Chapter 8, research administrators provide valuable insights about federal funding. Tyler Myatt, a grant writer, observed that despite federal funding's complexity, it provides the most systematic and predictable framework for research administrators to support faculty effectively through established templates, checklists, and compliance procedures. This predictability can be an advantage for researchers who invest time in understanding federal requirements.

Federal agencies also employ different mechanisms for distributing funds. Some, like NSF's EAGER program (EArly-concept Grants for Exploratory Research), support high-risk, high-reward projects that don't fit standard solicitations. As one researcher discovered, having a program officer suggest the EAGER mechanism after a conference conversation opened doors for innovative work that didn't align with any existing calls. These mechanisms reward researchers who build relationships with program officers and understand agency cultures beyond what's published in standard solicitations.

Working with federal agencies requires mastering their administrative requirements. Detailed budgets must account for every expense category according to federal guidelines. Indirect cost rates are typically nonnegotiable. Progress reports follow strict formats and deadlines. Data management plans must address federal requirements for sharing and archiving. While these requirements can feel burdensome, they also provide structure and accountability that can improve research quality.

The peer review process at federal agencies offers both challenges and opportunities. Review panels typically include researchers from related but not identical fields, requiring proposals that speak to broader audiences while maintaining technical sophistication. Understanding this reality helps explain why program officers often provide seemingly contradictory advice: be specific enough for experts but accessible enough for educated nonspecialists. See Chapter 12 for a detailed dive into writing for a reviewer audience.

Private Foundations: Mission-Driven Partnerships

Private foundations operate according to entirely different principles from federal agencies. Rather than serving broad public interests, foundations pursue specific theories of change aligned with their founders' visions or board priorities. Understanding these philosophical commitments is essential for determining fit.

The relationship-building process with foundations often begins years before any proposal submission. One senior researcher described spending years cultivating relationships with foundation program officers, including hosting site visits, providing informal research briefings, and demonstrating alignment with foundation values. During project execution, the program officer attended every team meeting, providing high-level direction to ensure the work advanced foundation priorities. This level of involvement can feel intrusive to academics accustomed to independence, but it's the price—and sometimes the benefit—of foundation support.

As you will see in Chapter 8, research administrators note that foundation funding presents unique challenges requiring different investigative skills. Julie Campos, a senior research administrator, explains how foundation funding often involves detective work: "Sometimes I'm told that we don't. There's not an RFA. And then I find out.... I start doing digging.... I will start poking around and doing some research online for that particular foundation. And then I might find out that actually, there is an RFA." This variability requires PIs and research administrators to uncover unstated requirements and informal application processes not immediately apparent.

Foundation funding processes vary dramatically. Some operate like federal agencies with open competitions and peer review. Others work more relationally, with program officers codeveloping ideas with researchers over months or years. In these cases, the written proposal merely documents agreements already reached through extensive dialogue. As one researcher observed, "We didn't write a proposal first. The program officer and I developed the idea together, then I wrote the research in a manner that matched the program's priorities."

Many foundations explicitly state they don't accept unsolicited proposals. Your only entry point might be submitting a letter of intent, typically just one or two pages, on which they'll base decisions about whether to invite a full proposal. These brief documents can determine access to millions of dollars in funding, making their careful crafting essential.

Elizabeth Carroll, a research administrator, observes an emerging trend that has particular implications for social scientists: "Foundations can often... require a video pitch. And a lot of these videos are high quality. So where they have a production team creating them." This requirement represents "a completely different skill set" that researchers rarely develop through traditional academic training. Even federal agencies are beginning to adopt these formats, with Elizabeth noting that "DARPA… they're asking for video pitches," indicating that skills traditionally associated with foundation funding may become more broadly applicable.

The advantages of foundation funding include greater flexibility in budget categories, fewer administrative requirements, and often more tolerance for project evolution as learning occurs. Foundations may fund advocacy, community organizing, or policy work that federal agencies cannot support. They might also provide general operating support rather than project-specific funding, offering sustainability that federal grants rarely provide.

However, foundation funding comes with its own constraints. Their theories of change may be rigid—a foundation committed to education reform through charter schools won't fund research on improving traditional public schools, regardless of merit. Board priorities can shift suddenly, eliminating entire program areas. The program officer who championed your work might leave, taking institutional memory and support with them.

State and Local Agencies: Solving Immediate Problems

State agencies rarely fund research for its own sake. Instead, they contract with researchers to solve specific, immediate problems using rigorous methods. This transactional approach differs fundamentally from federal or foundation funding models. The contract structure of state funding creates different dynamics from the start. Contracts specify explicit deliverables with concrete deadlines. A state transportation department doesn't want to advance knowledge about communication patterns—they want to know how to get drivers to slow down in work zones. This practical focus shapes every aspect of the relationship.

As research administrators in Chapter 8 emphasize, state funding occupies a particularly challenging middle ground. Julie Campos notes that state contracts frequently include provisions that can catch traveling researchers off guard, such as prohibitions on reimbursement for restaurant tips and requirements for every single receipt, creating administrative burdens that would be allowable under federal grants. "State funding often has the most restrictive travel policies I encounter," Julie explains. "Faculty who are accustomed to federal grant flexibility can find themselves personally responsible for legitimate business expenses that would be covered under NSF or NIH funding."

State agencies typically assign project managers who actively participate in research activities. These representatives attend regular team meetings, monitor progress against deliverables, and ensure projects stay on schedule. While this oversight might feel constraining, these project managers also serve as invaluable allies. When researchers need access to state employees for interviews or require data from state systems, project managers can open doors that would otherwise remain closed. Their emails carry authority that academic researchers lack.

The administrative requirements for state contracts often differ significantly from university norms. State travel regulations might prohibit reimbursement for tips, regardless of university policy. Invoice procedures may require detailed documentation linking every expense to specific contract tasks. These requirements aren't negotiable; they reflect accountability to state taxpayers and legislative oversight.

One unexpected requirement of state funding involves translating academic research for practitioner audiences. Researchers might need to present findings at conferences far outside their academic fields—emergency management associations, transportation summits, or public health gatherings. Success requires developing new communication skills to reach audiences who need practical guidance, not theoretical insights.

Finding state funding opportunities requires different strategies than federal searches. Rather than browsing comprehensive databases, researchers often learn about opportunities through professional networks in specific topic areas. A researcher studying flood communication connects with the state agency handling flood response. Someone examining educational disparities builds relationships with the state education department. These connections often develop through years of engaged scholarship within state boundaries.

City and local government funding operates similarly but on a smaller scale. Cities might establish partnerships with local universities for specific research projects. A city planning department might need help evaluating a new bike lane system. A county health department might want to understand vaccination hesitancy in specific communities. These projects tend to be smaller in scope but can provide valuable local connections and highly applied research experience.

Corporate Funding: Opportunities and Complexities

Another potential funding source that deserves careful consideration is corporate funding. While corporate partnerships can provide substantial resources and access to unique data or infrastructure, they come with distinct complexities that differ from traditional grant mechanisms. Publication restrictions represent one key consideration. Some corporations may want to review findings before publication, delay publication to protect competitive advantages, or restrict what findings can be published at all. These restrictions can conflict with academic norms around open scholarship and timely dissemination of findings. Before entering any corporate funding arrangement, carefully review any publication restrictions and consider whether they're compatible with your tenure requirements and scholarly values.

Intellectual property (IP) ownership creates another layer of complexity. Universities operate as nonprofit educational institutions with particular missions around knowledge creation and dissemination. Many corporate funders want to retain rights to any intellectual property generated through funded research, which can create fundamental conflicts with university policies. Some institutions will not allow you to accept corporate funding if the contract requires the university to assign IP ownership to the corporation. Here's where it gets particularly complicated: even if you believe your social science research won't generate any patentable IP, your institution's research administration team must still protect institutional interests. They're required to consider "what if" scenarios—what if some aspect of this research does generate commercializable IP? What if these findings lead to tool development or methodology that has market value? This explains why contract negotiations for corporate funding typically take much longer than federal funding—universities already have standard agreements with federal agencies, but each corporate contract must be negotiated from scratch.

A real-world example illustrates these challenges: During the COVID-19 pandemic, Keri was approached by a corporation that owned extensive workplace communication data showing how people used multiple platforms during the sudden shift to remote work. The corporation wanted to provide this rich dataset for analysis, which would have been invaluable for understanding communication patterns during a historic moment. However, after six months of attempted contract negotiations between her institution and the corporation, they couldn't reach agreement on terms that satisfied both parties. Despite the research opportunity, she ultimately had to decline and lost access to that unique dataset. But she has also had successful corporate partnerships that provided valuable resources and data. The key difference? In successful cases, we started conversations about contract terms early—before investing significant time in proposal development. We involved our research administration team from the beginning, and we allowed sufficient time for the negotiation process (often three to six months or longer). We also maintained realistic expectations about what terms our institutions could and couldn't accept.

If you're considering corporate funding, follow these guidelines:

- Contact your research administration office before you start developing the proposal—they need to know about corporate partnerships early
- Ask your research administrator what types of contract terms your institution typically accepts or rejects
- Build in three to six months (or more) for contract negotiation before any deadlines
- Get any verbal agreements or promises from the corporate partner in writing
- Be prepared to walk away if contract terms aren't compatible with your institution's requirements or your scholarly values
- Consider whether publication restrictions are acceptable given your career stage and tenure requirements

Corporate funding can work well when expectations align and sufficient time is devoted to the negotiation process. Just remember that the complexity of these arrangements requires extra planning, patience, and institutional support.

Cooperative Agreements: A Partnership Model

We've discussed grants and contracts, but another funding mechanism deserves attention: cooperative agreements. While these may be less common for early-career researchers, understanding this mechanism helps you recognize opportunities when they arise. A cooperative agreement represents a partnership model where the federal agency remains substantially involved in the project. Unlike traditional grants where the funder provides resources but has limited involvement in project execution, or contracts where the funder specifies exact deliverables but the contractor determines methods, cooperative agreements position the funding agency as an integral partner in various aspects of the research.

In a cooperative agreement, federal staff might do any of the following activities:

- Provide specialized technical resources or expertise not available elsewhere
- Give access to unique datasets, facilities, or populations
- Collaborate on data analysis using proprietary or highly sophisticated methods
- Participate in study design modifications based on emerging findings
- Coauthor publications resulting from the research

Cooperative agreements are particularly common in public health research, where agencies like the CDC might fund research while simultaneously providing access to surveillance systems, laboratory facilities, or specialized epidemiological expertise. However, they can occur across many research domains and at various funding levels. If you're considering a cooperative agreement opportunity, understand that you're committing to genuine partnership with the federal agency. This may mean more frequent communication and reporting than typical grants require, shared decision-making on key aspects of the project, and recognition that agency coauthors will contribute to and potentially modify research directions.

Box 3.3 The Funding Alignment Matrix: Evaluating Opportunities Systematically

This matrix helps you evaluate potential funding opportunities across multiple dimensions, making implicit judgments explicit and comparable. Use this tool for any opportunity requiring more than twenty hours of proposal preparation.

Instructions: Score each item from 1 (poor fit) to 5 (excellent fit).

RESEARCH ALIGNMENT

- Core questions match: How closely do fundable topics align with your research interests?
- Methodological fit: Does the funder support your preferred research approaches?
- Theoretical compatibility: Can you pursue theoretical development alongside practical goals?
- Population/context match: Does your work with specific populations fit their priorities?

PRACTICAL CONSIDERATIONS

- Budget adequacy: Does maximum funding cover true project costs including indirect?
- Timeline reasonableness: Do project periods allow for rigorous research and dissemination?
- Administrative burden: Are reporting and compliance requirements manageable?
- Institutional support: Does your institution have infrastructure for this funder?

CAREER ADVANCEMENT

- Publication potential: Can you publish findings in your target journals?
- Tenure/promotion value: Will your institution value this funding for advancement?
- Skill development: Will you gain valuable new competencies?

- Network building: Does this create important collaborative opportunities?

FUNDER FIT

- Mission alignment: Does your work genuinely advance funder goals?
- Competitive advantage: Do you offer unique qualifications for this call?
- Review panel fit: Will reviewers likely understand and value your approach?
- Past funding patterns: Has this program funded similar work before?
- University/institutional support: Does your organization have the facilities and resources that can enhance the quality and feasibility of the proposal?

SCORING INTERPRETATION

Examine how you rated each major category and the items within each one. The ratings are only meant to have you think strategically about a funding opportunity. If you do this same exercise with multiple opportunities, you can compare them and make informed decisions around which ones to pursue and in which priority.

Building Your Funding Portfolio

Experienced researchers rarely rely on single funding sources. Instead, they build diversified portfolios balancing different types of support, much like financial advisors recommend diversifying investments. A mature funding portfolio might include federal grants providing core support for basic research, foundation funding enabling community partnerships, state contracts generating quick wins and practical applications, internal seed grants exploring emerging ideas, and industry partnerships for specialized projects. Together, they create more impactful research than any single source would support. Portfolio thinking also helps evaluate imperfect opportunities. A state contract requiring extensive reporting might seem burdensome, but if it funds graduate students and provides access to crucial data, it might deserve a small portion of your time. The key is to ensure that no single funder dominates your research agenda.

Every experienced researcher has stories of spectacular mismatches—proposals that never should have been written, relationships that soured, projects that satisfied no one. These failures provide valuable learning if you're willing to examine them honestly. Common mismatch patterns include forcing theoretical research into applied frameworks, underestimating philosophical differences with funders, accepting severe underfunding hoping to "make it work," ignoring early warning signs about funder expectations, and pursuing prestige over genuine alignment.

One researcher spent six months writing an elaborate proposal for a foundation whose program officer seemed enthusiastic in initial conversations. Only after rejection did they realize the foundation's board had shifted priorities, something the program officer had hinted at but never stated directly. The lesson: pay attention to subtle signals and ask direct questions about funder stability.

The most successful researchers view funders as long-term partners rather than one-time ATMs. This shift in perspective changes everything about how you approach funding relationships. Start by delivering excellent work on initial grants, even small ones. Meet deadlines, communicate proactively about challenges, and produce high-quality deliverables. Program officers remember researchers who make their jobs easier. They're more likely to encourage future applications or suggest other opportunities.

Maintain relationships between grants through brief updates about publications, policy impacts, or media coverage. These touchpoints keep you visible without being burdensome. When new opportunities arise, program officers think of researchers they know and trust. Contributing to the funding ecosystem through proposal reviews provides invaluable education while building credibility. You'll see what excites reviewers, recognize common mistakes, and understand funder perspectives. This insider knowledge improves your own proposals immeasurably.

The Critical Importance of Following Guidelines

Across all funder types—internal, federal, foundation, or state—one principle remains paramount: follow the guidelines exactly. This seems obvious, yet violations remain among the most common reasons for proposal rejection. Kerk has heard more than once that if you can't follow guidelines during the proposal stage, how can funders trust you'll follow their rules during project execution?

Program officers at federal agencies deal with hundreds or thousands of proposals. An easy first cut eliminates those that don't follow basic formatting requirements, page limits, or submission procedures. This isn't bureaucratic rigidity—it's practical necessity and fairness to those who do follow rules. Foundation officers, even with smaller proposal volumes, still use guideline adherence as an initial quality filter. Be sure to read Chapter 13, "Writing Mechanics," for more details about how to make your proposals stronger.

The message is clear: read guidelines multiple times, highlighting different requirement categories. Create checklists ensuring you've addressed every element. Have research administrators and colleagues review your proposal specifically for guideline compliance. When in doubt, contact the program officer for clarification rather than making assumptions. The extra time invested in careful compliance pays dividends in avoiding easy rejections.

Conclusion

Finding the right funding match requires patience, strategy, and self-awareness about what compromises you're willing to make. Perfect alignment is rare; successful researchers learn to identify "good enough" matches that advance their work while serving funder goals. The key insight is recognizing that finding funding is just like finding journals—a process you've already mastered. Apply the same systematic thinking, relationship building, and strategic patience that you use in publishing. Study the landscape, understand different funder cultures, build relationships over time, and learn from both successes and failures.

Never submit anything without prior conversation with a program officer—unlike journal submissions, funding requires relationship building before proposal writing. Whether through formal channels or fish fry conversations, these interactions provide invaluable intelligence about fit, competitiveness, and funder priorities.

The colleague who forwards you mismatched opportunities means well but hasn't done the deep work of understanding alignment. Thank them, then do your own detective work. Use the strategies in this chapter—from systematic investigation to direct engagement with program officers—to find opportunities that genuinely fit your research. Most importantly, maintain perspective. Funding is a tool for advancing knowledge, not an end in itself. The best matches amplify your ability to contribute meaningful research while building toward long-term sustainability. With strategic thinking and patient persistence, you'll find your place in the funding world, supporting work that matters while maintaining your scholarly integrity.

4

Partnerships and Community Engagement

The landscape of external funding has fundamentally shifted toward recognizing partnerships as essential components of impactful research. While not all funded research requires a partnership approach, funding agencies increasingly prioritize projects that demonstrate meaningful collaboration with communities, organizations, and stakeholders who can both inform the research and benefit from its outcomes. These partnerships go beyond traditional academic collaborations, extending into genuine relationships with the communities that researchers study and serve. The stories of researchers who have successfully navigated this terrain reveal that building authentic partnerships requires time, trust, and a fundamental commitment to addressing real-world problems rather than purely theoretical questions.

The Evolving Role of Partnerships in Research Funding

Federal agencies, foundations, and other funding sources have recognized that research conducted in isolation from its intended beneficiaries often fails to achieve meaningful impact. This recognition has led to explicit requirements for community engagement, stakeholder involvement, and collaborative approaches in many funding opportunities. The National

Science Foundation emphasizes broader impacts and societal impacts, the National Institutes of Health prioritizes community-based participatory research (Satcher, 2005), and private foundations often require evidence of genuine partnership with the populations served.

However, the partnership requirement represents more than a bureaucratic checkbox. Effective partnerships fundamentally transform research from an extractive process—where academics study communities and then leave—into a collaborative endeavor where knowledge creation serves mutual goals. This transformation requires researchers to develop new skills, adopt different mindsets, and invest significant time in relationship building that may not immediately translate into traditional academic outputs.

From Theoretical Inquiry to Community Integration

Kerk's journey into the cyberinfrastructure community illustrates how academic research can evolve from purely theoretical inquiry into deep community engagement that ultimately enables sustained funding success. His story began with a dissertation focused on theoretical questions about technology adoption and diffusion. Initially approaching cyberinfrastructure—the computational systems and networks that support scientific research—from a detached academic perspective, Kerk did not start out with an intention for the group he studied to become his genuine community.

The transformation began with a simple interview question designed to capture anything missed: "Is there anything else you would like to tell me? Are there questions that you thought I should have asked?" This open-ended inquiry, intended merely to ensure comprehensive data collection, instead revealed a fundamental disconnect between academic interests and community needs. Respondents didn't offer theoretical insights; they posed practical questions about real challenges they faced. They wanted to know how to increase adoption of their technologies, how to sustain their infrastructure projects, and how to demonstrate impact to funders.

This feedback challenged Kerk to reconsider his approach. Drawing on grounded theory principles that emphasize letting findings emerge from data rather than imposing preconceived frameworks, he began orienting his research toward questions that mattered to the cyberinfrastructure community. This shift required more than changing research questions; it demanded authentic engagement with the community itself.

Acting on advice from a colleague—who pointed out that truly understanding the community required attending their conferences rather than conducting distant phone interviews—Kerk began participating in TeraGrid (later XSEDE, and now PEARC) conferences. Initially, financial constraints as a graduate student made this challenging, but once he secured his first NSF grant, he deliberately built conference participation into his research design.

This physical presence transformed everything. Kerk didn't just attend sessions; he conducted interviews on-site, recruited participants through snowball sampling, and, crucially, engaged in member checking by sharing his findings back with the community. This reciprocal approach, where research insights flowed back to benefit those studied, caught the attention of cyberinfrastructure community leaders. They began to see him not as an outside observer but as someone genuinely interested in their challenges and committed to helping address them.

Recognition grew organically. Community members started saying, "You need to talk to Kerk. He understands our adoption challenges." Invitations followed to join working groups, co-organize conference sessions, and participate in strategic planning efforts. When major cyberinfrastructure initiatives needed social science perspectives on their teams, Kerk's name surfaced repeatedly. His reputation as someone who cared about the community, understood their technical challenges, and could translate between social science insights and practical applications made him invaluable.

This integration wasn't without costs. Attending conferences, participating in working groups, and maintaining relationships required significant time and financial investment, activities that didn't directly count toward tenure at his institution. Colleagues questioned whether he was "wasting time" on service rather than focusing on traditional academic outputs. Yet this investment built the foundation for sustained research funding. When Kerk applied for his NSF CAREER award, he could assemble an advisory board of respected cyberinfrastructure leaders who genuinely supported his work because they had witnessed its value firsthand.

The relationships deepened over the years. One early interviewee became a close friend whose family Kerk knew personally. When this soft-money researcher faced elimination of his position, he reached out to Kerk for help transferring his active grant to another institution. The trust built through years of genuine engagement enabled Kerk to facilitate this transition, demonstrating how professional partnerships can evolve into meaningful personal connections that transcend individual projects. See the References for some of the meaningful research Kerk has published from these cyberinfrastructure projects.

Building Trust in Disaster Research

Keri's path to community-engaged research took a different route, emerging from direct experience with crisis and a commitment to ensuring research serves those most affected by disasters. Her journey began with an institutional communication audit, a seemingly straightforward service-learning project that revealed the complexity of truly understanding organizational life. When her graduate student returned from late-night data collection with employees who worked 24/7 shifts, the student's reaction was telling: "Thank you for this opportunity. I never want to do this again. I would rather work with data than actually collect data directly from people through field projects."

This student's honest response highlighted a fundamental divide in research approaches. Some scholars thrive on controlled experiments with undergraduate subjects, viewing human participants primarily as data sources. Others, like Keri, find meaning in understanding the lived experiences of people facing real challenges. The student's preference for "detached" research, focused on variables rather than the people, was perfectly valid but incompatible with the community-engaged approach that would define Keri's career.

Hurricane Harvey catalyzed Keri's deep dive into community partnerships. As a flood survivor herself, she felt compelled to contribute meaningfully to recovery efforts. However, she understood that showing up as an untrained volunteer would burden already-stressed communities. Instead, she sought to contribute through research that could genuinely help affected populations. An undergraduate student helped identify a church donating space for federal disaster assistance paperwork processing. The church's suggestion was practical: flood victims waited hours for assistance; perhaps they would participate in research interviews during the wait. This arrangement served mutual needs by providing data for research while offering flood victims an opportunity to share their experiences during an otherwise frustrating wait.

Keri's approach went beyond extraction. Noticing that many flood victims' phones were dying while they waited, she purchased phone chargers to share. This small gesture served the practical purpose of ensuring phones remained charged for the photo elicitation interviews her team was conducting while demonstrating care for participants' immediate needs. Every interaction reinforced that she saw participants as whole people deserving respect, not merely data sources. See the references for some of the meaningful research resulting from this project.

The trust built through such genuine concern yielded powerful moments. When one participant noticed the National Science Foundation funding acknowledgment on the consent form and questioned whether the government would access her data, the conversation that followed revealed both vulnerability and trust. After Keri explained data protection protocols and anonymization procedures, the woman chose to proceed with the interview because she trusted Keri to protect her story while ensuring it could contribute to improving disaster response.

Becoming Part of the Community Fabric

Both authors' experiences demonstrate that meaningful partnerships require moving beyond periodic engagement to becoming recognized members of the communities they study. For Kerk, this meant years of conference attendance, service on organizing committees, and consistent presence that led community members to say, "Oh, that's Kerk. He's the one who brings students to interview us about adoption challenges." His integration became so complete that conference organizers would offer quiet spaces for his research team's interviews, and participants would ask unfamiliar interviewers, "Are you one of Kerk's students?"

Keri's integration into emergency management communities followed a similar pattern of sustained engagement. Working with a community association conducting a wildfire evacuation drill (Stephens & Boettner, 2020; Stephens et al., 2023), she attended monthly planning meetings for over a year, driving through traffic to Lake Travis repeatedly. As the drill approached, meetings intensified to several times per week. This sustained presence demonstrated commitment that communities recognized and reciprocated.

The depth of these relationships became evident in continued invitations years later. The community that conducted multiple wildfire drills invited Keri to after-action reviews, celebrations, and planning sessions for future exercises. Seven years after initial engagement, invitations still arrive for community events because she's considered part of their extended network—someone who genuinely cares about their preparedness and resilience.

The Challenge of Extractive Research

Research has traditionally operated on an extractive model: researchers enter communities, collect data, publish findings in academic journals, and move on. Communities rarely benefit directly from participating, and research findings seldom address their practical challenges. This approach increasingly fails to meet funder expectations or community needs.

Both Kerk and Keri encountered explicit challenges to this model. When Kerk promised to share findings with research participants, one respondent expressed doubt and challenged whether the "academics" would just analyze problems or if they would offer actionable solutions.

Similarly, when Keri entered a room of county officials in rural Texas—having kept them waiting due to road construction, she faced direct questioning about her motives. A road crew supervisor stood up and demanded: "Why are you really here? What are your motives? How much money are you getting to do this project?" These moments of testing required honest responses. When Keri disclosed the million-dollar grant amount, audible gasps filled the room because the sum exceeded some communities' entire annual road budgets. Yet her honesty, combined with a genuine commitment to using funds to reduce flood risk in their communities, earned trust. "OK, I trust you now," the questioner said, sitting down. From that moment, she was treated as a community member rather than an outside researcher.

Solutions-Focused Research: Meeting Community Needs

The shift from problem identification to solution development represents a fundamental reorientation of research priorities. Traditional academic training emphasizes theoretical contributions and critical analysis of problems. Journal reviewers often explicitly state that practical solutions "aren't theoretical enough" for publication. Yet communities desperately need actionable insights that improve their daily lives. This tension requires researchers to become, in effect, bilingual, capable of producing theoretical insights for academic audiences while generating practical solutions for community partners. The theoretical framework remains important; for instance, Keri's work in Alaska examines how high-reliability organizing functions differently in extreme climates. But the driving questions focus on uncovering what works: "What's the magic? When you're constantly in crisis, dealing with severe weather, what makes it work?"

This solutions-oriented approach transforms research relationships. As one Alaskan community member explained, "When we have a real crisis, people just act. We come together. There's no politics.... The problems come when situations aren't acute." This insight—that effective emergency response emerges from immediate necessity while longer-term preparedness suffers from political fragmentation—offers both theoretical richness and practical guidance for improving community resilience.

Community Partners as Team Members: Bridging Research and Practice

Increasingly, funding agencies emphasize meaningful community engagement in research projects, creating opportunities for community partners to serve in formal roles beyond traditional advisory positions. These roles can range from advisory board membership to full co-PI status (see Chapter 5 for detailed definitions of these different roles), each bringing unique opportunities and challenges that require careful consideration and planning.

The integration of community partners into research teams reflects a broader shift in funding priorities. Agencies like the Patient-Centered Outcomes Research Institute (PCORI) have pioneered approaches where patients and community members serve as genuine research partners rather than merely subjects of study. Some proposals include researchers who have personal experience with certain diseases as co-PIs, while others involve patients without research backgrounds in similar leadership roles. Stakeholders increasingly participate in study design, including generating research questions and hypotheses, ensuring that research addresses real community needs and incorporates lived experiences from the beginning.

When community partners join research teams as co-PIs or coinvestigators, the administrative challenges can be substantial. Most community organizations lack the infrastructure that universities have developed for grant management. A community partner who has never interacted with federal funding agencies must navigate complex registration processes, create biosketches despite having no traditional academic credentials, and learn reporting requirements that seem second nature to academic researchers but can be overwhelming to newcomers.

One emergency management coordinator who joined one of Keri's research teams as a co-PI exemplified both the challenges and rewards of meaningful community partnership. Without a strong partnering university research administration team to help him obtain an NSF ID and navigate the institutional approvals required from his agency, his participation would have been impossible. The research administrator walked him through every step, from initial registration to final documentation. The process proved so challenging that the team maintained a backup plan to shift him to an advisory board role if they couldn't complete his coinvestigator establishment in time. They started months in advance but still weren't certain they would meet the deadline until the day before submission. Yet the effort proved worthwhile. When the grant was funded, the emergency manager's pride in being a co-PI on an NSF grant was palpable—he told everyone he encountered about this achievement. His involvement brought credibility and practical insights that strengthened the project immeasurably, and the team published many papers with him as a coauthor (e.g., Hughes et al., 2022; Peterson et al., 2019). His agency saw the value of the partnership and became more supportive of future collaborations, creating lasting benefits beyond the single project.

Not all community partners face equal challenges in formal research roles. Those with previous academic experience often transition more smoothly. An executive director of a museum who had previously served as a faculty member could readily compile an impressive biosketch and understand the institutional requirements. His academic background allowed him to translate between community and research contexts effectively, making him an ideal coinvestigator who brought both community connections and research expertise.

These contrasting experiences highlight an important principle: choose community partner roles based on genuine capacity and contribution, not just ease of administration. While it may be simpler to work with community partners who have academic backgrounds, the most valuable partnerships often come from engaging those deeply embedded in communities who bring perspectives and connections that no academic could provide. The key is providing appropriate support to enable their meaningful participation.

Additional considerations arise when community partners participate in human subjects research. If they will be part of data collection or analysis, they must complete the same human subjects training required of all researchers, such as Collaborative Institutional Training Initiative (CITI) training (CITI, n.d.). This requirement can create unexpected barriers. When working with community partners whose highest education levels were fifth and sixth grade, Keri made the difficult but ethical decision that they could not reasonably complete the complex training modules filled with academic jargon. Instead of forcing them through training they couldn't meaningfully complete, the team found other valuable roles for these partners that didn't require human subjects' involvement.

This situation illustrates the importance of thoughtfully considering what we ask of community partners. The goal is to build genuine partnerships that leverage everyone's strengths, not create situations where partners feel embarrassed or unable to contribute. Researchers must balance the desire for meaningful involvement with realistic assessment of capacity and the support available. Sometimes the most respectful approach involves finding alternative ways for community members to contribute their invaluable expertise without forcing them into ill-fitting academic structures.

The Time and Trust Investment

Building authentic partnerships requires substantial investment that often goes unrecognized in traditional academic reward structures. Both Kerk and Keri invested years developing relationships before seeing tangible research outcomes. Conference attendance, community meetings, relationship maintenance, and trust building consume time that could be spent on activities that "count" more directly for tenure and promotion.

The financial costs are equally real. Before securing travel funding through grants, researchers often pay personally to maintain community connections. Keri's drives to Lake Travis, Kerk's conference attendance, and countless other relationship-building activities required personal investment based on faith that meaningful partnerships would eventually emerge. Yet these investments yield returns that multiply over time. When Kerk needs letters of collaboration for new proposals, a simple request to his cyberinfrastructure network yields enthusiastic support. When Keri identifies community needs that align with funding opportunities, a phone call to established partners generates budget estimates and collaboration letters within days. The trust built through years of genuine engagement cannot be manufactured quickly when grant deadlines loom.

Sustaining Partnerships Beyond Project Cycles

Perhaps the greatest challenge in community-engaged research involves maintaining relationships beyond specific funding cycles. Communities rightfully grow skeptical of researchers who appear when grants are active and disappear when funding ends. An added challenge is setting partners' expectations, especially since most proposals are not funded on a first submission. A partner that thinks the funding is definitely going to come and then is disappointed when it doesn't (or worse, has planned for the funding and now doesn't have it) is not going to be one that can be a lasting partner across multiple projects.

Sustaining partnerships requires creative approaches to maintaining presence and demonstrating ongoing commitment even without active funding. We both want to emphasize that partnership obligations don't end with project completion. Communities that have shared their challenges and trusted researchers with their stories deserve continued engagement. This might mean attending community events without research objectives, providing informal consultation based on accumulated expertise, or simply maintaining personal connections that transcend professional relationships.

The sustainability challenge creates a cycle where researchers need continued funding to maintain community relationships that enable future funding success. This reality requires strategic thinking about funding portfolios, with overlapping projects that maintain community presence even as specific initiatives end. It also demands honesty with communities about funding constraints while demonstrating commitment that transcends any single grant.

Translating Partnership Success for Academic Recognition

While funding agencies increasingly value community partnerships, traditional academic reward structures often lag in recognizing this work. Time spent building relationships, attending community meetings, and developing trust may be dismissed as "service" rather than recognized as essential research infrastructure. Publications resulting from community-engaged research may take longer to produce and target different venues than traditional academic journals.

This misalignment requires researchers to become advocates for recognizing partnership work within their institutions. Documenting partnership activities, articulating their essential role in funding success, and educating tenure committees about changing funder expectations all become necessary tasks. Some institutions have begun recognizing community engagement as valuable scholarship, but widespread change remains slow.

The key is demonstrating how partnership-based research advances both academic knowledge and community well-being. When million-dollar grants flow from community relationships, when research findings directly influence emergency management practices, when communities themselves testify to research value, the impact becomes undeniable. We strongly believe this work deserves academic credit because it represents a legitimate and increasingly essential form of scholarship that funding agencies explicitly value.

The Ethical Imperative of Non-Extractive Research

Beyond funding success, partnership-based research responds to ethical imperatives about research's role in society. Academic research has contributed to its own credibility crisis by producing knowledge that seems irrelevant to public concerns. When communities see researchers arrive, extract data, and disappear without sharing findings or addressing real problems, they rightfully question academia's value.

Partnership approaches offer a different model where research serves mutual goals. Communities gain access to resources, expertise, and evidence-based solutions. Researchers gain authentic understanding, sustained access, and the satisfaction of contributing to meaningful change. Funders see their investments yielding both scientific advances and societal benefits.

This ethical dimension becomes particularly salient when working with vulnerable populations. Whether flood victims in Texas, rural communities in Alaska, or any group facing significant challenges, researchers bear responsibility for ensuring their work benefits those who share their stories and challenges. This responsibility extends beyond avoiding harm to actively pursuing positive impact.

Partnerships as Pathways to Impact

The experiences of successful partnership-based researchers reveal fundamental truths about external funding in contemporary academic environments. While not all research requires community partnerships, funding agencies increasingly recognize that sustainable impact emerges from genuine collaboration with those affected by research outcomes. Building such partnerships requires abandoning extractive research models in favor of sustained engagement, mutual benefit, and solutions-focused approaches.

The journey from theoretical inquiry to community integration, exemplified by Kerk's cyberinfrastructure work, shows how openness to community needs can transform research trajectories and enable sustained funding success. Similarly, Keri's evolution from institutional communication audits to disaster research partnerships demonstrates how personal commitment and authentic care create possibilities for meaningful impact.

These partnerships demand significant investments of time, money, and emotional energy that may not align with traditional academic reward structures. They require researchers to become bilingual, producing theoretical insights for academic audiences while generating practical solutions for community partners. They challenge researchers to maintain relationships beyond funding cycles and to view communities as genuine partners rather than data sources.

Yet the rewards—both tangible and intangible—justify these investments. Letters of collaboration flow readily from established partners. Funding proposals gain credibility from demonstrated community support. Research findings achieve real-world impact because they address genuine needs identified through sustained engagement.

Perhaps most importantly, researchers experience the satisfaction of work that matters: scholarship that advances knowledge while improving lives.

As funding landscapes continue evolving toward partnership models, researchers who develop authentic community relationships position themselves for sustained success. But beyond strategic considerations, partnership-based research offers something more profound: an opportunity to ensure academic scholarship serves society's needs. In an era when academia faces credibility challenges and funding constraints, demonstrating research value through community impact becomes not just advantageous but essential.

The stories shared here illustrate that building meaningful partnerships is neither quick nor easy. It requires patience, humility, and genuine commitment to community well-being. It demands skills beyond traditional academic training and time investments that may not immediately yield publishable outputs. Yet, for researchers willing to make these investments, partnerships open doors to funding opportunities, create possibilities for meaningful impact, and ultimately transform both communities studied and researchers themselves. The trust earned through years of authentic engagement becomes the foundation for research that truly matters—scholarship that serves both academic advancement and human flourishing.

The next chapter delves deeply into the various roles researchers can play on externally funded projects. You have already heard us throw around terms like *principal investigator* (PI) and *advisory boards*; that chapter provides detailed examples of what each role entails. As you read that chapter, consider your goals with external funding. Which of these roles fits your career right now, and which roles might you want to expand into for the future?

5

Understanding Different Roles and Responsibilities

In the world of funded research, roles are more than titles—they signal responsibility, authority, recognition, and labor expectations. Understanding the distinctions among principal investigator (PI), co-PI, senior personnel, advisory board member, and other roles is essential for social scientists who want to navigate interdisciplinary projects effectively, advocate for their contributions, and make strategic career decisions. The role you accept on a grant team will determine not only your day-to-day responsibilities but also how your contributions are recognized in databases, how much control you have over project direction, and what benefits you receive from the collaboration.

Before committing to leading your own grant as a principal investigator, it is valuable to understand the ecosystem of roles available on grant teams. Each role comes with different expectations, benefits, and challenges. For tenure-track faculty and graduate students, starting in a supporting role can provide valuable experience while minimizing risk and allowing you to learn the complexities of grant management without bearing full responsibility for project administration.

This chapter explores the full spectrum of grant roles, from entry-level positions that provide learning opportunities to senior leadership positions that require sophisticated project management skills. We will examine the strategic considerations for choosing roles at different career stages, the unique challenges social scientists face in interdisciplinary collaborations, and the pathways from token participation to meaningful intellectual contribution.

Consultant Role: A Low-Risk Entry Point

The term *consultant* can have many different meanings. At some institutions, the term refers to individuals who are paid as an individual (not as a subcontractor) and who are not at the PI's institution. At other times, the term refers to a specific contributor to grants and they can be located at the same institution as the investigators. These individuals often bring in expertise without the full responsibility of a PI or co-PI. This arrangement frequently emerges because large collaborative projects cannot accommodate everyone as a co-PI—NSF grants typically allow only one PI plus four co-PIs maximum. For early career scholars, consulting on a grant can provide valuable experience while bringing funding to a new position, creating an immediate positive impression with colleagues and administrators.

Noga, an assistant professor of linguistics, started her grant journey as a consultant on a Department of Education project studying bilingual education. The $50,000 consulting fee over two years provided summer salary and research funds while teaching her about federal grant management without the full administrative burden. This experience allowed her to observe how project timelines unfold, how budgets are managed, and how reporting requirements work, all while contributing to her specialized expertise in language acquisition.

The consultant role offers several advantages for tenure-track faculty. First, it carries minimal administrative burden, allowing you to focus on your specific contribution rather than managing the entire project. Second, it provides flexibility in time commitment, which is crucial when you are balancing teaching loads, coursework, or other research obligations. Third, it offers an opportunity to learn grant management processes without bearing full responsibility for project success or failure. Finally, it creates potential for authorship and publication opportunities without the extensive project management that comes with leadership roles.

However, consultant roles also come with limitations that early-career faculty should understand. Your level of control over project direction may be minimal, and you may have little input into decisions that affect your work. Additionally, consultant roles may not carry the same prestige or recognition as PI or co-PI positions when it comes to tenure evaluation, though they still demonstrate your ability to secure external funding.

A critical decision consultants face is whether it is possible or desirable to route payment through their university or receive it directly. When payment goes through the university, the institution takes indirect costs—often a substantial percentage—but the researcher gains institutional recognition for bringing in funding. Direct payment provides higher personal compensation but no institutional credit. This creates potentially awkward situations with university administrators who may prefer not to know about payments that bypass university indirect costs. Some senior researchers create elaborate mechanisms for these arrangements, such as establishing business-like limited liability corporations to receive grant funds. In such a case, they can also pay consultants directly. Whether consultants get paid directly or through their institution is much more complicated than making a personal decision. They need to consider if institutional resources are being used, and if they are, the payment almost certainly must go through the university. They also need to consider the following potential issues: the tax implications for the researcher who is receiving additional income, and the percentage of their time they will spend on the project and if that can affect their other university obligations. While getting paid as a consultant is possible, it's important to talk about it with someone who understands the university's regulations around these issues.

Advisory Board Member: Providing Strategic Guidance

One of the other roles that researchers can serve in funded projects is as an advisory board member. This opportunity typically arises when a colleague familiar with your work reaches out to say they're assembling a grant proposal that will include an advisory board. Usually consisting of three to ten people, these boards provide strategic guidance and expertise to the project team without the day-to-day involvement required of investigators.

For funded research projects, advisory board members are often compensated, though the amounts are typically modest. You might receive $500 for meeting twice a year for an hour each time and reviewing proposal documents or providing specific feedback. While this may not seem like substantial compensation, the real value lies elsewhere. Advisory board participation offers an excellent way to observe the entire grant process unfold, contribute your expertise to meaningful projects, and build relationships with research teams—all while maintaining a manageable time commitment.

When asked to serve on an advisory board, think carefully about whether you can genuinely contribute to the project. Your participation might be sought for various reasons: expertise in a particular research method, theoretical framing, community connections, or subject matter knowledge. The best advisory board experiences occur when the PI is explicit about exactly what they need from you. Clear expectations make it easier for board members to provide valuable contributions and feel comfortable committing to the role.

Advisory board members are typically asked to provide a letter of collaboration or support as part of the grant application. Best practice for PIs is to be very explicit about expectations, telling potential board members exactly what will be asked of them and where their expertise fits into the project. This clarity helps advisory board members understand the commitment involved, and depending on the funding source, the board member may be able to write a more detailed letter of support.

For social scientists new to the grant process or those interested in collaborating with a particular team, advisory board membership represents an excellent opportunity. Even experienced PIs have learned that advisory board service can lead to deeper involvement in future projects. When advisory board members prove themselves to be helpful, insightful, and collaborative, they often find themselves invited to participate in subsequent proposals as senior personnel or even co-PIs. This progression reflects how experienced PIs often use advisory board positions to build relationships with potential collaborators, essentially providing a low-risk way to assess compatibility before entering into more formal partnerships.

Senior Personnel Role: Contributing to a Specific Part of the Project

Being senior personnel often allows for focus on a specific project component without broad administrative burdens. Because key leadership positions (PI/co-I) are often limited in number, senior personnel roles are an excellent way to extend the expertise of the full project team. People in these roles often contribute biosketches and have other documents required for their participation in the proposal. After receiving the award and conducting the research, senior personnel can sometimes have more publication freedom with fewer obligatory coauthors, and can still receive indirect cost credit if funding is routed through their institution.

The senior personnel role can provide valuable experience and funding, but it requires careful negotiation about authorship, recognition, and the specific deliverables for which you will be responsible. It is important to clarify upfront how your contributions will be acknowledged in publications and presentations, and to ensure that your work is visible to the broader scholarly community.

The senior personnel designation can emerge when co-PI slots are filled but a researcher is still doing significant work on the project. This frequently happens on large multimillion-dollar center grants spanning multiple institutions where all the co-PI slots are taken before additional institutions join. Even when functioning essentially as a co-PI, senior personnel are not typically listed among the project leadership listed in databases, creating a disconnect between actual contribution and official recognition. While you may be doing co-PI-level work, external reviewers examining your CV may not understand the scope of your contribution if you are listed only as senior personnel. This makes it crucial to document your actual contributions carefully and to ensure that your role is accurately described.

Senior personnel status can sometimes result from strategic decisions about project presentation. A researcher might initially be listed as a co-PI on a proposal, but as the collaboration grows, they may be moved to senior personnel so a more established researcher can be elevated to co-PI. Such decisions aim to present the strongest possible team on paper to enhance funding chances. This role change can occur despite bringing additional collaborators to the project, highlighting how power dynamics and strategic considerations can override contribution levels in role assignments.

Co-PI Role: Shared Leadership, Shared Challenges

Co-PIs (also called Co-I's with some funders) are part of the leadership team along with the PI. They shoulder significant responsibility and leadership, though still with less control than the PI, particularly over budget decisions. In multi-institutional collaborations, being a sub-awardee can make someone a PI at their own institution, while collaborative proposals can effectively double the number of PI/co-PI slots by having each institution submit connected proposals. Co-PIs typically have significant input into project direction and are expected to contribute to all major project decisions. This increased responsibility comes with greater potential rewards, including stronger authorship opportunities and more significant recognition for the project's success. However, it also means greater accountability if the project encounters problems or fails to meet its objectives.

One critical challenge co-PIs face is securing clear agreements about fund distribution. When co-PIs are from different colleges within the same university, they may need formal letters establishing that funds will transfer directly to them; otherwise, they may not have control over the funds supporting their specific projects, and indirect costs might remain entirely with the PI's college. This may or may not be an issue depending on your institution and how those indirect costs are used to support your college and your research.

Mikel, an economist studying labor markets, learned this lesson as a co-PI on a multimillion-dollar NSF grant. Despite contributing 30 percent effort to the project, he discovered that all indirect cost returns went to the PI's engineering college, leaving his economics department without resources to support his grant work. This created tension with his department chair and complicated his ability to secure course releases and research support. Mikel had to negotiate retroactively to ensure that his department received appropriate indirect cost returns, a process that strained relationships and created an unnecessary administrative burden.

Social scientists serving as co-PIs on STEM projects face unique challenges as disciplinary outsiders. Many describe feeling like they are functioning as the PI of a social science project despite being only a co-PI or senior personnel on the larger grant. This isolated role means being the only person driving the social science components with no colleagues to consult, doing all the training, and taking full responsibility for students working on social science aspects. This isolation is compounded by the need to educate STEM colleagues about social science methods and terminology, including basic distinctions like the difference between interviews and surveys that engineering collaborators might use interchangeably.

For tenure-track faculty, co-PI roles can provide excellent training in project leadership while sharing the burden with more experienced colleagues. The key is to ensure that the partnership is genuinely collaborative and that your contributions are appropriately recognized and rewarded.

PI Role: The Buck Stops Here

The principal investigator bears ultimate responsibility for project success, managing both the scientific direction and administrative details. At least 50 percent of a PI's time on grants is typically spent on administration rather than research. The administrative burden grows substantially once staffing is involved, with a notable difference between managing one graduate student versus multiple graduate students, postdocs, and staff members.

PI roles come with the greatest potential rewards but also the highest risks. As PI, you have ultimate control over project direction, budget allocation, and personnel decisions. You also bear full responsibility for ensuring that the project meets its objectives, stays within budget, and complies with all reporting requirements. This level of responsibility can be overwhelming for early-career faculty who are still learning to manage their own research programs while juggling teaching and service obligations.

The PI role also requires sophisticated project management skills that are rarely taught in graduate school. You must coordinate multiple team members, manage complex budgets, navigate institutional bureaucracy, and maintain relationships with program officers at funding agencies. These skills take time to develop, and mistakes can have serious consequences for both the project and your career.

PIs face unique challenges with budgeting and staffing that extend well beyond typical academic management. When team members underperform, the PI must still deliver promised outcomes to funding agencies and external partners. This might mean staying up all night to complete a report after someone drops the ball—external partners do not care about internal staffing issues; they just need deliverables on time. The comparison to restaurant ownership is apt: if your chef quits unexpectedly, you have to walk into the kitchen and start cooking. This responsibility extends to managing graduate students who, once funded for a semester, typically cannot be removed even if they stop contributing. In such situations, the university often provides no backup plan, leaving the PI to complete the work while still paying for nonperforming staff.

The PI must also navigate different authorship norms across disciplines, which becomes especially complicated on interdisciplinary projects. In social sciences, faculty are often first authors and authorship order matters significantly. In STEM fields, the PI typically appears as the last author, signifying lab leadership. Following STEM conventions may impress program officers and build credibility for future funding but could hurt evaluation by social science colleagues who do not understand this convention. This creates difficult strategic choices, especially for untenured faculty who need to satisfy both funding agencies and promotion committees with different and sometimes contradictory expectations about publication and authorship.

Managing Multiple Principal Investigator (MPI) Arrangements

The National Institutes of Health (NIH) and some other agencies use the term *multiple principal investigators* (MPI) to describe grants with more than one PI, each with equal authority and responsibility. (Note that NIH also uses *program director* or *project director* (PD) as synonymous with PI in some contexts.) When a proposal includes multiple PIs, the funding agency expects a clear management plan addressing how decisions will be made when PIs disagree. This requirement is essential infrastructure for successful collaboration. Consider the practical scenario: if you have two PIs who disagree about a major study design modification or how to address a reviewer concern, how will you resolve it? With three PIs, you might use a majority-rules approach. With two PIs, you need a different conflict resolution mechanism—perhaps a pre-identified third-party arbiter, or a policy of deferring to whichever PI has primary expertise in the area under dispute.

Your management plan should address the following types of things:

- How major decisions will be made (methodology changes, hiring decisions, budget reallocations)
- How routine decisions will be made (scheduling, minor purchases, student supervision)
- Communication frequency and mechanisms among PIs
- What happens if one PI leaves the institution or can no longer participate
- How credit and authorship will be determined

Be realistic in your management plan. Don't promise weekly meetings among PIs at different institutions if your schedules won't support it. Don't claim consensus decision-making if you actually plan to divide responsibilities by expertise area. Reviewers appreciate honest, practical management plans that reflect how the team will actually work together.

External Evaluator Role: Objective Assessment with Limitations

Another role social and behavioral scientists can play in funded projects is as an external evaluator. These professionals can have a role in the development and writing of the proposal, and if the funding is awarded, they typically assess project outcomes and processes while maintaining independence from the research team (see Boulmetis, 2025, as a comprehensive resource). Though methodologically similar to research, evaluation serves a different purpose. External evaluators measure performance metrics to demonstrate whether the team successfully completed what was proposed to the funding agency. They function as objective assessors rather than research contributors, focusing on whether promised deliverables were achieved with high-quality results.

The external evaluator role comes with significant limitations for social scientists accustomed to research-focused positions. Unlike research, evaluation data is typically not collected with IRB approval for academic publication. The data collected for evaluation may have no IRB protocol associated with it, eliminating publication possibilities from the outset. Even when data might theoretically be publishable, there may be strong resistance to publishing negative evaluations that could reflect poorly on the project and its leaders. This creates fundamental restrictions on research productivity.

The value of serving as an external evaluator comes primarily from the experience and compensation rather than research output. This makes the external evaluator position fundamentally different from other grant roles that might generate publications or dissertations. For social scientists considering various pathways to grant involvement, this distinction is critical for career planning, especially for early-career researchers who need publications for promotion and tenure. The decision to take on this role should be made with clear understanding of its benefits and limitations, and you should be trained in this type of rigorous methodology.

Graduate Student and Postdoc Roles: Learning While Contributing

Graduate students and recently minted PhDs can get involved in funded research by being hired as a research assistant (RA) or a postdoctoral scholar (postdoc). Quite often investigators have already secured the funding, so the project goals and objectives are set before they hire these early career roles. In these roles, the RAs and postdocs' primary duties are to carry out the funded project as described in the proposal, which serves as a contract between the PI/university and the funder. In other words, RAs and postdocs often do not have the flexibility to deviate from the project tasks as designed. See also Chapter 11 focused on helping graduate students get their own funding where they do get to design their own research project.

Graduate students and postdocs can significantly benefit from grant involvement. Being on a funded team provides graduate students and postdocs with experiences they can put on their CVs, thus demonstrating skills that others at their career stage may not have. Grant work provides valuable professional development, especially when students can participate in writing proposals and understanding budgeting decisions. These opportunities are most beneficial when senior team members are transparent about budgets and decision-making processes, actively teaching the grant process rather than simply assigning tasks.

However, several challenges can arise with student involvement that require proactive management by the researchers. Some students treat grant projects as individual work, attempting to publish findings without proper acknowledgment of funding sources or team contributions. Faculty report discovering student poster presentations using project data without attribution or acknowledgment of the funding source. More extreme situations can develop when students leave projects (through graduation or other commitments) but still expect to be included in publications even if they were only involved in data collection. These situations highlight the importance of clear communication about ownership, credit, and responsibilities from the beginning of any student's involvement with funded work.

Disciplinary differences compound these challenges significantly. In STEM fields, advisors typically appear on all student papers, and dissertations often comprise three to four publishable papers derived from collaborative lab work. In communication and other social sciences, students frequently produce solo-authored dissertations with optional advisor inclusion, but only after the dissertation has been completed. Some faculty strategically direct students toward projects that can become grant proposals, having them develop thesis work that later transforms into funding applications. This approach has successfully generated funded projects but can raise questions about idea ownership and credit when the student's work is part of a multi-investigator funded project—issues that may be interpreted differently across disciplines and by individual students.

Working with graduate students on funded projects requires clear communication about expectations from the outset. Students in social sciences often face competing priorities between their individual academic goals and grant deliverables. Many have been trained in an academic culture that prioritizes independent scholarship, sole-authored publications, and dissertation work over collaborative project obligations. This fundamental disconnect can lead to situations where students fail to deliver promised output despite having received funding, leaving principal investigators to complete the work themselves to meet contractual deadlines.

Specifying deliverables, acknowledgment requirements, and deadlines is essential for accountability. Beyond paperwork, faculty need to explicitly discuss how grant funding differs from traditional academic work—emphasizing that grant money comes with specific obligations that must be fulfilled. Students must understand that when they accept funding, they are making a professional commitment to produce certain outputs according to an established timeline, regardless of their other priorities.

The postdoc role is not a student role; it is closer to a temporary professional staff position, and it should involve more substantial responsibility. Postdocs should take a much more active role in grant writing as part of their professional development. They can also handle significant grant administration, particularly valuable given most social scientists' lack of formal project management training. Engineering departments often include project management in their curriculum, producing graduate students skilled at tracking deadlines and organizing collaborative work. Social science students typically lack this training, creating another gap that must be addressed for successful grant management. Finally, postdocs often have advanced methodological skills and expertise that make them ideal to conduct analyses on their own and train graduate students on their team. Postdocs are learning to become faculty members or professional researchers, and working on a funded project is an ideal way for them to have a successful social science career.

Navigating Last-Minute Invitations

Throughout your academic journey, you might receive urgent invitations to join grant proposals at the last minute. These situations present both significant opportunities and potential pitfalls that require careful strategic thinking. Remember in Chapter 1, you learned about having a travel suitcase ready with key documents; these situations clearly demonstrate the importance of having that suitcase ready if you choose to join the team. Understanding how to evaluate and respond to these invitations is a crucial skill for social scientists at all career stages who are building their networks and establishing their reputations in the grant-funding ecosystem.

Last-minute invitations typically unfold with a team of researchers, often from STEM fields, having nearly completed their grant proposal when they suddenly realize they need a social science component. With the deadline looming—sometimes days away—they reach out with an urgent invitation that can feel both flattering and overwhelming. The timing reflects the reality that many interdisciplinary teams underestimate the complexity of integrating social science perspectives into their projects until late in the proposal development process.

Understanding the Dynamics Behind Last-Minute Invitations

These last-minute scenarios can emerge from reviewer feedback on previous submissions, conversations with program officers who suggest that a proposal would be strengthened by adding social science expertise, or from members of the team who have heard about your work. Teams may have initially planned to handle the social science components themselves or assumed such expertise was unnecessary for their technical project. When they discover otherwise, they face the challenge of finding qualified social scientists willing and able to contribute meaningful input on very short notice.

The academic reward system contributes to these dynamics. STEM researchers often face pressure to focus on technical innovation and may view social science components as add-ons rather than integral parts of their research design. This can lead to proposals where social science contributions feel disconnected from the core technical work, limiting both the intellectual value of the collaboration and the potential for meaningful contributions from social science team members.

Program officers at funding agencies and funding calls increasingly recognize the importance of interdisciplinary approaches and may specifically encourage or require teams to include social science expertise. However, this guidance can come late in the proposal development process, after technical teams have already invested significant time and effort in developing their approaches. This creates pressure to find social science collaborators quickly rather than investing the time needed to develop truly integrated interdisciplinary approaches.

The Double-Edged Nature of Last-Minute Opportunities

For early career scholars, these invitations generally provide valuable learning experiences despite their limitations. The opportunity to observe how established researchers frame their work, structure proposals, and respond to reviewer feedback represents an informal apprenticeship in grant culture that can accelerate your learning curve significantly. Consider Kevin, an assistant professor of public policy, who received a call five days before an NSF deadline from an engineering team working on a Smart and Connected Communities proposal. The team received reviewer feedback indicating their previous submission lacked adequate attention to social and behavioral factors affecting technology adoption. Despite the rushed timeline and his limited familiarity with their technical approach, Kevin agreed to join. The experience taught him valuable lessons about NSF proposal structure, review criteria, and the importance of broader impacts sections. More importantly, it led to ongoing collaborations and a properly integrated proposal the following year that resulted in significant funding for his research program.

However, these late-stage invitations often reveal fundamental misunderstandings about social science contributions. Teams frequently view social scientists as merely responsible for social media outreach, public engagement activities, or other "broader impacts" components rather than core intellectual contributors. This misconception reflects a broader lack of understanding about the theoretical and methodological sophistication that social scientists bring to interdisciplinary projects. There is often an assumption that social science work involves primarily promotional messaging or community outreach rather than rigorous empirical research requiring specialized training and expertise.

Strategic Responses by Career Stage

When considering last-minute invitations, adapt your approach strategically based on your career stage and professional goals.

- **Graduate students** face challenges because they may lack experience evaluating collaboration quality or leverage to negotiate better terms. However, they also have more flexibility in time allocation and fewer competing professional obligations. Graduate students should seek guidance from advisors when considering these opportunities and view them primarily as learning experiences rather than major career opportunities.
- **Early-career faculty** occupy a middle position with more experience than graduate students but still benefit significantly from networking and learning opportunities. They should be more selective than graduate students but more open than senior faculty to participating in imperfect collaborations offering genuine learning opportunities and relationship-building potential.
- **Mid-career faculty** have more leverage to insist on meaningful integration and should generally avoid participating where they're clearly being added as an afterthought. However, they may still find value if opportunities lead to ongoing collaborations or provide access to new funding streams aligning with career goals.
- **Senior faculty** have the most leverage and should generally insist on full integration from the beginning or decline to participate. However, they may choose to participate as a form of service to the field or to mentor junior colleagues involved in projects.

Box 5.1 Making Last-Minute Invitations Work for You

If you decide to accept a last-minute invitation, several strategies can help maximize benefits while minimizing risks:

1. **Insist on seeing the entire proposal**, not just the section you're expected to contribute. Understanding the overall project design, goals, and approach helps assess

whether your contributions can be meaningful and whether the collaboration has genuine success potential.

2. **Clarify the deliverables** you're committing to both during proposal development and if funded. Many last-minute invitations are vague about expectations, leaving room for later misunderstandings. Be explicit about what you can and cannot contribute, given time constraints and other professional obligations.
3. **Ensure adequate budget allocation** for your participation. Last-minute additions often result in insufficient budgets that don't reflect the true scope of expected work. If the budget is inadequate, negotiate for additional resources or scale back expected contributions accordingly.
4. **Use the experience strategically** to build relationships for future collaborations. Even if the immediate collaboration is imperfect, it may lead to ongoing relationships with researchers who value your expertise and may involve you more meaningfully in future projects.

Adaptive Strategies for Success

When you have decided to join the last-minute proposal writing, you need to be adaptive and flexible. Consider temporarily setting aside some disciplinary identity concerns and methodological preferences to be maximally cooperative. With only days remaining, teams lack bandwidth for substantive revisions or methodological debates—they need someone willing to fill a perceived gap efficiently and professionally. By demonstrating cooperative spirit in constrained circumstances, you may earn invitations to future collaborations with greater involvement from the outset.

For those seeking to transform last-minute invitations into meaningful collaborations, one effective approach involves requesting permission to substantially reshape the proposal—not just adding a paragraph about social science but integrating social science perspectives throughout. This means including research questions, aims, and hypotheses as core intellectual contributions, not just add-ons to technical work. While this may not always be possible given time constraints, proposing such integration demonstrates your value as a true research partner rather than a service provider.

Common Pitfalls and How to Avoid Them

Several pitfalls can undermine the value of participating in last-minute grant collaborations:

- **Overcommitting without understanding scope**: The urgency can lead to hasty agreements creating unrealistic expectations. Always clarify expected time commitment and deliverables before agreeing to participate.
- **Dramatically altering your research agenda**: While some adaptation is necessary, major departures from established expertise likely result in superficial contributions that don't serve career development or project success.
- **Failing to evaluate alignment**: Not every last-minute invitation is worth accepting. Be selective about which opportunities align with professional goals and development needs.

The key to successfully navigating last-minute invitations lies in maintaining realistic expectations while being strategic about which opportunities to pursue. These collaborations are rarely perfect, but they can provide valuable learning experiences and relationship-building opportunities for scholars who approach them with clear goals and appropriate boundaries. By understanding the dynamics creating these situations and developing strategies for evaluating and responding to them, social scientists can use last-minute invitations as stepping stones to more meaningful collaborative relationships and funding opportunities.

Strategic Considerations Across Career Stages

As you consider different grant roles throughout your career, several factors should guide your decision-making process. How much time can you realistically commit given your teaching load, research obligations, and other professional responsibilities? What level of administrative support does your institution provide for grant management? How will this role be valued in your annual reviews, tenure evaluation, or promotion considerations? What skills do you hope to develop through this experience? How does this role align with your publication timeline and long-term research goals?

The answers to these questions will help you make strategic decisions about which roles to pursue and when. Early in your career, advisory board, consultant, senior personnel, and co-PI roles may provide the best balance of learning opportunities and manageable risk. These positions allow you to gain valuable experience with grant processes while limiting your administrative responsibilities and financial exposure. As you gain experience and develop your project management skills, PI roles become more attractive and feasible.

For graduate students, grant involvement should be viewed primarily as professional development with the potential for funding and publication opportunities. The focus should be on learning how grants work, understanding the responsibilities involved, and building relationships that may prove valuable in future career stages. Graduate students should be cautious about taking on too much responsibility too quickly, as their primary obligation remains completing their degree requirements successfully.

Early-career faculty face different considerations as they balance grant opportunities with tenure requirements. See Chapter 9 for a detailed discussion of funding opportunities while in a tenure-track or early-career job role. Publications typically remain the primary currency for tenure evaluation, so grant activities must ultimately support rather than detract from publication productivity. The timing gap between receiving grants and producing publications can be particularly challenging for untenured faculty who need to demonstrate consistent scholarly output throughout their probationary period.

Mid-career and senior faculty have more flexibility to pursue ambitious grant projects and leadership roles (see Chapter 10), but they also face increasing expectations for mentorship and service. Senior scholars may find value in serving as external evaluators or consultants on projects led by junior colleagues, providing expertise while supporting the next generation of researchers.

Building Meaningful Collaborations

The most successful grant collaborations begin well before proposal writing. Authentic engagement in problem definition, research design, and theoretical framing from the earliest stages produces not only more competitive proposals but also more scientifically rigorous and impactful research. While last-minute invitations can serve as entry points to these collaborations, the goal should be moving toward earlier, more substantive engagement in future partnerships.

Building these relationships requires patience, strategic thinking, and often significant upfront investment of time and energy. Social scientists may need to attend conferences outside their disciplines, participate in working groups, or volunteer their expertise on pilot projects to demonstrate their value to potential collaborators. This relationship-building work is rarely rewarded directly but can be essential for creating opportunities for meaningful interdisciplinary collaboration.

The progression from advisory board member to co-PI exemplifies how strategic relationship building can create opportunities over time. When you prove yourself as a valuable advisory board member—offering insights that genuinely improve the project, being responsive to requests for input, and demonstrating collaborative spirit—principal investigators remember. They think of you when developing new proposals and may invite you to take on more substantial roles in future projects. This organic progression often leads to more successful collaborations than jumping directly into leadership roles with unfamiliar teams.

Conclusion: Making Strategic Choices

Understanding the different roles available on grant teams empowers social scientists to make strategic choices about their involvement in funded research. Each role comes with distinct advantages, challenges, and requirements that must be carefully weighed against your career stage, institutional context, and professional goals. Whether you are a graduate student seeking valuable learning experiences, an early-career faculty member building toward tenure, or a senior scholar looking to make significant research contributions, there are pathways for meaningful participation in the grant ecosystem.

The key is approaching these opportunities with clear eyes about what each role entails, honest assessment of your capabilities and constraints, and strategic thinking about how each experience fits into your broader career trajectory. By understanding the full spectrum of grant roles and using what you learned in Chapter 1 about Grant Readiness, you can be more prepared to navigate the complex world of funded research more effectively and build a sustainable, impactful research program that advances both your career and your field. Remember that your path through these various roles need not be linear—you might serve as a PI on one project while simultaneously participating as an advisory board member on another, or step back from leadership roles during particularly demanding career phases. The flexibility to adapt your grant involvement to your changing circumstances and goals represents one of the great advantages of understanding this full ecosystem of roles.

Now that you better understand the different roles you might play on a grant, the next chapter delves into one of the most overlooked issues in pursuing and receiving external funding: the roles you need others to play on your project. Considering how you will accomplish the project while writing the proposal is essential, so you will want to begin with the hiring end in mind.

6

Begin with the Hiring End in Mind

The notification arrived on a Friday morning. After months of waiting, Anika Müller finally received word that her Kresge Foundation grant was funded. The euphoria lasted approximately ten minutes… just long enough for reality to set in. She had budgeted for a postdoctoral researcher, two graduate students, and an undergraduate research assistant, but had no idea how to actually hire them, what paperwork was required, or how long the process would take. More troubling still, she didn't know what she didn't know. "I thought getting the grant was the hard part," Anika told a colleague later. "I had no idea that managing the grant would be ten times more complex than writing the proposal."

This sentiment echoes across the experiences of countless social scientists who successfully secure external funding only to discover they're woefully unprepared for what comes next. Unlike STEM colleagues who often have firsthand experience with established lab structures and institutional knowledge about grant management, social scientists typically build their research operations from scratch, learning through costly mistakes what should have been clear from the beginning.

Stephen Covey's (2020) principle of "begin with the end in mind" has never been more relevant than in externally funded staffing decisions. Before writing a single job position description or posting a single job advertisement, you need to understand the full lifecycle of each position you're creating. What will the hiring process entail? How long will it take? What are the hidden costs beyond salary? What institutional rules govern these positions? How will you evaluate performance? When and how will positions end?

This chapter addresses these critical questions, drawing from decades of combined experience making—and learning from—staffing mistakes. We'll explore each major category of externally funded positions, from undergraduate researchers to administrative staff, examining not just the obvious considerations but the hidden complexities that can derail even well-funded projects. Most importantly, we'll help you understand why beginning with the end in mind isn't just good advice—it's essential for grant success.

The Hidden Time Cost of Managing People

Before exploring specific staffing categories, we need to address a fundamental reality that catches most new PIs off guard: managing people takes enormous amounts of time. Some experienced researchers without dedicated staff support estimate spending at least 20 percent of their time—a full day per week—on what could be called "project administration." This includes hiring, training, weekly meetings, progress monitoring, conflict resolution, and report writing. None of this time contributes directly to research outputs. This administrative burden doesn't scale linearly. Managing three team members doesn't take three times as long as managing one—it often takes five or six times as long due to coordination complexity, interpersonal dynamics, and communication overhead. When managing six concurrent externally funded projects during particularly busy periods, we have found ourselves creating formal orientation sessions for research assistants each semester, complete with documentation packages and structured onboarding processes.

The implications are profound. When you budget for staff in your grant proposal, you're not just committing funds, you're committing substantial portions of your own time. This time commitment must be factored into your decision-making about how many people to hire and when to bring them on board. The entrepreneurial mindset shift required here is significant: you're no longer just a researcher but a small business owner managing human resources, project timelines, and complex deliverables.

Consider developing systems early that can minimize this burden over time. Create comprehensive onboarding checklists, document standard procedures, establish regular meeting rhythms, and invest in project management tools. The time spent developing these systems pays dividends as your team grows and projects multiply. Perhaps most importantly, recognize that managing people isn't optional—it's an essential component of modern externally funded scholarship. The sooner you accept this reality and develop appropriate skills and systems, the more successful your research will be.

Understanding Institutional Constraints and PI Eligibility

Every institution has its own byzantine rules governing employment, and these rules profoundly affect your staffing plans. At some universities, hiring a postdoc requires a comprehensive salary study to ensure equity across the institution. For smaller institutions where there were not many prior postdocs, this process, which might involve contacting other universities in the region to gather comparison data, can take months to complete. At others, the process resembles hiring an assistant professor, complete with search committees and extensive HR requirements.

One constraint involves PI eligibility restrictions. Consider the case of a professional-track faculty member at a large state university. Despite being a full-time lecturer with a PhD and years of research experience, she discovered she lacked PI-eligibility status when trying to apply for grants to build her CV. This created a Catch-22: she needed grants to advance her career, but her institution wouldn't allow her to apply for them. The institution's perspective focuses on long-term accountability. Universities argue they need someone permanent who will be responsible if issues arise years after a grant ends. They worry about continuity if a lecturer leaves mid-project. While these concerns have merit, they create systemic barriers for capable researchers trying to advance their careers. The result is a two-tier system where some faculty can pursue external funding while others cannot, regardless of their qualifications or research capabilities.

These institutional variations extend far beyond postdocs and PI eligibility. Graduate student appointments might be limited to either teaching or research at some institutions, while others allow split appointments. International students face different restrictions than domestic students. Work-study students may have specific limitations on the types of work they can perform. Some institutions have different rules for who can serve as PI on different types of grants—a research scientist might be eligible for some funding mechanisms but not others.

Understanding these constraints before you write your budget can prevent painful surprises later. Schedule a meeting with your HR department before writing any grant proposal that includes personnel. Come prepared with specific questions: What are the true costs of each position type, including benefits and overhead? What is the typical timeline from posting to start date? What are the rules about undergraduate employment hours? Can students work additional hours during breaks? What documentation is required for each position type? Who has PI eligibility at your institution, and are there pathways for others to gain this status?

Box 6.1 "Institutional Constraints on Hiring Checklist"

A living document that captures all the rules, rates, and restrictions that govern employment at your institution. We believe this is essential before writing a budget.

Create what we call an "institutional constraints on hiring checklist" that you can reference for future proposals. This living document should capture all the rules, rates, and restrictions that govern employment at your institution. Update it annually, as these rules change frequently and without much fanfare. Understanding who can serve as PI, who can be hired, and under what conditions will save countless hours of frustration later.

Postdoctoral Researchers: The Advanced Team Members

Postdocs represent one of the most valuable—and most complex—staffing categories in externally funded research. They bring advanced skills and independence but require different management approaches than students. They're employees, not students, which means they need office space, computers, travel funds, and annual evaluations. They are also trainees who should be receiving mentorship toward becoming an independent researcher, and detailing their training plan is an important part of some funding proposals. Yet many PIs approach postdoc hiring with the same attitude they might bring to recruiting graduate students.

The learning curve for postdoc management can be steep. New PIs often discover that the job description hastily written when trying to hire becomes the exact criteria for annual evaluation—a connection they hadn't anticipated. Experienced researchers have learned through painful experience never to hire a postdoc for less than two years, and ideally three. The reasoning is compelling: Year one involves learning your systems and projects while trying to maintain their own research agenda from their dissertations. Year two brings full productivity but they are also on the job market, looking for a full-time position, which will directly impact the time they can spend on funded projects. Offering a third year can often provide a win-win situation for everyone because then they are more experienced, efficient, and can mentor others while maintaining productivity.

The Challenge of Postdoc Recruitment

Finding the right postdoc extends beyond identifying intellectual capability. One cautionary tale involves a brilliant postdoc who, despite being well-published and intellectually gifted, proved to be a poor fit for the team. This individual constantly questioned the value of the funded research, likely because in their social science graduate program, they had not been exposed to external funding. Thus, they preferred to pursue their own agenda rather than the project's stated goals. They were also reluctant to mentor undergraduate and graduate students, activities the PI wrote into broader impacts of the funded proposal.

This experience, repeated in various forms across many research groups, teaches valuable lessons about postdoc recruitment. During interviews, ask specifically about their willingness to mentor students, their flexibility in pursuing grant-defined research questions, and their long-term career goals. Be explicit about your expectations: Will they need to help with grant reporting? Will they supervise students? What are the project's nonnegotiable research questions? Look for candidates who understand that externally funded research requires balancing personal research interests with project deliverables. Ultimately, the postdoc position was funded to advance the project, not the postdoc's individual research agenda.

Consider structuring postdoc positions with built-in evaluation points. A two-year appointment contingent upon successful completion of year one provides both parties with a graceful exit if the fit isn't right. This protects you from being locked into a long-term relationship with someone who isn't advancing the project's goals while giving postdocs fair notice if they need to seek other opportunities. Make evaluation criteria clear from the beginning, linking them directly to the initial job description to avoid surprises later.

Space and Infrastructure Needs

The practical requirements of postdoc positions often catch PIs off guard. Stories abound of physical office space issues. Postdocs may need to share offices, sometimes with their supervisors—arrangements that please neither party. Beyond the obvious privacy and professionalism concerns, such arrangements can create awkward power dynamics and limit both parties' ability to work effectively. Beyond space, postdocs need appropriate infrastructure. They require computers capable of handling research tasks, software licenses, and travel funds for conferences and professional development. Many grant budgets include postdoc salaries but forget these essential supports. Failing to budget for these items means scrambling to find funds from other sources or asking postdocs to work without proper resources—neither option is fair or conducive to productivity.

Graduate Students: The Backbone of Social Science Research Teams

Graduate students often represent the most common type of staffing, offering a balance of capability, commitment, and cost-effectiveness for externally funded research. However, their integration into funded projects requires careful consideration of both institutional rules and individual development needs. The complexity begins with understanding what graduate student employment costs. Most PIs are shocked to discover the true expense of graduate student support. Beyond the stipend, you must budget at least for tuition and fringe benefits (such as health insurance). The total cost (not including indirect costs on all staffing budget items) can be double the stipend amount or more, depending on tuition rates. Moreover, these costs change annually, and what you budgeted in your proposal may not cover actual expenses by the time you're hiring several years later. Researchers have shared stories with us of how their two-year-old budget fell short by nearly $5000 per student per year due to tuition increases and benefit changes.

Institutional rules governing graduate student appointments vary dramatically and can create unexpected challenges. Some universities require students to be either teaching assistants or research assistants, never both. Others allow split appointments but require complex coordination between departments. At a university where a college has a PhD shared among five departments, a single administrator must balance requests from five departments for teaching assistants, research assistants funded by grants, and general assistantship positions. This person performs what colleagues call "magic" each semester, but continuity isn't guaranteed—you might have different students each term.

The challenge becomes more complex when institutional priorities conflict with research needs. A PI might need a student to work twenty hours per week on research, but the department needs teaching assistants. The compromise—a split appointment—means the student juggles competing demands, often to the detriment of both roles. When students have ten hours allocated to teaching a new course preparation and ten hours for complex research tasks, something inevitably suffers. The PI gets a distracted, overworked researcher, while undergraduate students get an overwhelmed, underprepared instructor.

Summer Unpredictability: A Perennial Challenge

Summer employment of graduate students presents unique challenges that many PIs don't anticipate. While the academic year brings structure and predictability, summer employment is often chaos. Students frequently want to travel or return home for extended periods, sometimes with little notice. Even when students are not traveling, visa restrictions might limit their work hours or require special paperwork. One research team discovered this unpredictability the hard way when three of their five graduate researchers announced in May that they wouldn't be available for summer work. The timing was catastrophic—data collection was scheduled to begin in June, and training new researchers would take weeks. The PI scrambled to reorganize the project timeline, ultimately delaying deliverables and frustrating community partners who had arranged their schedules around the original timeline.

Even when students commit to summer work, institutional rules create complications. Some universities require students to enroll in a minimum number of credit hours even during summer, forcing PIs to supervise independent studies simply to meet bureaucratic requirements. Students might choose to enroll in six course credits when you've only budgeted for three, forcing you to cover the difference or risk losing a valuable team member. These decisions often happen at the last minute, leaving PIs scrambling to find additional funds or restructure project budgets.

The solution requires planning for uncertainty, which we fully acknowledge can be difficult. Build flexibility into project timelines, avoiding critical summer deadlines when possible. Create overlapping responsibilities so no single student's absence derails the project. Most importantly, have frank conversations with students early in the spring semester about summer plans, making clear the project's needs while respecting their autonomy. Some PIs now require written commitments by March for summer employment, though even these aren't binding if students' circumstances change.

Setting Clear Expectations and Evaluation Processes

One of the most common sources of conflict with graduate students involves unclear expectations about work schedules and commitments. Many students assume their research appointments follow the academic calendar, disappearing the moment they submit their last final exam. This assumption, while understandable, can derail projects with tight timelines or summer data collection plans. Some students may be paid for a specific number of hours per week (e.g., twenty hours or forty hours) but need flexibility to take off for vacation.

Fundamentally, clear communication between the PI and the team is essential, and enacting an evaluation process is another way to codify expectations. Evaluation processes help PIs to reflect on student performance regularly rather than letting problems fester. It gives students clear feedback about their progress and areas for improvement. Perhaps most importantly, it creates accountability on both sides—students understand their work will be assessed, while PIs must justify their evaluations with specific examples.

However, implementing evaluations raises its own challenges. Evaluations take time, coordination, and documentation. PIs who know they'll continue working with students—in classes, on committees, or in small departments—may hesitate to provide honest feedback. The power dynamics are complex: a critical evaluation might poison a relationship that needs to continue for years. Some PIs admit to avoiding evaluations entirely rather than navigating these difficult conversations, though this ultimately serves no one well.

Undergraduate Researchers: High Reward, High Investment

The integration of undergraduate researchers into externally funded projects represents both tremendous opportunity and significant challenge. Success stories abound—undergraduates who become coauthors on major publications, who develop innovative methodological approaches, who bring fresh perspectives that transform project directions. Yet for every success story, there are tales of frustration: students who disappear mid-semester, who produce work requiring complete revision, who treat research positions as just another campus job rather than a learning opportunity. The key to success lies in recognizing that undergraduate researchers require different management approaches than graduate students. They need more structure, clearer guidelines, and step-by-step training. They also need different types of motivation and recognition. While graduate students understand how research experience builds their CVs, undergraduates might not see the connection between today's data entry and their future careers.

Some institutions have developed robust infrastructure supporting undergraduate research. These might include offices of undergraduate research that provide training workshops, presentation opportunities, and funding for conference travel. One successful model involves requiring all undergraduate researchers to present posters at campus research fairs. New researchers present as first authors with experienced undergraduates as second authors, creating natural mentoring relationships while providing tangible outcomes for both students and PIs.

This structured approach serves multiple purposes. It gives students concrete goals and deadlines. It creates peer learning opportunities where experienced undergraduates pass on both technical skills and professional norms. It provides material for grant reports—funding agencies love seeing undergraduate involvement in research. Most importantly, it transforms undergraduate research from an isolated experience into a community endeavor.

Success with undergraduates also requires honest assessment of your capacity to provide necessary training and supervision. Training an undergraduate to conduct qualitative interviews might take weeks of role-playing, feedback, and gradual independence. Teaching statistical analysis requires not just software instruction but conceptual understanding of research design. If you're already overwhelmed with other responsibilities, bringing on untrained undergraduates might create more burden than benefit.

The administrative requirements add another layer of complexity. Universities often limit undergraduate work hours, sometimes cumulatively across all campus positions. One PI discovered mid-semester that a promising research assistant suddenly couldn't work because she'd exceeded the total allowed hours by taking a second campus job. A conversation about an undergraduate student's overall campus involvements may help prevent similar issues unexpectedly.

The Social Media Team Challenge

Many PIs, recognizing the importance of research dissemination and public engagement, have attempted to leverage undergraduate interest in social media for project communication. The results often illustrate the vast gulf between undergraduate social media fluency and scientific communication needs. Students who expertly navigate TikTok, Instagram, and other platforms for personal use often struggle to adapt these skills for research dissemination.

The fundamental disconnect stems from different conceptual frameworks about social media's purpose. Undergraduate students often approach social media through an influencer lens—seeking engagement, likes, and viral content. They think about peer audiences and entertainment value. When asked to create research-focused content, they might produce posts that trivialize findings, misrepresent methodology, or fail to consider the diverse stakeholders interested in the research.

Keri learned this lesson when a member of her undergraduate research team began live-tweeting research meetings. The students thought they were providing exciting "behind-the-scenes" content, similar to what they'd seen from their favorite influencers. They didn't understand that brainstorming sessions contain provisional ideas, dead-end hypotheses, and confidential information about upcoming studies. Keri discovered the social media posts only when a colleague mentioned seeing "interesting ideas" from her lab online. She immediately had a conversation with the student, and it was obvious they had no idea what they were doing could be a problem, so they apologized and stopped immediately.

Even with clear guidelines, the challenge persists. Students struggle to understand the multiple audiences for scientific social media: funding agencies looking for impact evidence, potential collaborators assessing research quality, institutional leaders evaluating productivity, peer researchers considering collaboration, and community partners seeking practical applications. Crafting messages that resonate with these diverse groups while maintaining scientific accuracy requires sophisticated understanding of both science and communication.

Some PIs have found success by reconceptualizing the student role. Rather than expecting students to create science communication content, they leverage student expertise differently. Students might research how similar labs use social media, analyze engagement patterns with different types of content, or monitor discussions about related research topics across platforms. This approach uses their platform knowledge while acknowledging their limited science communication experience.

The time investment required to properly manage social media teams often exceeds the benefits. PIs report spending hours reviewing and revising content, only to essentially rewrite everything. One researcher calculated they could create better content in less time than they spent managing their social media team. Yet the pressure to maintain an active social media presence—from institutions, funders, and peers—makes abandoning these efforts difficult. Moreover, funders like to see involvement of undergraduate students in research teams through activities that are appropriate for their capabilities, and the desire to demonstrate such undergraduate involvement can create a dilemma for some PIs.

Research Scientists and Staff Positions

Beyond students and postdocs, grants sometimes support professional research staff. These positions, though rare in social sciences, offer unique advantages and challenges. Research scientists can pursue entire careers in these roles, unlike postdocs who are expected to move on. This creates different dynamics and expectations that PIs must carefully navigate.

The ideal research scientist combines technical expertise with a collaborative mindset. They need to be accomplished enough to contribute meaningfully and to desire a non-faculty career path. They must respect the PI's leadership while maintaining their own professional identity. Most challengingly, they must accept the inherent job insecurity with what is often called soft funding, meaning their position depends entirely on continued grant funding, which is never guaranteed.

Finding such individuals requires careful recruitment and clear communication. During interviews, discuss frankly the position's dependence on external funding. Explore their comfort with uncertainty and their backup plans if funding disappears. Assess their willingness to support the PI's vision while contributing their own expertise. Look for candidates who see themselves as part of a team, understanding that everyone's success depends on collective achievement.

For early-career PIs without extensive funding portfolios, hiring research scientists presents unique challenges. How can you promise stable employment when your own funding extends only two or three years? How do you retain talented staff when industry offers higher salaries and better job security? The answer often involves creative approaches: encouraging staff to pursue their own small grants, building collaborative relationships where they're valued partners rather than just employees, and being transparent about funding realities while working to secure longer-term support.

Alternative Full-Time Research Positions

Given the structural challenges of academic calendars and competing obligations, some social scientists have explored alternative staffing models that complement traditional graduate student appointments. One possible approach involves hiring recent graduates with bachelor's or master's degrees as full-time research scientists or research associates. These positions, typically lasting one to two years with possible extensions, serve individuals seeking intensive research experience before pursuing doctoral studies.

This model addresses specific project needs better than trying to align with graduate student availability. When projects require consistent full-time attention—particularly those with tight deadlines or intensive data collection periods—having dedicated staff can ensure continuity. These positions offer recent graduates invaluable benefits: hands-on research experience, mentoring from established scholars, and strong letters of recommendation for future doctoral applications. For PIs, these staff members can provide focused attention during critical project phases, complementing the broader contributions that graduate students make to research teams. One researcher who uses this model told us that the role is ideal for recent graduates looking to gain research experience before pursuing a PhD, creating a win-win situation for both the project and the individual's career development.

The key is recognizing that different staffing models serve different purposes within a research portfolio. Graduate students can bring theoretical sophistication, longer-term continuity, and deep engagement with scholarly questions. Full-time research staff offer intensive focus during critical periods and dedicated attention to project logistics. Many successful PIs with funding sources that allow these varied types of research roles use a combination approach. This allows them to match staffing decisions to specific project needs and timelines. Understanding your university's job classifications for these positions—whether called research scientists, research associates, or other titles—and having funding certainty for at least a year makes this option viable when project demands require concentrated effort beyond what traditional academic appointments can provide.

Administrative Support: The Missing Piece

Perhaps no area of grant management frustrates social science PIs more than the lack of administrative support. Unlike large centers with dedicated administrative staff, most social scientists cobble together partial solutions that never quite meet their needs. Yet administrative support can make the difference between a smoothly functioning research program and constant crisis management. The tasks that administrative support might handle are numerous: expense reports, travel arrangements, room reservations, speaker payments, meeting scheduling, note-taking, deadline tracking, file management, and basic communication coordination. For PIs trying to juggle research, teaching, and service obligations, offloading these tasks can free up hours each week for actual intellectual work.

Some fortunate researchers benefit from partial administrative support—perhaps eight to ten hours per week shared with other faculty. Even this limited help can be transformative. When possible, hiring an experienced administrator brings not just task completion but institutional knowledge: whom to contact for various issues, how to navigate bureaucratic requirements, which rules are firm and which allow flexibility. Their deep understanding of institutional culture can solve problems that would take faculty hours to untangle.

For truly large projects, some PIs secure funding for project managers. These positions transform project efficiency. A skilled project manager becomes the operational backbone of complex research: scheduling meetings across multiple institutions, ensuring deliverables stay on track, managing communication between team members, maintaining organized file systems, and even helping with community partnership development. One project manager described to us how her support of a multi-site study saved the PI an estimated fifteen hours per week in administrative tasks.

Creative Solutions for Administrative Support

Given funding constraints, PIs must be creative in securing administrative support. General administrative support is typically not allowed on grant budgets because funders often believe it should be covered by indirect cost returns to the institution. If they are allowed, they need to be very carefully justified as being entirely focused on the funded project in a highly specific role.

Some strategies for securing administrative support have proven particularly effective when they are allowed by the specific funding mechanism. Cost-sharing positions across multiple grants or PIs spreads the financial burden while providing more stable employment. Hiring recent graduates as project coordinators offers mutual benefits—they gain professional experience while providing dedicated support. Partnering with other faculty to jointly fund positions creates economies of scale. One innovative approach involves hiring retired university staff for part-time positions. These individuals bring decades of institutional knowledge, understand university systems, and often seek flexible, part-time work. Their experience navigating bureaucracy proves invaluable when facing complex administrative challenges. They know whom to call, which forms to file, and how to phrase requests for maximum effectiveness.

However, creative staffing solutions can still encounter unexpected political challenges. When one junior faculty member hired a full-time project coordinator using grant funds, senior colleagues questioned why they had dedicated support when the department shared a single administrator. The resentment was palpable: "Must be nice to have your own secretary," one colleague commented, not understanding the position was grant-funded and project-specific, not general administrative support.

Managing Politics and Professional Jealousy

The politics surrounding building externally funded research teams deserve explicit acknowledgment. Success in securing grants and building research teams can induce complex interpersonal dynamics within departments and institutions. Colleagues who've never pursued external funding may not understand why you need dedicated staff, why you're buying equipment, or why you have different time constraints than they do. The jealousy can manifest in subtle and not-so-subtle ways. Colleagues might question your commitment to teaching when you buy out teaching obligations. They might resent your ability to attend conferences when travel funds are tight. They might minimize your research contributions, suggesting you're "buying" publications with grant money rather than earning them through scholarship. These attitudes, while frustrating, often stem from misunderstanding rather than malice.

Some PIs report more serious political challenges. Attempts to hire external staff might be blocked by administrators who don't understand project needs. Requests for space might be denied because others have waited longer. Graduate student assignments might mysteriously change, with your funded researchers reassigned to teaching duties. In extreme cases, colleagues might actively undermine grant activities they perceive as threatening to departmental culture or resource allocation.

Navigating these politics requires diplomatic skill and strategic thinking. Build alliances with colleagues who understand external funding, even if they don't pursue it themselves. When needed, educate department administrators, chairs, and deans about how grant activities benefit the entire institution through indirect cost recovery, graduate student funding, and institutional reputation. Most importantly, maintain perspective. The goal isn't to eliminate all political friction—that's impossible in academic environments. Instead, focus on building sufficient support to protect your research activities while minimizing unnecessary conflicts. Choose battles carefully, recognizing that today's opponent might be tomorrow's necessary ally.

The Entrepreneurial Mindset Shift

Perhaps the most fundamental challenge in managing externally funded research teams involves the required mindset shift. Traditional academic training prepares scholars for independent research, peer review, and classroom teaching. It doesn't prepare them to run what amounts to small businesses within university structures. This entrepreneurial aspect of modern academic life catches many social scientists unprepared. The shift begins with recognizing that securing external funding transforms your role. You're no longer just a researcher pursuing intellectual questions. You're now an employer responsible for hiring, training, and managing staff. You're a budget manager tracking expenses and ensuring compliance with sponsor requirements. You're a project manager coordinating timelines and deliverables. You're a diplomat navigating institutional politics and building collaborative relationships.

This entrepreneurial mindset requires different skills than traditional scholarship. You need to think strategically about resource allocation, making difficult decisions about which positions to fund and when. You must balance short-term project needs with long-term sustainability, perhaps sacrificing immediate productivity to build systems supporting future growth. You need to accept risk, knowing that grants might not be renewed and positions might disappear. The business analogies extend further. Like entrepreneurs, PIs must be comfortable with uncertainty and rapid change. A key team member might leave for another opportunity, requiring quick recruitment and training of replacements. Institutional rules might change mid-project, forcing creative adaptations. Funding priorities shift with political administrations, requiring pivot strategies. Success requires resilience, creativity, and willingness to learn from failures.

Yet this entrepreneurial mindset shouldn't completely override scholarly values. The goal isn't to become a business executive who happens to work in academia. Rather, it's to develop hybrid capabilities: maintaining rigorous scholarly standards while building organizational capacity to support research. The most successful PIs integrate entrepreneurial thinking with academic values, creating research operations that are both intellectually vibrant and organizationally sustainable. This integration manifests in practical decisions. When hiring, balance immediate technical needs with long-term team development. When allocating resources, consider both project deliverables and student training opportunities. When facing conflicts, weigh business efficiency against educational mission. The tension between entrepreneurial and academic mindsets never fully resolves; it requires constant navigation and thoughtful balance.

Building Sustainable Teams Despite Constant Turnover

The academic research enterprise faces turnover rates that would cripple most industries. Undergraduate researchers graduate after a year or two. Graduate students complete their degrees. Postdocs move to faculty positions. Even staff members eventually seek more stable employment or they find a higher-paying position in the same institution. This constant churn creates enormous administrative burden and threatens project continuity.

Successful PIs develop strategies to manage this reality. They create overlapping positions so knowledge transfers between generations of researchers. They document everything obsessively, creating detailed protocols, training materials, and project histories. They build training into project timelines rather than expecting immediate productivity. Most importantly, they accept that managing turnover is part of the job, not an unfortunate distraction.

Documentation strategies prove particularly crucial. One effective approach involves requiring all team members to maintain detailed research logs, documenting not just what they did but why they made specific decisions. These logs become invaluable when training new team members or reconstructing project history. Another strategy involves creating video tutorials for common procedures, allowing new team members to learn at their own pace while ensuring consistency.

The portfolio approach to funding (discussed more in Chapter 18) helps tremendously with turnover management. When you have multiple grants with staggered timelines, you can move experienced personnel between projects as needed. You can promise longer-term employment by combining funds from multiple sources. You can maintain critical mass even as individuals come and go. This requires careful planning and often complex negotiations with institutional administrators, but the stability gained justifies the effort.

Some PIs have developed innovative approaches to knowledge management. Some maintain things like a project wiki where all team members contribute to documentation. Others might use collaborative platforms where departing members create "transition documents" detailing their responsibilities, key contacts, and ongoing projects. These systems require initial investment but pay long-term dividends in preserved institutional memory.

Beginning with the End in Mind: Practical Implementation

Stephen Covey's principle transforms from abstract advice to concrete necessity in externally funded staffing. Before posting any position, consider its entire lifecycle. When will you recruit? How long will training take? When will the person become productive? When will they likely start job searching? How will the position end? These questions shape every aspect of position management.

- For postdocs, this might mean structuring two-year appointments with evaluation at year one, recognizing that year two involves job searching. Build in time for knowledge transfer before they leave. Plan for overlapping positions if project continuity is crucial. Document expectations clearly from the start, linking job descriptions to evaluation criteria to avoid later conflicts.
- For graduate students, understand institutional constraints about summer employment, hourly limitations, and benefit requirements. Plan for the reality that students have competing demands on their time and loyalty. Create structured onboarding processes, recognizing you'll need to train new students regularly. Accept that summer productivity will vary wildly based on student availability and motivation.

- For undergraduates, recruit strategically based on expected graduation dates. A junior who can work for two years provides better return on training investment than a senior graduating in months. Create peer mentoring systems where experienced undergraduates train newcomers. Develop projects with natural break points aligning with semester boundaries.

This planning extends to practical matters. If you need someone productive by September, work backward through the timeline. Account for institutional hiring delays, background check requirements, and training needs. Build in buffer time for the unexpected—the perfect candidate who needs visa sponsorship, the institutional hiring freeze that delays everything, the key team member who announces an unexpected departure.

Conclusion: From Overwhelm to Strategic Management

The complexity of externally funded staffing can overwhelm even experienced researchers. The hidden costs, institutional rules, interpersonal dynamics, and administrative burden far exceed what most new PIs anticipate. Yet thousands of social and behavioral scientists successfully manage externally funded teams, advancing knowledge while providing valuable training opportunities for the next generation.

Success requires accepting several difficult truths. Managing people will consume enormous time—plan for it rather than resenting it. Institutional rules will complicate every decision—learn them rather than fighting them. Turnover will create constant challenges—develop systems to manage it rather than hoping it won't happen. Politics and jealousy may emerge—navigate carefully rather than ignoring them. Administrative support will be insufficient—find creative solutions rather than accepting limitations.

The entrepreneurial mindset shift, while challenging, opens new possibilities. By thinking strategically about team building and accepting the business and administrative aspects of research management, PIs can create thriving research operations that multiply their impact. This doesn't mean abandoning scholarly values—rather, it means developing additional capabilities that support and enhance scholarly work.

Most importantly, success requires perspective. Every challenge in managing externally funded teams connects to a larger purpose: advancing knowledge while training future scholars. The undergraduate who struggles today might become tomorrow's innovative researcher. The postdoc who requires extensive mentoring might go on to establish their own successful research program. The administrative systems you build might support decades of future research.

7

Understanding Pre-Award and Post-Award

The shift from thinking about research as a continuous flow to understanding it as distinct pre-award and post-award phases represents more than administrative categorization—it fundamentally transforms how researchers approach their work. This distinction, while initially seeming bureaucratic, actually provides a framework that enhances research quality, planning, and execution in ways that benefit both the researcher and the institution. Pre-award is considered the planning and writing of the grant up to submission, while post-award represents everything from receiving notice of an award to closing the grant.

The Transformative Power of Thinking in Phases

Before engaging with external funding, most researchers conceptualize their work as an uninterrupted journey from idea generation through IRB approval, data collection, analysis, and publication. This organic flow feels natural and allows for flexibility and adaptation. However, external funding introduces a critical demarcation point that changes everything: the moment you receive the award.

This separation into pre-award and post-award phases forces a level of planning rigor that many researchers have never experienced. During the pre-award phase, you must anticipate every aspect of your project's execution—from personnel needs to equipment purchases, from timeline constraints to potential obstacles. This isn't just bureaucratic box-checking; it's comprehensive project design at a level that makes your research more robust and achievable.

The transformation is profound. Without this framework, research planning often remains loose and adaptable, with the assumption that adjustments can be made as needed. While flexibility has its merits, it can also lead to inefficiencies, missed opportunities, and inadequate resource allocation. The pre-award/post-award structure demands that you think through every detail because once you transition to post-award, your resources are largely fixed. If you haven't planned for something in pre-award, you likely won't have the money or approval to do it in post-award.

This constraint, rather than being limiting, becomes liberating. It forces researchers to develop clearer project scopes, more realistic timelines, and better-defined outcomes. The rigor required for external funding often makes researchers better at designing and executing all their research, even projects without external support.

Pre-Award: Building Your Research Foundation

The pre-award phase encompasses everything needed to secure funding, from initial conceptualization through proposal submission. Some universities have dedicated pre-award staff who specialize in helping faculty navigate this complex landscape, while others combine these roles into a single staff member. One of the biggest roles these research administrators play is helping with budget development. See Chapter 15 for a detailed discussion of budgets. Understanding what these professionals do—and don't do—is crucial for building effective partnerships.

The Reality of "Grant Writers"

One of the most persistent misconceptions in academia is the role of the "grant writer." Faculty often hear this term and assume these professionals will write their research narratives, crafting compelling scientific arguments and designing methodologies. This fundamental misunderstanding can lead to frustration and missed opportunities for meaningful support.

In reality, grant writers don't write your science—you do. As the investigator, you possess the deep theoretical knowledge, methodological expertise, and vision that drives the research. A skilled grant writer serves multiple crucial functions. They ensure format compliance, checking that your proposal adheres to often-byzantine funder requirements regarding margins, fonts, page limits, and section organization. They read your narrative with fresh eyes, identifying areas where jargon might obscure meaning or where arguments need strengthening for nonspecialist reviewers. Grant writers can also understand the bigger picture institutional opportunities and help you leverage those in your application. They spot opportunities to weave in institutional strengths, can introduce you to potential collaborators, and to institutional members who may be willing to offer advice that can strengthen your competitive position.

Visual Communication Through Graphics

The power of visual communication in grant proposals cannot be overstated, yet many researchers underestimate its importance. Sometimes, researchers have access to graphic designers who can transform rough sketches into professional visualizations that clarify complex concepts and enhance proposal readability. Creating effective graphics requires researchers to first crystallize their ideas visually—an exercise that often reveals gaps or disconnections in the research plan itself. The process of sketching out your research design, even crudely, forces you to identify relationships, sequences, and dependencies that might remain hidden in text-based descriptions.

One particularly successful example involved hiring an architecture student to create a visual representation of a complex community engagement project. The resulting graphic not only strengthened the proposal but became a cornerstone of project communication. Note that Figure 7.1 provides a caption that clearly gives the "take-away message." Too many figure captions are simply descriptions (e.g., "Data from Experiment") without telling reviewers what the figure is conveying in support of the overall argument in the proposal. In the project where Figure 7.1 was used, after it was funded, this single image appeared on the

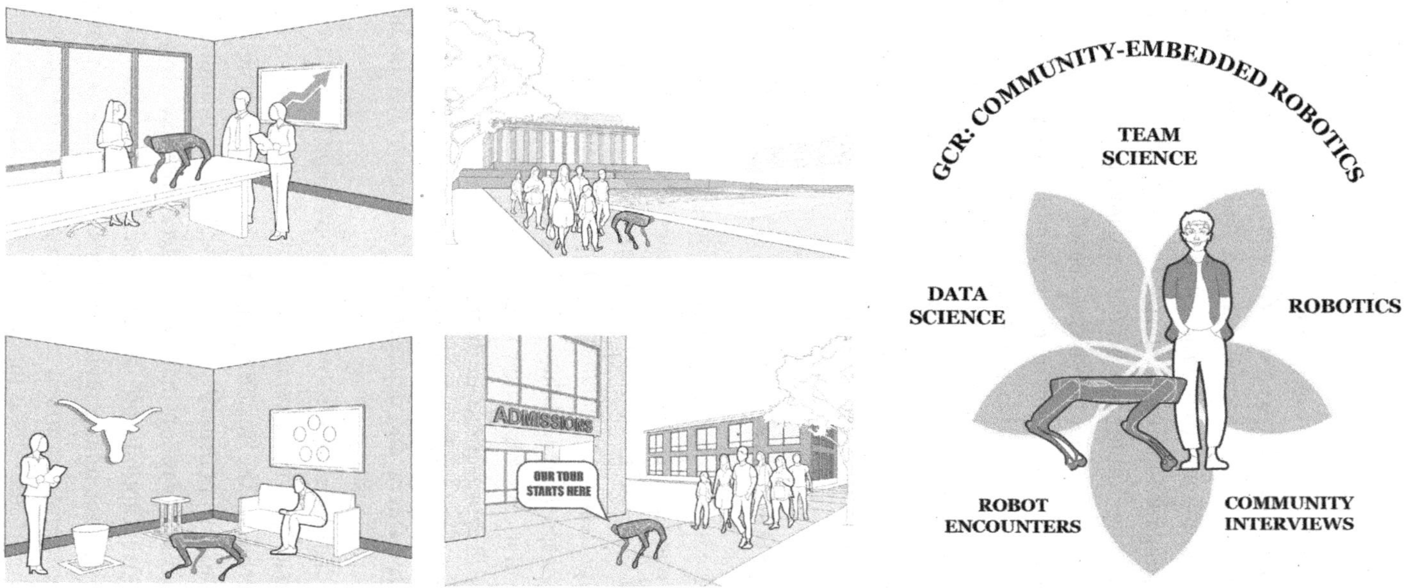

Figure 7.1 Project visualization useful in proposal and for websites explaining project. Reproduced with permission of the designer, Sarah Kay Stephens.

project website, in every presentation, and in progress reports. It became the visual shorthand that helped diverse stakeholders quickly understand the project's scope and approach.

This multiplier effect—where proposal materials serve ongoing project needs—illustrates why investing in quality graphics during pre-award pays dividends throughout the project lifecycle. A well-designed conceptual model or project workflow diagram created for your proposal often becomes essential for team coordination, stakeholder communication, and dissemination activities.

Templates, Timelines, and Coordination

Experienced pre-award professionals maintain extensive libraries of templates and examples that can dramatically streamline proposal development. These resources include everything from email scripts for initial program officer contact to formatted biosketches for different funding agencies. For researchers new to external funding, these templates provide crucial scaffolding that demystifies the grant-seeking process.

Timeline management represents another critical pre-award function. Skilled administrators create detailed schedules that account for all proposal components while building in buffer time for the inevitable complications. They understand faculty work patterns—recognizing that academics often work in intensive bursts rather than steady progress—and design timelines that accommodate these rhythms while ensuring deadlines are met.

In multi-investigator proposals, pre-award staff become invaluable coordinators. They can reach out to collaborators for required documents, track submission progress, and diplomatically nudge team members who fall behind. This project management function frees principal investigators to focus on scientific content while ensuring all administrative pieces come together smoothly.

Post-Award: Executing with Excellence

The transition from pre-award to post-award marks a fundamental shift in your relationship with research administration. The collaborative brainstorming and creative problem-solving of proposal development give way to a focus on compliance, accountability, and careful resource management. This isn't a reduction in support quality—it's a necessary evolution that ensures your project meets all legal and fiduciary obligations.

Account Setup and Financial Infrastructure

Post-award administration begins with establishing the financial infrastructure for your project. This involves creating account numbers, setting up approval hierarchies, and ensuring all university systems recognize your new funding. Be sure to read more about these procedures in Chapter 16, You Got the Grant: Communicating Your Success. While seemingly mundane, this foundational work enables everything that follows.

The complexity of account structures often surprises new investigators. Funds must be allocated to specific categories—salary, fringe benefits, travel, supplies, equipment—with varying rules governing each. Understanding these categories and their restrictions from the outset prevents frustration later when you discover that money can't always be moved freely between accounts.

Compliance and Ongoing Management

Post-award administrators serve as your guides through the maze of compliance requirements that accompany external funding. They ensure you maintain required training certifications, submit progress reports on schedule, and document expenses appropriately. This isn't bureaucracy for its own sake; it is protection for both you and your institution during the audits that inevitably occur.

The timeline management function continues in post-award, though with a different focus. Administrators send reminders about approaching grant expiration dates, flag when spending rates suggest potential problems, and help navigate no-cost extension requests when projects need additional time. Their institutional memory about specific funder requirements and preferences can be invaluable when facing unexpected challenges.

The Art of Rebudgeting

One of the most valuable post-award services involves rebudgeting—the process of moving funds between budget categories as project needs evolve. Despite careful planning, research rarely proceeds exactly as anticipated. Perhaps you budgeted for equipment that proves unnecessary, or fringe benefit rates changed, leaving excess funds in that category. Rebudgeting requires understanding both institutional policies and sponsor requirements. Some funders allow significant flexibility, while others require approval for even minor changes. Post-award administrators know these rules and can guide you through the approval process, often handling sponsor communications on your behalf.

A common scenario involves excess funds accumulating in fringe benefit accounts. When institutional rates decrease or personnel changes occur, these accounts can build substantial balances that can't be used for their original purpose. Skilled administrators help identify these accumulations early and facilitate moving funds to areas of greater need, such as additional personnel support or participant compensation.

Account Closure and Final Reconciliation

As grants near their end dates, post-award support becomes crucial for ensuring clean closures. This involves reconciling all expenses, chasing down final receipts, and ensuring all transactions clear before accounts close. The complexity of university purchasing systems means that what seems like a simple transaction can take weeks to fully process. Post-award staff understand these timelines and help researchers avoid the common pitfall of discovering unpaid expenses after accounts close. They provide crucial reminders about deadlines for final purchases and help expedite processing when time grows short.

Making the Choice: Is External Funding Right for You?

After understanding the comprehensive nature of pre-award and post-award administration, it's important to acknowledge a fundamental truth: external funding isn't for everyone, and that's perfectly acceptable. The administrative responsibilities, compliance requirements, and time investments are substantial. Some researchers may find that these demands detract from the joy and productivity of their research.

Small-scale internal grants can provide adequate support for many research projects without the extensive administrative overlay. These funding sources allow researchers to maintain focus on the intellectual work they love while avoiding the entrepreneurial and managerial aspects of large external grants. Social scientists and humanities scholars have conducted high-quality, impactful research for decades without external funding, so the decision to seek it should be driven by the research you want to conduct.

For those who do choose to pursue external funding, recognizing that you're essentially committing to run a small business within the university helps set appropriate expectations. You'll need to develop new skills in project management, personnel supervision, and financial oversight. While these capabilities can enhance your research impact and open new opportunities, they also require time and energy that could otherwise go toward pure research activities.

Looking Ahead: Learning from the Research Administrators

Understanding pre-award and post-award functions provides the foundation for building successful relationships with research administrators. The next chapter, Chapter 8, takes you behind the scenes to hear directly from four experienced research administrators about their career paths, daily challenges, and perspectives on building effective faculty partnerships. Through their stories, you'll discover how these professionals view their work, what makes faculty collaborations successful or frustrating, and how to maximize the support available at your institution. Their insights reveal the human side of research administration—the dedication, expertise, and genuine desire to see faculty succeed that motivates their work.

These administrators will share candid observations about common faculty mistakes, the importance of timing and preparation, and how appreciation and recognition can enhance the support you receive. Their perspectives will help you see research administrators not as bureaucratic obstacles but as knowledgeable allies in your research journey. By understanding both the systematic framework of pre-award and post-award administration and the human elements that make these partnerships work, you'll be better positioned to navigate the complex world of external funding successfully. Whether you ultimately choose to pursue major grants or stick with smaller funding sources, this knowledge will help you make informed decisions about your research future.

8

Inside the World of Research Administration

Research administration, and the related concept of research development, are critical yet often invisible components of the academic research enterprise. While faculty members focus on developing innovative research ideas and conducting studies, research administrators work tirelessly behind the scenes to ensure that the complex machinery of grant funding operates smoothly. Through an in-depth exploration of the experiences of Julie Campos, an experienced research administrator at the University of Texas at Austin, Tyler Myatt, former grant writer at Texas Tech University's College of Media & Communication and current content director with Hanover Research, Cory Blackwell, an assistant director with thirteen years of experience at Texas Tech University's Office of Research Services and Elizabeth Carroll, who works in Texas Tech's central Research Development and Communications Office, we gain valuable insights into this essential profession that bridges the gap between researchers' scientific ambitions and the practical realities of securing and managing external funding.

These essential professions (referred to as research administration in this chapter) remain largely misunderstood, particularly by faculty in the social sciences, who often receive less institutional support and training for grant-seeking compared to their STEM counterparts. Understanding the world of research administration is crucial for social scientists seeking to build successful partnerships that can significantly enhance their research funding success while making the complex landscape of grant funding more navigable and less overwhelming.

The Accidental Profession and Its Evolution

Perhaps no aspect of research administration is more telling than how people enter the field. The pathways into research administration are as diverse as they are unexpected, reflecting a profession that draws talented individuals from across disciplines and career backgrounds. Tyler Myatt's journey exemplifies this pattern perfectly. His entry into research administration began at a party where he was "complaining about how much I hated public accounting" to a friend who suggested he might enjoy grant work. Intrigued by the possibility of working with academic research rather than corporate finances, Tyler took a fifteen-hour graduate certificate course in grant and proposal writing—a relatively modest educational investment that opened an entirely new career path. He was subsequently recruited by Texas Tech's College of Media & Communication and spent nearly a decade becoming an expert in research development, ultimately supporting millions of dollars in successful grant applications.

The transition from accounting to research administration proved surprisingly seamless for Tyler, who discovered that his financial background provided crucial skills for budget development and cost analysis that many faculty found intimidating. "I found that social science faculty, in particular, often viewed budgeting as the most intimidating part of any proposal," Tyler reflects. "My accounting background allowed me to translate complex budget requirements into accessible formats and help faculty understand the financial implications of their research plans." This translation ability became one of his most valuable services, enabling faculty to focus on research design while ensuring their projects were financially realistic and compliant with sponsor requirements.

Similarly, Elizabeth Carroll's transition into research administration demonstrates how skills from seemingly unrelated fields prove surprisingly valuable in grant management. Her background in linguistics and international student services, particularly her extensive experience with federal immigration documentation, provided unexpected preparation for the regulatory complexity and compliance requirements that characterize grant administration. Her work supporting international students through complex federal processes translated directly to helping faculty researchers navigate the equally complex world of grant funding regulations and requirements.

Elizabeth's linguistic training proved particularly valuable in understanding the precise language requirements that characterize different funding announcements. "Grant solicitations often use very specific terminology that has particular meanings within the funding agency context," she explains. "My background in linguistics helped me understand how subtle differences in wording could signal different expectations or requirements." This attention to linguistic precision became crucial when helping faculty craft proposals that aligned precisely with funder expectations and demonstrated clear understanding of program priorities.

Cory Blackwell's path illustrates another common entry route through public service. After working for Texas Parks and Wildlife Department for eight and a half years, he pursued an MBA at night school while working full-time, graduating in 2010. When family considerations led him to seek a more stable position with less travel, he discovered research administration through job searching with keywords like "budgeting." As he explains, "I really just happened into the research administration field. I didn't really know anything about it, but the skills that were required were the skills that I had picked up through my MBA." His background in geography, anthropology, and business, combined with his public service experience, provided an ideal foundation for supporting faculty research endeavors. Starting as an entry-level research administrator in October 2012, Cory has worked his way up through the proposal team over thirteen years to become an assistant director, demonstrating the career advancement possibilities within the profession.

This pattern of "accidental entry" reflects what Julie Campos observes: "We jokingly say that nobody started out to be a research administrator." People arrive through diverse pathways—from accounting, international affairs, linguistics, library sciences, education, and countless other fields—bringing varied skill sets that prove valuable in unexpected ways. Elizabeth notes that within the national research administration organizations, "there is no clear path that brought everyone into research development," highlighting how the profession attracts individuals with diverse backgrounds and experiences.

Julie's own path into research administration began in financial management within university settings, where she developed expertise in complex financial systems and regulatory compliance that proved directly applicable to grant management. Her experience managing large budgets and ensuring compliance with federal regulations in other university contexts provided a solid foundation for understanding the financial and regulatory aspects of research funding. "What I discovered was that research administration combined my interest in supporting academic excellence with my skills in financial management and regulatory compliance," Julie explains. "It allowed me to contribute directly to scientific advancement while using the analytical and organizational skills I had developed throughout my career."

The professionalization of research administration has evolved significantly over recent decades, transforming from an informal support function to a sophisticated profession with formal education programs, certification requirements, and robust professional networks. Julie Campos holds a Certified Research Administrator (CRA) credential, which required passing a rigorous four-hour examination covering all aspects of research administration from pre-award through post-award management. This certification must be maintained through continuing education, with requirements recently updated from every five years to every three years, requiring eighty hours of professional development activities. Remarkably, as Julie notes with some irony, this exceeds the continuing education requirements for many other professions, including law.

The research administration community maintains robust professional networks through organizations like the National Council of University Research Administrators (NCURA), the Society of Research Administrators International (SRA International), and the National Organization of Research Development Professionals (NORDP). These organizations host annual conferences that provide crucial opportunities for professional development and informal knowledge exchange.

Understanding Institutional Structures and Support Models

Research administrators operate within institutional infrastructures that vary significantly across universities, creating a complex landscape that faculty must learn to navigate. Understanding these structural variations is crucial for social scientists seeking to identify the right type of support for their specific needs and career stages. The differences between centralized and decentralized models, specialized versus generalist support, research development versus administration, and college-level versus university-wide services create different opportunities and constraints that significantly affect the types and quality of support available to faculty.

At Texas Tech University, Cory works within a centralized model where the Office of Research Services handles all externally funded research grant proposals for the entire university. Their team manages caseloads divided by colleges and departments, with each team member assigned to particular sets of departments and colleges. This centralized approach ensures consistency in institutional policies and procedures while allowing for specialization based on experience levels and management responsibilities.

The training and development of new team members represents a significant investment. Cory describes how "for the first six to twelve months, we review all of the budgets that our newest team members prepare, and all of the proposals that they're submitting." This systematic approach ensures quality control while building expertise, though it requires substantial time investment from experienced administrators. The office's approach to hiring emphasizes transferable skills rather than prior research administration experience: "We really focus on the skills and abilities you need to do the job, then we focus on job training."

Elizabeth also works within a centralized model where the Research Development and Communications Office reports directly to the vice president of Research and Innovation. This centralized structure focuses primarily on large center-type grants and institutional strategic initiatives, providing specialized expertise for complex, multimillion-dollar proposals that require coordination across multiple colleges and significant infrastructure support. There is a similar centralized structure at the University of Texas as well. This level of coordination and project management support would be difficult for individual colleges or departments to maintain, but it becomes feasible when provided through a centralized office with dedicated resources and specialized expertise.

In contrast, Tyler's embedded role within the College of Media & Communication represented a decentralized model where research administrators work directly within individual colleges or departments.

This embedded approach allowed Tyler to provide comprehensive support to faculty across all grant-seeking activities, from small foundation grants to major federal awards. His college-level position enabled him to develop deep, long-term relationships with faculty members, understanding their individual research trajectories, career goals, and specific support needs.

The embedded model offers significant advantages for building sustained relationships and providing personalized support. Tyler describes how his nine years in the college allowed him to develop intimate knowledge of faculty research programs. This deep familiarity enabled him to provide anticipatory support, understanding faculty career trajectories and research evolution in ways that allowed him to identify relevant opportunities and provide strategic guidance that extended well beyond individual proposal development.

Tyler's embedded position also allowed him to develop resources specifically tailored to the needs of social science faculty in his college. "I have templates for everything you want. I have a template for a concept paper that you can use to approach a program officer. I have a script for the email if you're nervous about the first introduction to the program officer," he explains. These resources addressed the specific knowledge gaps that social science faculty often face, providing structured guidance for activities that STEM faculty might handle intuitively based on their doctoral training.

However, the embedded model also has constraints that became apparent when Tyler moved to supporting larger, university-wide grants. Individual colleges may lack the resources to support extremely complex proposals or may not have expertise in certain types of funding mechanisms. The embedded administrator may become overwhelmed during busy proposal seasons or may lack the specialized knowledge needed for particular types of awards.

This structural variety means that faculty often struggle to understand who does what and when to engage different types of support. Tyler frequently found himself copied on emails intended for the Office of Research Services, while faculty would sometimes approach central offices for services his college office provided. The confusion about institutional support structures is compounded by the fact that many universities maintain hybrid models that combine centralized and decentralized elements, often with overlapping responsibilities and different areas of specialization. Some institutions have centralized pre-award support but decentralized post-award management. Others maintain specialized centers for particular types of funding while providing general support through college-level offices. Understanding these institutional variations requires faculty to invest time in learning their specific institutional landscape and building relationships with appropriate administrators at different organizational levels.

For social scientists, understanding these institutional variations is particularly important because they may need more comprehensive support than STEM faculty who typically receive grant-seeking training throughout their doctoral programs. Identifying the right research administrator—whether embedded in their college, centralized at the university level, or specialized in particular funding types—can significantly impact their grant-seeking success. The key is understanding not only which services are available but also which administrator or office is best positioned to provide the type and level of support needed for specific career stages and grant types.

The Multifaceted Role Revealed

At its core, research administration involves navigating the intricate landscape of grant funding from proposal development through post-award management, but the complexity of this role becomes apparent when examining the daily realities that research administrators face and the diverse skill sets they must maintain to support faculty success effectively. The role extends far beyond the paperwork processing that faculty often assume defines research administration, encompassing strategic intelligence gathering, project management, education and skill-building, compliance oversight, and relationship facilitation that enables successful collaborative research.

Julie Campos explains that her typical day is driven by deadlines and the need to juggle multiple proposals simultaneously, each with its own unique set of rules and requirements. She has a systematic approach including using detailed checklists to manage complexity while ensuring that nothing falls through the cracks. The systematic nature of her work reflects years of experience in identifying potential problems before they occur and developing reliable processes that can handle the inevitable complications that arise during proposal development.

Julie's approach to prioritization reveals the strategic thinking required for effective research administration. This prioritization is not arbitrary but reflects understanding of institutional priorities, faculty career needs, and the relative complexity and potential impact of different types of proposals. A federal proposal may require weeks of intensive support and coordination, while a small foundation grant might need only basic compliance checking and submission assistance.

The position demands exceptional ability to switch contexts rapidly while maintaining attention to detail across multiple complex projects. On any given day, Julie might work on a multimillion-dollar federal grant requiring extensive compliance documentation, a foundation proposal with unique formatting requirements, and a state grant with specific regulatory restrictions, all while managing deadlines for different sponsors and coordinating with faculty who have varying levels of experience and different support needs.

Research administrators serve as strategic intelligence gatherers, staying current with funding landscapes that change rapidly and often unpredictably. This intelligence function requires constant vigilance and sophisticated understanding of how different funding agencies operate, how their priorities evolve, and how these changes affect research opportunities for faculty.

Project management also has become central to effective research administration, particularly as proposals become more complex and collaborative. This evolution reflects the growing recognition that successful grant development requires coordinated effort across multiple stakeholders, often with competing priorities and schedules. Tyler's project management responsibilities included creating and maintaining detailed timelines that accounted for faculty schedules, institutional review processes, and sponsor requirements.

Elizabeth describes similar responsibilities at an institutional scale: "We help faculty in organizing the meetings. So, we can serve as a project manager in the development of it… maintaining regular communication with the lead on a project with other individuals on a team." Her office's project management becomes particularly crucial for interdisciplinary or multi-institutional proposals where coordination challenges multiply exponentially and where faculty may lack experience managing large, complex collaborative projects. Moreover, this larger-scale context requires creative problem-solving within the constraints of institutional security policies and federal compliance requirements.

Another role research administrators can serve in some institutions involves education and skill-building for faculty, particularly in areas where traditional academic training provides insufficient preparation for the grant-seeking process. Elizabeth emphasizes that "writing for proposals for funding requires a different skill set versus what you typically see in publishing.... You have to really sell the idea." The distinction between academic writing and grant writing represents a fundamental challenge that many faculty struggle with, particularly those in fields where persuasive writing may be less common than analytical or descriptive writing. Grant writing requires faculty to make explicit arguments about significance, feasibility, and impact that may be implicit or understated in traditional academic writing.

Many centralized research administration offices address this educational need through structured programming that builds both skills and community among faculty. These offices engage in activities such as running regular writing groups, helping faculty set goals, answering questions, and bouncing off ideas. Writing groups provide both practical support and informal mentorship opportunities, creating communities of practice that help faculty develop grant-seeking skills over time while building professional relationships that can support future collaborations.

Building Effective Faculty Partnerships

The relationship between research administrators and faculty researchers forms the cornerstone of successful grant management, but building these partnerships requires understanding and effort from both parties, along with recognition that effective collaboration can significantly enhance both the quality of proposals and the likelihood of funding success. These partnerships develop over time through repeated interactions, shared successes, and mutual understanding of respective expertise and constraints.

The contrast between well-prepared faculty and those who engage late or without adequate preparation is striking. Julie describes faculty who arrive with complete understanding of sponsor requirements, realistic timelines, and clear communication about their needs as enabling efficient, high-quality collaboration. "They know to read the solicitation carefully, they understand what documents they need to provide, and they give me realistic deadlines for reviewing their work," she explains. "This allows me to provide much more substantive feedback and support because I'm not spending time tracking down basic information or explaining fundamental requirements."

Faculty who attempt to bypass administrative processes create additional complications. Cory notes that some faculty "will submit proposals without going through our office" to private foundations where direct submission is possible, but "then the award comes in, and they want us to process it, and we find that there's conditions that we can't accept with the award, and we end up having to decline an award that we could have accepted if they had gone through us beforehand." These situations highlight the importance of institutional oversight in ensuring that awards align with university policies and capabilities.

Communication style plays a crucial role in these partnerships, requiring sensitivity to sometimes delicate dynamics between administrative expertise and academic authority. Julie has developed a careful approach to working with diverse faculty personalities: "My approach is always just to be as respectful as possible, to entertain whatever thought they might have, and to present my counter to that.... I never want to appear to be a know-it-all." This diplomatic approach helps navigate situations where administrators may have more knowledge about funding mechanisms while faculty have deeper expertise in their research areas.

Tyler stresses the importance of setting clear expectations early in partnerships: "Early on I went into a few of these projects, where we got through a full draft or two revising before the PI realized that I wasn't a subject matter expert, because I didn't communicate that well enough because I was inexperienced." This experience taught him the importance of establishing realistic boundaries and expectations from the beginning of working relationships.

A significant but often overlooked aspect of faculty-administrator partnerships involves recognition and appreciation, which can substantially impact the quality and extent of support that faculty receive. Cory's insights reveal how appreciation creates positive feedback loops that benefit both parties and ultimately enhance research success. "We notice the appreciation of our faculty, and it's something that, I mean, it gets around the office," he explains. "So we have the faculty who appreciate us get a lot of word-of-mouth through the office, and so they end up getting a lot of really good support."

The key insight for faculty is that simple acknowledgments and appreciation can significantly enhance their working relationships with research administrators. This appreciation doesn't require elaborate gestures but can be expressed through timely communication, realistic expectations, acknowledgment of administrators' expertise, and recognition of the complex work involved in proposal development and submission.

Timing Matters

Timing emerges as perhaps the most crucial factor in successful partnerships, with early engagement enabling higher-quality support and better outcomes for all involved. All four administrators emphasize this principle, though they also recognize that academic schedules and opportunity timelines do not always allow for ideal planning. Julie provides specific deadlines for different proposal components: "I think faculty appreciate having dates.... It helps them to organize their brain [about] when things need to be done, and it helps them not to be last-minute."

Julie's approach to timeline management reflects understanding of both administrative requirements and faculty work patterns. She creates structured schedules that account for the time needed for substantive review and revision while recognizing that faculty often work in intensive bursts rather than steady, incremental progress. "I try to build in buffer time for unexpected complications while still maintaining realistic expectations about when different components need to be completed," she explains.

Elizabeth reinforces this from her central office perspective: "The longer that we have before a proposal is due, that makes for a more productive relationship, just that we have the time to be able to provide as much service as possible." When faculty engage late in the process, "the quality suffers.... Our Grant editors, which is one of our largely used services, they may not even have the time capacity to look at something." Elizabeth's experience illustrates how timing affects not just the quality of individual proposals but also the types of services that can be provided.

These timing challenges are compounded by the volume of proposals that offices handle simultaneously. As Cory explains, faculty "don't realize that our office may be submitting dozens of proposals that day, and I think some faculty they don't take into account how many proposals and faculty we work with. They think that once they reach out to us, we're completely focused and only working on their proposal. And that's just not the way it operates."

Additional timing complications arise from technological security requirements that didn't exist in earlier eras of research administration. Cory notes that sponsor portals "have gotten a lot more restrictive on access" and "a lot of these require multifactor authentication for us to log into now." These security measures mean that "sometimes just getting logged into a sponsor portal to work on a proposal can take five to ten minutes to go through those steps," adding unexpected delays that faculty may not anticipate when calculating submission timelines.

Early engagement allows for iterative development, strategic planning, and comprehensive review that significantly enhance proposal competitiveness. Late engagement often limits support to basic compliance checking and formatting assistance, missing opportunities for substantive improvement that could make the difference between funding and rejection.

Looking Across Disciplines to See External Funding Differences

The external perspective that research administrators provide proves valuable precisely because they understand funder priorities and reviewer expectations while maintaining some distance from the detailed technical content. Tyler explains how this perspective enabled him to help faculty position their work more effectively: "I could look at a proposal and immediately see whether the significance was clearly articulated for a nonspecialist audience, whether the broader impacts were compelling, and whether the research plan would make sense to reviewers from related but not identical fields."

Tyler's experience working across different disciplinary contexts reveals important distinctions in partnership development and the types of support that prove most valuable for different faculty populations. When he moved from college-level support to working on large, university-wide grants, he found that "STEM faculty are taught… how to write grants and to navigate especially federal funding landscapes, but they just know it better." This difference meant that his role with STEM faculty became "much more of a project management role" focused on coordination and compliance rather than education and skill-building.

The budget scale differences between disciplines also affect the types of support needed and the expectations for proposal development. Cory provides specific comparisons: STEM projects typically involve "$200,000 to $300,000 per year for a three- to five-year project," while social science projects more commonly request "$50,000 to a $100,000 per year for one to two years." These scale differences affect everything from budget complexity to institutional overhead calculations to the level of infrastructure support required. Submission frequency also varies dramatically between disciplines, affecting both faculty experience levels and administrative workload patterns. Cory estimates that "a STEM type faculty might submit four or five major proposals per year, and a couple of small ones," while "a social science faculty might submit one major a year or every other year, and then two or three smaller ones per year." This frequency difference means that STEM faculty develop familiarity with proposal processes through repeated exposure, while social science faculty may need more comprehensive support for each submission due to less frequent engagement with grant-seeking activities.

The distinction in faculty preparation levels significantly affected the nature of partnerships Tyler could develop. With experienced STEM faculty, partnerships often focused on efficiency, coordination, and strategic positioning rather than fundamental education about grant-seeking processes. With social science faculty, partnerships required more comprehensive support across all aspects of proposal development, from identifying appropriate opportunities through post-award planning.

Elizabeth observes that social scientists bring a different perspective to collaboration that creates opportunities for particularly productive partnerships: "Social scientists are eager to reach out to us to be able to be integrated on projects to get involved earlier on versus added on to a project… really being able to shape the proposal itself, instead of just being an add-on." This eagerness for meaningful collaboration contrasts with some STEM collaborations where social scientists may be added late in the process to address specific requirements rather than being integrated into the fundamental design of research projects.

This desire for substantive involvement creates opportunities for research administrators to provide more comprehensive support while helping social scientists contribute meaningfully to interdisciplinary projects. Understanding this dynamic allows administrators to position social science collaborators more effectively and helps social scientists articulate their potential contributions more persuasively.

Supporting Diverse Institutional Contexts

One of the most significant challenges in research administration involves working with institutions that have varying levels of research infrastructure, creating disparities that affect collaborative research projects and limit opportunities for faculty at these institutions. These disparities manifest in multiple ways, from differences in administrative expertise and support staff to variations in technological infrastructure and compliance oversight that can significantly impact the success of multi-institutional collaborations.

When collaborating with subcontractors from under-resourced universities, Julie often finds herself in an educational role that extends well beyond her primary institutional responsibilities: She describes situations where administrators from under-resourced institutions lack access to the professional development opportunities, specialized training, and peer networks that larger institutions can provide. "I might be working with someone who is handling all aspects of research administration single-handedly, from pre-award through post-award, often while juggling other responsibilities like sponsored programs administration or compliance oversight," she explains. "They simply don't have the bandwidth to stay current with constantly changing regulations or to attend professional conferences that could enhance their knowledge."

The educational role Julie finds herself in requires significant additional time and effort but is essential for project success. "I might spend hours walking someone through basic compliance requirements or helping them understand budget development principles that I take for granted at my institution," she notes. "But if I don't provide this support, the entire collaborative project suffers, and the faculty at the under-resourced institution lose valuable opportunities to participate in funded research." This absence of specialized support creates additional workload for administrators at institutions with more developed research support offices who must step in to fill gaps if collaborative projects are to succeed.

Tyler Myatt's evolution from college-level to university-wide support gave him perspective on resource variations even within a single institution, illustrating how support needs and capabilities can vary dramatically across different organizational contexts. At the college level, he was often "a one-man show" handling everything from opportunity identification to budget development to proposal review and post-award support. As he moved to supporting larger, multi-institutional grants, he observed how some institutions simply lacked the infrastructure for complex proposal development.

The challenge of supporting institutions with limited research infrastructure is compounded by the fact that many funding agencies expect all participating institutions to meet the same standards of compliance and project management regardless of their internal capacity. Tyler observed how this expectation could create unfair disadvantages for faculty at institutions with fewer research support resources: "A faculty member at a small teaching college might have a brilliant research idea and real expertise in their field, but they're competing against faculty from R1 institutions who might have resources to hire professional grant editors, dedicated budget specialists, and comprehensive compliance support."

Julie actively mentors research administrators from under-resourced institutions, both formally through conference presentations and informally through ongoing professional relationships. "I try to make myself available to answer questions or provide guidance when colleagues from under-resourced institutions are dealing with situations they haven't encountered before," she explains. "We all benefit when the research administration community is stronger, and that requires sharing knowledge and supporting professional development across institutional types."

For social scientists, understanding these resource disparities is important because social science research often involves collaborations across diverse institutional types, including community colleges, teaching-focused universities, and specialized research institutions that may have limited research administration infrastructure. Social scientists seeking to build collaborative relationships should be prepared to help identify and address support needs at partner institutions, potentially including research administration support in collaborative budgets or seeking funding mechanisms that provide capacity-building resources for under-resourced institutions.

Navigating Funding Complexity

Research administrators must manage diverse requirements across different funding sources, each with its own rules, expectations, and compliance standards, requiring them to maintain expertise across multiple regulatory frameworks while adapting quickly to changing requirements and emerging opportunities. See Chapter 3 for detailed descriptions of the various types of funding social scientists and humanities scholars typically receive. The complexity of the funding landscape has only increased over time as funding agencies have developed more sophisticated requirements and as interdisciplinary collaboration has become more common.

While federal grants follow predictable patterns that experienced administrators can navigate efficiently, foundation funding presents unique challenges characterized by variability that requires different strategies and skills than federal grant applications. Julie describes the detective work often required when working with foundation funding: "Sometimes I'm told there's not an RFA. And then I start digging.... I will poke around and do some research online for that particular foundation. And then I might find out that actually, there is an RFA." This variability requires research administrators to be skilled investigators, often uncovering requirements and systems that are not immediately apparent and helping faculty understand the sometimes hidden expectations that characterize foundation funding.

The foundation funding challenge is further complicated by the relationship-based nature of many foundation grants, which operate on informal networks and personal connections that may be completely unfamiliar to faculty accustomed to the more systematic processes of federal funding. Julie describes situations where foundation requirements are communicated through informal channels or where application processes depend on preliminary conversations with program officers that must be initiated months before formal deadlines. "I might discover that what appears to be an open application process actually requires a letter of intent or preliminary proposal that isn't mentioned in the official guidelines," she explains. "Or I find out that successful applicants typically engage with the foundation through conference presentations or advisory board participation that creates relationship foundations for future funding."

State funding occupies a particularly challenging middle ground, often combining federal-style complexity with additional restrictions and reporting requirements that differ significantly from both federal and foundation standards. Furthermore, requirements can vary significantly not just between states but even between different agencies within the same state government. Julie describes working with Texas state agencies that have completely different budget categories, reporting requirements, and compliance standards despite all being part of the same state system. "I might work on a grant from the Texas Education Agency that has one set of requirements and then immediately switch to a Department of Transportation grant that operates under completely different rules," she notes.

The Strategic Partnership Model

A fundamental tension exists in research administration between the need to be flexible and responsive while operating within strict regulatory frameworks, and this tension captures the essence of what makes research administration both challenging and essential for institutional success. Julie captures this balance perfectly: "Our job is all about being flexible and able to pivot but recognizing that much of our job is following hard-and-fast rules." This duality manifests in numerous ways throughout the research administration process, from mobilizing resources quickly for sudden funding opportunities to adapting existing processes when regulations change mid-stream, all while ensuring compliance and maintaining quality standards.

The balance between flexibility and rules becomes particularly evident during crisis situations or when unexpected opportunities arise. Julie describes situations where major funding announcements are released with tight deadlines, requiring rapid mobilization of resources and expertise while ensuring all compliance requirements are met. "We might have forty-eight hours to pull together a letter of intent for a major center grant, which means coordinating with faculty across multiple departments, ensuring all institutional commitments are realistic and approved, and making sure we understand any special requirements that could affect our approach," she explains. This requires both systematic preparation and the ability to adapt quickly to unexpected circumstances.

Tyler's philosophy that research administration should "take things off researchers' plates" rather than add bureaucracy captures the essence of effective partnership and illustrates how research administrators can become force multipliers for faculty productivity. His approach evolved from simple administrative support to comprehensive project management: "Project management ultimately became the main thrust of my role." This evolution reflects how research administrators can enhance faculty effectiveness while enabling researchers to focus on their core competencies in research design, implementation, and dissemination.

Tyler's project management approach required understanding not just administrative requirements but also faculty work patterns, research timelines, and the complex interpersonal dynamics that characterize successful collaborative research. "I learned that effective project management in the academic context requires different skills than project management in business settings," he reflects. "Faculty have different work rhythms, competing priorities, and collaborative styles that require flexible approaches while still maintaining systematic progress toward proposal deadlines."

The partnership model requires mutual understanding, respect, and clear communication about roles, expectations, and capabilities. Tyler learned through experience that effective partnerships require administrators to take responsibility for clear communication: "I will always put it more on us than I will on the researchers, because we are there to help" while also expecting faculty to engage early and communicate clearly about their needs and constraints. This approach acknowledges that research administrators have professional responsibility to facilitate successful collaboration while recognizing that faculty have competing demands and may lack familiarity with administrative processes.

Elizabeth emphasizes that effective partnerships require administrators to have "the courage to speak up to faculty with suggestions" because "we have a perspective that would still be useful, and beneficial." This willingness to provide constructive feedback and alternative perspectives, when delivered respectfully and appropriately, can significantly enhance proposal quality and competitiveness. The key is developing sufficient trust and mutual respect so that faculty welcome administrative input rather than viewing it as interference.

Box 8.1 Who Are the Research Administrators and Developers at Your Institution?

Take some time to ask your department, school, college, and university about the research enterprise support you have available. Even if you think you know your contacts, or are working with them actively, go beyond your current network. There could be resources available that you can only use when seeking a multimillion-dollar gift or a large foundation award. Write down what you learn here:

____

____

____

The emotional investment that research administrators develop in faculty success becomes evident in their responses to funding outcomes. Cory describes how "we do take a lot of pride when we see awards come in. You know we feel like we were a part of it, and it is very special to us to see awards come in." Conversely, "we get disappointed. When declinations come in, we get really sad when faculty don't get their projects awarded, and that makes us want to help them work to improve the proposal for the next round." This personal investment in faculty success drives administrators to provide comprehensive support that extends beyond basic compliance to include strategic guidance for improving competitiveness over time.

The experiences of all four administrators highlight particular challenges and opportunities in supporting social science research that have important implications for faculty career development and research success. Tyler's observation that "STEM faculty are taught… how to write grants and to navigate especially federal funding landscapes, but they just know it better" while "it's not social scientists' fault. It's just not part of the curriculum" points to systemic gaps in doctoral training that research administrators can help address through targeted support and skill-building programs.

This training gap creates both challenges and opportunities for building effective partnerships with social science faculty. While social scientists may require more foundational education about grant-seeking processes, they also often bring different perspectives and collaborative approaches that can enrich the partnership experience. There is often an eagerness for substantive partnerships that creates opportunities for research administrators to provide more comprehensive support while helping social scientists contribute meaningfully to interdisciplinary projects and enhance their visibility within collaborative research teams.

Conclusion: The Essential Partnership

Research administration represents a critical bridge between the academic world of ideas and the practical world of funding and compliance, requiring professionals who can navigate complex regulatory frameworks while maintaining focus on enabling scientific discovery and innovation. Through the insights provided by Julie Campos, Tyler Myatt, Cory Blackwell, and Elizabeth Carroll, we see that effective research administrators must be part detective, part diplomat, part educator, and part strategic advisor, combining diverse skills and knowledge areas to support faculty success across multiple dimensions of the research enterprise.

The profession has evolved dramatically from an informal, learn-as-you-go field to an increasingly professionalized discipline with formal education programs, rigorous certification requirements, and robust professional networks. Yet at its heart, research administration remains fundamentally about relationships—between administrators and faculty, between institutions, and between researchers and funding agencies. These relationships form the foundation upon which successful collaborative partnerships are built and sustained over time, creating the trust and mutual understanding necessary for effective support of complex research endeavors.

Tyler's reflection that "the overwhelming majority [of research administrators] are trying to make the process easier, and they're trying to make you more competitive as best they can" captures the fundamental motivation that drives effective research administration. This commitment to research success, combined with the expertise to navigate complex systems and the flexibility to adapt to changing conditions, makes research administrators essential partners in the scientific enterprise and valuable allies for faculty seeking to build successful research careers. Beyond the technical and procedural aspects of research administration lies a deeper sense of purpose that motivates many professionals in the field. Cory's reflection on his work at Texas Tech reveals the personal investment that research administrators often develop in their institution's research mission:

> I take a lot of honor and pride in working for Texas Tech University. Like I said, I've always been kind of focused on public service and wanting to provide support in different ways, and being an alumn[us] of Texas Tech, I especially took a lot of honor in working for this office, and it means a lot to me to see the university's overall growth and development.

Understanding and appreciating the often-invisible work of research administration is essential for anyone involved in the research enterprise, from graduate students writing their first grant proposals to senior faculty managing multiple research projects and complex collaborative relationships. When the partnership between researchers and research administrators works well, it enables researchers to focus on pushing the boundaries of knowledge while ensuring that all complex administrative requirements are met and that opportunities for success are maximized.

9

Early Career and Tenure-Track Success

The New Faculty Funding Reality Check

You met Dr. Sarah Martinez in the introduction to this book. During graduate school, her PhD program in cultural studies emphasized theory and ethnographic methods but never mentioned grants. She focused on developing rigorous research skills and building a strong publication record. When she landed a tenure-track position at a regional state university, she learned that they required her to apply for $75,000 in external funding or risk not having a successful third-year review. Suddenly, Sarah found herself facing a completely new challenge she had never been trained to handle, with a ticking tenure clock that felt impossibly urgent.

Arjun, a political scientist studying electoral behavior, experienced a different version of this challenge. He was hired at an institution where grants weren't initially expected, but during his second year, the university announced its aspiration to achieve Research 1 status. Overnight, the informal culture shifted. Suddenly, colleagues were talking about funding requirements that hadn't existed when Arjun interviewed.

As described in Chapter 1, scholars engage with grants at three levels: exposure (understanding the landscape), knowledge (knowing what would be required), and action planning (actively preparing to pursue funding). This chapter addresses early-career researchers and tenure-track faculty who need to move quickly from exposure through knowledge to action planning while balancing the competing demands of their positions.

Whether you were hired with explicit funding expectations or find yourself at an institution with evolving priorities, the foundation-building approach remains the same: understand your context, develop targeted skills, and build sustainable practices that serve your long-term career goals. The key insight for early-career scholars is that grant readiness doesn't mean immediately writing proposals. Just as you wouldn't attempt complex statistical modeling without proper training, you shouldn't dive into grant writing without understanding the landscape, processes, and unwritten rules that govern success.

Know Your Terrain: Institutional Assessment

Before pursuing any external funding, you must decode what your institution actually values and requires. This varies dramatically across universities, and the official story often differs from reality. Some institutions now explicitly include funding requirements in faculty contracts, specifying minimum dollar amounts or application expectations within the first few years. These requirements typically focus on applications rather than awards—a crucial distinction that provides flexibility in planning.

Other institutions maintain unwritten expectations that faculty should pursue external funding, communicated through departmental culture rather than formal policies. Still others place little emphasis on grants at all, though this category is shrinking rapidly as budget pressures mount.

Written requirements tell only part of the story. The real expectations emerge through careful observation and targeted conversations. Sarah Martinez, the faculty member with a requirement to apply for $75,000 in external funding, discovered this when she started paying attention to which colleagues received course releases, salary increases, and public recognition. The pattern was clear: grant-active faculty were rewarded, regardless of what the official guidelines emphasized. Understanding institutional signals requires systematic investigation. Contract language might state "expected to apply for $50k in external funding by year 3," while tenure guidelines could require "evidence of funding for promotion." Department culture often reveals itself in casual comments like "everyone here writes proposals—even if they fail" or administrative messaging about becoming "a top-tier research university."

Box 9.1 Self-Check: What Are Your Institution's Real Expectations?

- Is funding mentioned in your offer letter or contract?
- What kinds of awards do recently tenured colleagues hold?
- Who receives public praise, course releases, or raises?
- Do tenure guidelines prioritize proposals or awards?

The most revealing signals are often hidden understandings—who actually gets rewarded through course releases, raises, and public praise? Maria, an anthropologist studying urban poverty, learned this lesson when she secured a prestigious Wenner-Gren Foundation grant in her second year. The eighteen-month fieldwork commitment meant fewer publications during a critical review period, but her department chair assured her the grant would compensate. However, when external reviewers evaluated her tenure case, they noted her "thin" publication record compared to other anthropologists at her career stage.

This experience illustrates a crucial principle: get tenure in your field, not just at your university. External letter writers—typically scholars from your disciplinary community—evaluate cases according to field norms, not necessarily your institution's specific criteria. Understanding both local and disciplinary expectations is essential for effective decision-making.

Never rely on a single source of advice about tenure expectations. Seek perspectives from multiple senior colleagues, both within your department and in your broader field. Department chairs change, deans move on, but your disciplinary community remains relatively stable.

Building a Fundable Research Agenda

Developing a research agenda that can attract external funding while serving your scholarly goals requires thoughtful planning from day one. The good news is that many elements of fundable research align perfectly with excellent scholarship: well-designed projects, methodological rigor, and clear contributions to knowledge are valued by both funders and academic journals.

The challenge lies in learning to articulate your work's significance in terms that resonate with funding agencies while maintaining your intellectual integrity. This doesn't mean abandoning your research interests—it means learning to identify and emphasize the aspects of your work that address broader societal needs and funding priorities. This is something we also stressed in Chapter 3.

Zihan, an assistant professor of public health, initially struggled with this translation process. He had spent years developing expertise in the social determinants of health in urban communities, focusing on structural inequalities and community resilience. When he began exploring grant opportunities, he discovered that most health funders were primarily interested in projects with direct clinical or biomedical applications. Rather than abandoning his core interests, Zihan learned to reframe his work purposefully. He began emphasizing how his research on social determinants could inform community interventions and policy recommendations that would ultimately improve health outcomes. He highlighted the practical applications of his theoretical insights while maintaining the methodological rigor and community engagement that defined his scholarly identity.

This reframing process required Zihan to develop what we referred to in Chapter 2 as a "multilingual scholarly capacity"—the ability to communicate the same research in different languages depending on the audience. For his disciplinary colleagues, he emphasized theoretical contributions to public health scholarship. For funding agencies, he highlighted policy implications and intervention potential.

For community partners, he focused on practical benefits and collaborative decision-making.

Box 9.2 Translating Your Research for Funders

Disciplinary Language	Funders' Language
Theoretical contribution	Societal impact
Narrative analysis	Evidence-based intervention
Cultural critique	Policy relevance
Participant observation	Community-engaged research

The key to building a fundable research agenda is starting with projects that genuinely excite you intellectually, then learning to identify their broader significance and potential applications. Begin by reflecting on your core research questions: What problems are you most passionate about addressing? What unique perspectives do you bring to these issues? How does your work fit into the broader landscape of your field? From there, map out a trajectory of projects that build on each other over time. Consider how each project contributes to your larger vision while aligning with potential funding opportunities. This approach ensures that grant-funded work advances your scholarly goals rather than distracting from them.

Robert, a psychology professor studying adolescent development, exemplifies this deliberate approach. His core research interest focused on peer relationships and social identity formation during the teenage years. When he began exploring funding opportunities, he discovered that NIH was particularly interested in research addressing adolescent mental health and risky behaviors. Robert didn't change his research focus, but he learned to emphasize how peer relationship dynamics affected mental health outcomes and decision-making processes that could lead to risky behaviors. His NIH R03, small research grant proposal, maintained his theoretical sophistication while highlighting potential applications for intervention development and clinical practice.

The feedback process proved crucial for Robert's success. His initial proposal draft focused primarily on basic research questions about social identity formation. His mentor encouraged him to strengthen the connections to mental health outcomes and potential community applications. By incorporating this guidance while maintaining his core research interests, Robert crafted a proposal that satisfied both funding agency priorities and his scholarly goals.

Creating a Publication Pipeline

Creating a well-managed publication pipeline becomes essential when incorporating grant-funded research into your portfolio. The challenge for early-career scholars is to ensure that grant work contributes to rather than detracts from your publication productivity. Grant-funded research often operates on longer timelines than traditional academic publishing, and funders may expect different types of outputs than those valued for tenure.

The solution is to maintain a diversified research portfolio that includes both grant-funded and independent projects. Track your research from concept through publication to identify potential productivity gaps before they become problematic. Create a visual pipeline showing projects at different stages: conceptual development, data collection, analysis, writing, under review, and in revision.

This pipeline approach helps you see where grant-funded work fits into your overall productivity plan. If a major grant will consume two years of data collection time, ensure you have other projects moving through the pipeline to maintain consistent publication output during that period. Consider creating spreadsheets to monitor each project's status and timeline to identify potential gaps in productivity before they become problematic. This visual representation helps you see where grant-funded work fits into your overall productivity and whether you have adequate non-grant-dependent publications in the pipeline to sustain your tenure case.

Box 9.3 Sample Research Pipeline Tracker (Stages + Outputs)

Project Title	Stage	Output Goal
"Urban Youth & Media"	Data Collection	Journal article (AJS)
"Voting & Race"	In Writing	Conference paper
"Education Equity"	Under Review	Policy brief + article

Balancing Teaching, Research, and Service

One of the most significant challenges for tenure-track faculty is balancing the competing demands of teaching, research, and service while building grant readiness. It can be all too easy to get caught up in the immediate demands of course preparation, grading, and committee work, leaving little time for the critical work of developing your research agenda and pursuing grant opportunities.

Consider the case of Sakura, an assistant professor of education who found herself overwhelmed during her first year. She was teaching two new course preparations and serving on the university's curriculum committee. The combination of detailed lesson planning, extensive grading, and committee meetings left virtually no time for research activities, much less grant preparation.

Sakura's experience illustrates a common trap: allowing urgent tasks to crowd out important but less immediate activities. Course preparation and grading have clear deadlines that create immediate pressure, while research and grant development operate on longer timelines that make them easy to postpone. However, establishing a strong research agenda and funding pipeline is crucial for your long-term success and advancement in the field. The solution requires treating research and grant preparation as nonnegotiable commitments rather than activities you'll pursue "when you have time."

Protecting Your Research Time

Block dedicated research time in your schedule and protect it as fiercely as you would teaching obligations. This might mean declining nonessential committee assignments, limiting office hours, or saying no to social events during critical writing periods. Be proactive in communicating your needs and boundaries to colleagues and students. Consider using time tracking methods, such as those taught through the National Center for Faculty Development and Diversity (NCFDD) curriculum, to keep yourself honest about where you spend your time and where you might be wasting time. This systematic approach helps identify opportunities to create dedicated grant-focused time without compromising essential responsibilities.

Box 9.4 Time Protection Tactics That Work

- Use calendar blocks labeled "Class Prep" and "Research—Do Not Schedule."
- Say no to "nonstrategic" service roles in year one.
- Schedule recurring writing sprints with a colleague.
- Use apps like RescueTime to track screen distractions.

Finding Teaching-Research Synergies

Look for opportunities to integrate your research interests and projects into your courses, whether through developing new syllabi, incorporating research-based assignments, or involving students in your grant-funded work. Not only can this help you make the most of your limited time and resources, but it can also enrich your teaching and mentoring while helping you build a pipeline of future collaborators and research assistants. The key is being selective about which synergies to pursue. Not every research interest translates well into undergraduate coursework, and not every course topic connects meaningfully to your funding goals. Focus on high-impact connections that genuinely advance both your teaching and research objectives.

Purposeful Service Commitments

While service is an important part of your role as a faculty member, it's essential to be selective in the commitments you take on, especially in your early years. Look for opportunities that align with your research interests and goals, such as serving on grant review panels or committees related to your area of expertise, rather than spreading yourself too thin with unrelated or low-impact activities.

Serving on grant review panels, for example, provides invaluable education about funding processes while fulfilling service requirements. Editorial board positions in your field can strengthen your publication network while building reviewing skills. Avoid committee assignments that consume substantial time without clear professional benefits, especially those unrelated to your research area.

Patricia, a criminologist, exemplified thoughtful service selection throughout her early career. She declined general university committees in favor of opportunities that supported her research goals: reviewing for criminology journals, serving on American Society of Criminology committees, and eventually joining grant review panels for the Bureau of Justice Statistics. These service activities strengthened her professional network and funding knowledge while fulfilling advancement requirements.

Finally, don't hesitate to leverage institutional resources and support. Take advantage of the resources available to you as a new faculty member, such as startup funds, grant-writing workshops, or mentoring programs. Don't be afraid to ask for help or guidance from colleagues, department chairs, or research support staff—they are there to support your success and can often provide valuable insights and connections.

Building Your Support Network

Success in early career grant seeking depends heavily on relationships and mentorship. Unlike graduate school, where advisors provide structured guidance, new faculty must proactively build support networks that can provide advice, feedback, and collaboration opportunities. Start by identifying multiple mentors rather than relying on a single advisor. Different mentors can provide expertise in various areas: research methodology, grant writing, career navigation, work-life balance, and discipline-specific knowledge. This diversified approach protects you from the limitations or biases of any single perspective.

Seek mentors both within your institution and in your broader disciplinary community. Internal mentors understand local culture, expectations, and resources, while external mentors provide perspective on field norms and opportunities beyond your current institution. Conference networking, professional association involvement, and collaborative research projects can help you build these external relationships.

Zhi, a digital humanities scholar in a traditional history department, illustrates the importance of diverse mentorship. When she secured a prestigious National Endowment for the Humanities (NEH) Digital Humanities Advancement Grant for $150,000, her departmental colleagues dismissed it as "not real historical research." Zhi had to work hard to educate her colleagues about the value of digital humanities approaches while seeking mentorship from scholars at other institutions who understood her field.

Zhi's experience highlights another crucial point: not all senior faculty prioritize junior colleagues' advancement equally. Learn to distinguish genuine mentors from those with competing agendas or limited understanding of current career requirements. Effective mentors demonstrate consistent interest in your success, provide honest feedback, and make time for substantive conversations about your career development.

Peer networks prove equally valuable for early career grant seeking. Connect with other junior faculty facing similar challenges, both at your institution and through professional associations. These relationships provide emotional support, practical advice, and potential collaboration opportunities. Consider forming or joining grant writing groups where participants share work-in-progress, provide feedback, and maintain accountability for application deadlines. These groups can be discipline-specific or interdisciplinary, depending on your institution's size and your research interests.

Building relationships with institutional research staff represents another crucial networking priority. See Chapters 7 and 8 in this book for a detailed description of what these staff do and how they are often segmented into those who help you get the grant (pre-award), and those who help you fulfill the grant (post-award). Pre-award and post-award administrators can provide invaluable guidance about funding opportunities, application requirements, and institutional procedures. These staff members often have insights about successful approaches and common pitfalls that can save you significant time and effort.

When You Show Up to the Table

We want to share a scenario that illustrates lessons applying regardless of your career stage, but especially early in your career. An assistant professor attended his first meeting about a potential collaboration—an internal grant worth $10,000 that the lead department saw as a "dating period" to see if the team worked well together before pursuing larger external funding. In that meeting, the faculty member made a strategic misstep: he expressed that internal grants were not prestigious enough to be worth his time, despite being an assistant professor who needed to build his track record and relationships.

Yes, external grants typically carry more prestige than internal ones because they bring indirect costs that universities value, involve competitive review processes, and demonstrate ability to secure funding from outside sources. But internal grants serve crucial functions that external grants cannot. They let you discover who you work well with before committing to multiyear collaborations. They provide pilot data that strengthens future external proposals. They help you learn to work as an interdisciplinary team in lower-stakes environments. They demonstrate productivity and collaborative capacity to tenure committees. They're often more flexible than external grants with strict requirements. Dismissing internal grants as not prestigious enough, especially early in your career, closes doors before you understand what is on the other side. It signals to potential collaborators that you're more interested in credentials than in building relationships and conducting good research.

So, how do you show up to these meetings prepared to advocate for yourself while keeping possibilities open? Think carefully before attending about how much time you realistically have to commit to a new project. Understanding your motivations matters too. Why are you considering this opportunity? To build relationships? To learn new methods? To develop pilot data for future proposals?

Remember that initial meetings are exploratory. You don't need to fully commit in first conversations. You can say things like "This sounds interesting, let me think about how it fits with my current priorities" or "I'd like to understand more about the time commitment before I commit." Look for ways to contribute ideas and show interest in the collaboration's potential without overcommitting or rigidly defining your boundaries before you understand the full picture.

Practical Approaches for Career-Stage Success

Despite the challenges of balancing multiple responsibilities while learning grant-seeking skills, tenure-track faculty can successfully incorporate grants into their career development. Several approaches prove particularly effective for early-career scholars:

- **Seek multiple perspectives**: Never rely on a single source of advice about tenure expectations or funding approaches. Triangulate information from various senior colleagues, both within your department and in your broader field.
- **Be teachable**: Take feedback seriously, especially early in your career. The mark of successful early-career scholars is how well they listen to and incorporate feedback. Listen carefully to guidance, ask clarifying questions, and adjust your approach accordingly.
- **Understand the time investment**: Grants require significant time commitments for both application development and post-award management. Budget time accordingly, consider course buyouts when possible, and recognize that administrative tasks will consume substantial time beyond the research activities themselves.
- **Stack small wins**: Balance ambitious long-term goals with shorter-turnaround outputs. When joining grant-funded projects, prioritize components that will yield publications in your field's preferred venues relatively quickly.
- **Communicate your timeline**: When working on interdisciplinary teams, clearly communicate your tenure requirements to collaborators. Senior colleagues often willingly adjust publication plans to support junior team members when they understand the stakes and timeline pressures.

- **Build trusted relationships**: Learn to identify senior scholars who genuinely want you to succeed and who can provide honest guidance about institutional expectations.

Patricia, the criminologist mentioned earlier in this chapter, exemplified a portfolio approach that many successful early-career scholars adopt. She pursued a mix of funding opportunities: small dissertation completion fellowships from professional associations when she was a graduate student, and during her tenure-track, both mid-sized grants from government agencies and larger awards from major funders. This diversified approach provided steady funding while building her grant-writing skills incrementally and demonstrating sustained success to tenure reviewers.

When the Rules Change: Flexible Response

Even with the best planning, some tenure-track faculty find themselves facing changed funding expectations partway through their probationary period. When this happens, you need a crisis response plan that prioritizes immediate needs while building sustainable practices for the future. Imagine you're three years into your tenure-track position when your dean announces that all faculty seeking tenure must now demonstrate success in obtaining external funding. This wasn't part of your initial expectations, but it's now a reality you must address with limited time remaining.

Understanding Your Timeline and Options

First, assess your situation realistically. How much time do you have until tenure review? What specific funding expectations have been communicated? Are you being evaluated on applications, awards, or both? These details fundamentally shape your options.

If your institution tracks grant submissions rather than awards, you have important flexibility. Focus on opportunities that allow you to demonstrate grant-seeking activity without overwhelming your already packed schedule. Not all grants require equal effort—some foundation grants need only two to five pages while federal grants might require extensive technical writing and supporting materials.

Focused Retooling Under Time Pressure

The natural impulse when facing sudden funding pressure is to immediately start writing proposals. This is exactly the wrong approach. Instead, invest in focused education first. Attend grant writing workshops, study successful proposals in your field, and build relationships with program officers and potential collaborators.

Consider the story of Kenji, a literature professor who discovered new funding expectations in his fourth year. His initial panic led him to spend six months writing an elaborate NEH proposal without training or mentorship. The proposal was rejected with reviews indicating fundamental misunderstandings about program priorities. Instead of immediately trying again, Kenji stepped back and invested in education. He attended grant writing workshops, studied successful proposals, and built relationships with program officers. His second application succeeded—not because he was a better writer, but because he understood what success required.

Focus and Prioritization

When operating under crisis timelines, focus intensively on opportunities specifically designed for early career scholars or faculty at institutions like yours. These programs often have less competition and more realistic scope expectations than flagship programs designed for established researchers.

Consider collaborative opportunities that allow you to contribute expertise without bearing primary responsibility for project leadership. Many experienced grant writers welcome collaborators who bring specialized knowledge or methodological skills. These partnerships provide valuable learning experiences while meeting institutional funding requirements.

Priority management becomes absolutely crucial. You may need to temporarily reduce research productivity in other areas, streamline teaching preparations, or decline service commitments to create space for intensive grant preparation. These trade-offs feel uncomfortable but represent necessary investments in meeting new institutional requirements.

Preparation Time Pays Off!

Kerk's story about his early-career highly prestigious award illustrates the type of serious preparation that can really pay off. Knowing that the NSF CAREER award allows only three attempts, Kerk began preparing a full year before he was eligible to apply. Although he had already drafted his one-page project summary, he waited a year on the advice of his university's grant administrator after securing a solo-PI NSF VOSS grant (a specific funding call that was available through the NSF in the early 2000s called Virtual Organizations as Sociotechnical Systems). During that extra year, Kerk took a highly strategic approach: he requested six successful CAREER proposals—two from faculty in his liberal arts university, two from others in his organizational communication field, and two from researchers working on cyberinfrastructure. He also attended an NSF CAREER writing workshop hosted by the Computer and Information Science and Engineering (CISE) Directorate, his target funding program, where he received feedback on his summary from five different program officers.

Kerk didn't stop there. He secured letters of collaboration from seven respected scholars and practitioners to form a project advisory panel, as he has kept his relationships with all of them active for several years. Then he studied ten more CAREER proposals—five funded and five rejected—provided during the workshop. By the time he submitted his proposal the following year, he had refined every component of the research, education, and broader impacts plans. His effort paid off: he received the CAREER award on his first try. The lesson? Thoughtful, systematic preparation—grounded in feedback, mentorship, and peer examples—can make all the difference.

Your Grant Readiness Action Plan

With foundational understanding in place, develop a concrete implementation plan tailored to your specific timeline and circumstances.

The approach differs significantly depending on how much time you have until tenure review and what level of funding expectations you face.

Box 9.5 Mini-Action Plan: First Six Months on the Tenure Track

1. Identify three possible mentors and schedule intro meetings.
2. Draft a one-page research agenda (and test its "fundability").
3. Sign up for an institutional grant workshop or find workshops from funders or the American Association for the Advancement of Science.
4. Explore internal grant databases and set alerts.
5. Track your weekly time use for two to three weeks to diagnose time sinks.

If you have three or more years until tenure review, prioritize education and careful planning over immediate applications. Use this time to build knowledge, skills, and relationships that will support long-term success. Attend grant writing workshops, study successful proposals in your field, and develop relationships with program officers and potential collaborators. Focus on small, manageable funding opportunities that allow you to learn the process without overwhelming your schedule. Internal institutional grants, professional association awards, and small foundation grants often require fewer complex applications while providing valuable experience with proposal development, budget preparation, and project management.

With two years until tenure review, balance education with targeted applications to funding opportunities that align closely with your research agenda and career timeline. Prioritize applications to programs that support early career scholars or offer relatively quick turnaround times between application and award notification.

If you have less than two years until tenure review, focus on applications to programs specifically designed for early-career scholars, which often have less competition and more realistic scope expectations. Avoid large, multiyear grants that could consume substantial time during your critical pre-tenure period.

Throughout this process, maintain detailed records of your grant-seeking activities. Document applications submitted, feedback received, and lessons learned from each experience. This information will prove valuable for tenure review materials and future funding applications.

Create a realistic timeline that accounts for your teaching and service obligations while protecting dedicated time for grant development. Most successful funding applications require months of preparation, from initial concept development through final submission. Starting early and maintaining consistent progress prevents the last-minute scrambling that often leads to weak proposals or missed deadlines.

Building Sustainable Grant-Seeking Practices

Whether you're planning from your first year or adapting to changed expectations, the ultimate goal is to develop sustainable grant-seeking practices that serve your long-term career goals. The habits and relationships you develop as an early-career scholar will shape your funding success throughout your academic career.

Develop systems for staying informed about funding opportunities and agency priorities. This might include subscribing to funding newsletters, following funding agencies on social media, attending agency webinars, and maintaining organized files of relevant funding announcements. Create templates and standard materials that can be adapted for multiple applications rather than starting from scratch each time. Develop modular research descriptions, budget templates, and biographical statements that can be customized for different funding opportunities while maintaining consistency in your professional presentation. Build collaborative relationships purposefully, focusing on partnerships that genuinely enhance your research capacity rather than diluting your scholarly focus. The most productive collaborations emerge from shared intellectual interests and complementary expertise rather than convenience or funding requirements alone.

Maintain perspective on the role of grants in your overall career plan. External funding should enhance your research capacity and scholarly impact, not become an end in itself. The most successful scholars use grants thoughtfully to pursue research questions they're genuinely passionate about while building resources and relationships that support long-term productivity.

Remember that grant seeking is inherently iterative and often involves multiple rejections before success. Every application provides learning opportunities, even when unsuccessful. The skills you develop, relationships you build, and knowledge you gain through the process have value beyond any individual funding award.

By approaching early-career grant seeking with deliberate thinking, realistic expectations, and commitment to continuous learning, you can build the foundation for sustained funding success while maintaining focus on your core scholarly goals. The investment you make in building these capabilities early in your career will pay dividends throughout your academic journey.

10

Building Labs, Centers, and Social Science Institutes

Just as Dr. Elena Ivanova was settling into her fall semester routine, her college dean stopped by her office. After fifteen years as a successful architecture professor studying urban poverty and community resilience, she thought she understood the academic landscape. The visit from her dean changed everything: "Elena, I'd like to discuss an exciting opportunity. The university is establishing a new Center for Community Innovation, and we believe you'd be the perfect director."

What Elena didn't know—what she couldn't have known from her traditional academic training—was that this "exciting opportunity" would require her to become something she'd never imagined: an entrepreneur within the university walls. The expectation wasn't just to lead research, but to build a self-sustaining enterprise through external funding, develop revenue streams, manage complex budgets, and navigate institutional politics in ways her scholarly training had never addressed. Within two years, she would need to make the center financially independent or return to regular faculty duties.

Elena's situation reflects a growing reality for mid-career and senior social scientists. Whether they are thrust into these roles by institutional changes or actively seeking new challenges, scholars increasingly find themselves at a crossroads where traditional academic paths diverge into uncharted territory. The shift from individual researcher to leader of a lab, center, or institute represents more than a career advancement—it's a fundamental transformation of professional identity that many are unprepared to navigate.

The Changing Landscape of Academic Research Leadership

Universities across the country are fundamentally reimagining their research enterprises. Consider the recent restructuring at a major state university, where the vice president for Research now reports directly to the president rather than the provost. The new role description reads like a venture capitalist's job posting: 1. Growing our research portfolio and sponsored funding, 2. Cultivating a venture-oriented mindset to identify and invest in strategic opportunities, and 3. Collaborating closely with our research commercialization office. This isn't the research leadership model that existed even a decade ago.

For social scientists who spent their careers focused on theoretical contributions and peer-reviewed publications, this shift can feel disorienting. The traditional markers of success—journal articles, book publications, conference presentations—suddenly seem insufficient. Now institutions expect research leaders to think like entrepreneurs, advocate like lobbyists, and manage like CEOs, all while maintaining their scholarly productivity.

This transformation affects scholars at various career stages differently. Some, like Elena, find themselves unexpectedly recruited for leadership roles based on their research reputation, with little understanding of what the position truly requires. Others actively seek these opportunities as a natural evolution of their research programs, only to discover the vast gap between their preparation and the role's demands. Still others watch from the sidelines, uncertain whether to pursue similar paths or maintain their traditional faculty roles.

The challenge is particularly acute for social scientists because, unlike some of our STEM colleagues who often grow up in grant-filled environments with clear models of lab leadership, we typically lack exposure to these entrepreneurial research structures. A chemist might join a well-funded lab as a graduate student, learning grant management and research administration through osmosis. A mass communication scholar or historian rarely has such opportunities, making the transition to research leadership feel like learning a new language without a helpful online tutor.

Understanding the InGroup/ OutGroup Dynamic

A crucial insight for social scientists entering research leadership roles is recognizing that we often operate as members of an outgroup (Brewer, 1999) in the broader university research enterprise. This isn't a matter of intentional discrimination or conscious bias. Rather, it reflects the natural dynamics that occur when groups with different backgrounds, training, and perspectives come together. The ingroup—typically STEM researchers and administrators with similar backgrounds—shares common assumptions about how research works, what constitutes valuable contributions, and how resources should be allocated. They've grown up in a culture where multimillion-dollar grants are normal, where lab structures are well established, and where the path from graduate student to lab director is clearly marked. Social scientists are different from them because they may not understand our methods, our contributions, and our potential for interdisciplinary research leadership.

A public relations scholar developing expertise in crisis messaging might be seen as someone who could contribute to a disaster response communication team, but not as someone who could lead a major interdisciplinary initiative. An anthropologist studying innovation adoption might be valued for providing "broader impacts" to a technology grant, but not considered for the principal investigator role. These assumptions about what social scientists are "capable of handling" create invisible barriers to research leadership opportunities.

One senior engineering professor, when asked about including social scientists in a major infrastructure grant, responded candidly: "I know they do important work, but I'm not sure they understand the complexity of managing large-scale funded research. Maybe they could handle the community engagement component?" This well-meaning comment reveals the subtle ways outgroup dynamics shape opportunities and expectations.

Breaking through these assumptions requires deliberate strategy. Successful social science research leaders learn to demonstrate value in terms the ingroup understands while maintaining their disciplinary integrity. They become multilingual scholars, translating their expertise into language that resonates with different audiences without compromising their intellectual commitments. They build relationships slowly and strategically, proving their capacity for leadership through incremental successes rather than expecting immediate recognition.

The Identity Transformation: From Scholar to Research Entrepreneur

Taking on research leadership roles requires more than adding administrative duties to your existing responsibilities. It demands a fundamental shift in professional identity that many scholars find challenging to navigate. You're no longer just a faculty member who happens to run some grants—you're becoming what universities increasingly call an "intrapreneur," building entrepreneurial ventures within institutional walls.

This transformation affects multiple dimensions of academic and often your personal life. The comfortable rhythm of semesters organized around teaching and writing gives way to the relentless demands of funding cycles, budget management, and personnel decisions. While typical faculty appointments are for nine months, externally funded projects require work and management twelve months a year. The autonomy of individual scholarship transforms into the complexity of team leadership and collaborative negotiation. Perhaps most challenging, the clear metrics of academic success—publications, citations, teaching evaluations—become muddied by new expectations around revenue generation, partnership building, and organizational sustainability.

Consider how this identity shift played out for Dr. Marcus Chen, a political scientist who built a successful career studying electoral behavior and public opinion. When he accepted the directorship of his university's new Center for Democratic Innovation, he expected to continue his research with additional resources and broader impact. Instead, he found himself spending 70 percent of his time on activities he'd never anticipated: negotiating contracts with foundation partners, managing conflicts between faculty affiliates who wanted center resources, developing revenue-generating training programs, and constantly pitching the center's value to skeptical administrators. He had to accept that he was no longer primarily a political science professor. He was running a small business inside the university, with all the pressures and responsibilities that entails. Some days, he felt more like a CEO than a scholar, and that was hard to reconcile with his academic identity.

This identity transformation often creates tension with colleagues who remain in traditional faculty roles. They may not understand why you're suddenly unavailable for committee work, why you're hiring staff instead of teaching extra courses, or why you're spending time courting donors instead of writing journal articles. The informal support networks that sustain traditional faculty—department meetings, conference gatherings, writing groups—may no longer fit your new reality, leaving you isolated at precisely the moment you most need guidance and community.

Pathways to Research Leadership

Social scientists typically encounter research leadership opportunities through three primary pathways, each with distinct challenges and possibilities. Understanding these pathways helps scholars make informed decisions about whether and how to pursue such roles.

Many social scientists find themselves recruited for research leadership positions based on their scholarly reputation, with little warning or preparation. Universities seeking to establish new interdisciplinary initiatives often look to respected senior faculty who can bridge different fields and bring credibility to emerging programs. The offer seems flattering—recognition of your scholarly contributions and an opportunity for broader impact—but the reality often proves more complex than anticipated. These unexpected transitions carry particular risks because scholars enter without adequate preparation or realistic expectations. Universities may provide minimal guidance beyond "make it self-sustaining within three years," leaving new directors to figure out funding strategies, organizational structures, and management approaches through trial and error. The learning curve is steep, and mistakes made early can disadvantage the enterprise for years.

Other scholars consciously evolve toward research leadership as their programs expand. What begins as a single grant grows into multiple funded projects, necessitating more formal organizational structures. A small research team becomes a lab, which eventually expands into something larger. This evolutionary pathway offers advantages—you learn incrementally, building skills and relationships over time—but also presents challenges in recognizing when you've outgrown existing structures and need more formal institutional recognition and support.

Keri exemplifies this evolutionary journey. After achieving tenure and securing external funding, she realized she needed to create organizational structures to manage multiple grants effectively. First, she created a lab structure, something she had experience with as an undergraduate biochemistry major and something social science colleagues at other institutions had done. Starting with just a name, Organizing Practices through Technology, Information, & Communication, or OPTICLab, she gradually built a comprehensive research operation—developing a website, creating educational videos, organizing research teams, and establishing a clear brand identity. On June 10, 2020, she held a lab meeting where the title of the meeting was "Why a Lab?" and she explained this structure to all the graduate students working on her projects.

But as her funding portfolio expanded, she recognized she had outgrown the lab model. The opportunity to become codirector of the Technology and Information Policy Institute provided the next evolutionary step. Joining her colleague, Sharon Strover, who had decades of experience running an institute and getting external funding, made a tremendous difference in how she approached external funding. Keri was able to partner with Sharon and learn from her experience, while having some basic research infrastructure support.

Some mid-career scholars deliberately seek research leadership roles as a strategic career move. After achieving tenure and establishing their scholarly reputation, they look for new challenges and opportunities for broader impact. This pathway allows for more intentional preparation—attending leadership workshops, studying successful models, building relationships with potential funders—but still requires navigating the substantial gap between traditional academic training and entrepreneurial research leadership.

Building Your Research Enterprise: Models and Mechanisms

Successfully establishing a research organization requires understanding different models and their implications. While universities often distinguish between labs, centers, and institutes, the reality is that these definitions vary dramatically across institutions. What one university calls a lab might qualify as a center elsewhere. Some institutions have rigid requirements—specific funding thresholds, formal approval processes, dedicated space allocations—while others allow faculty considerable flexibility in establishing and naming their research groups.

Box 10.1 Am I Building a Lab, Center, or Institute?

Rather than focusing on formal definitions, consider the functional aspects of your research organization and see if there are specific guidelines to follow at your current institution. Ask yourself:

- What am I trying to accomplish?
- How many people will I employ?
- What kinds of projects will I pursue?
- What infrastructure do I need?

These practical questions matter more than whether you call yourself a lab, center, or institute. The key is understanding your own institution's specific requirements and culture.

Some universities actively discourage certain organizational forms, using funding thresholds or bureaucratic barriers to limit proliferation of centers and institutes. One researcher we talked to explained that the rhetoric at his institution was that to have a center, you needed a certain level of funding. The university made it sound so difficult that he never pursued it, even though his funding profile probably qualified. When he reflected on this he wondered if the ambiguity was intentional; they may not have wanted too many centers competing for resources.

One successful model found across disciplines is a Lab/Center/Institute with several faculty and staff PIs who are all bringing in their own funding and running it through the research structure. For example, if there are five faculty who are contributing to the sustainability of the research structure, there will be more indirect costs being returned to that structure, and over time, that structure might adopt support practices similar to a college or even a university. Some major soft money–funded Centers have their own pre- and post-award support, provide project management to all affiliated faculty and staff, and might receive a higher percentage of indirect cost returns because they are shouldering some of the research administration costs.

Funding Mechanisms for Social Science Research Leadership

Unlike STEM fields with clear pathways to multimillion-dollar federal grants, social scientists must creatively combine multiple funding streams to build sustainable research enterprises. Institutions often have dedicated staff who focus on securing private funding from donors and approaching foundations for research funding. There may be specific rules to follow when approaching foundations or donors, and these staff can help researchers navigate the best approaches to build successful relationships. Understanding these diverse mechanisms and their respective advantages and limitations becomes important for long-term success.

Federal funding remains an option but requires strategic positioning. While NSF and NIH budgets for social science research pale compared to their STEM allocations, opportunities exist for social scientists who can articulate their work's relevance to agency missions. The key lies in framing social science expertise as essential to addressing complex societal challenges rather than competing directly with STEM proposals. Successful social science research leaders often position themselves as leaders of interdisciplinary teams, leveraging their skills in human behavior, social systems, and community engagement to secure funding for projects with broader impacts.

Foundation support offers particular promise for social science and humanities research enterprises. Private foundations often prioritize social change, equity, and community impact—areas where social scientists and humanists excel. However, foundation funding requires different skills from federal grant writing. Foundation officers expect clear theories of change (Funnell & Rogers, 2011), evidence of community partnerships, and demonstrable pathways to real-world impact. Building relationships with program officers, understanding foundation priorities, and aligning research agendas with foundation missions become essential skills.

Donor cultivation represents an increasingly important but often uncomfortable frontier for academic researchers. Universities expect research centers to cultivate individual and corporate donors, yet few social scientists receive training in fundraising. The skills required—relationship building, storytelling, making "the ask"—feel odd to scholars trained in theoretical argumentation and empirical analysis. Furthermore, the rules around who can directly approach a corporate or foundation donor can vary, and it is common to require a research leader to work with a university development professional to seek these types of gifts.

Successful research leaders learn to translate their scholarly work into compelling narratives that inspire philanthropic investment, often partnering with university development offices to identify and cultivate potential donors. One center director we talked with explained that his university has an enormous development operation focused on foundation relationships. He had no idea these resources existed until three years into his job role as a center director. Now he regularly works with them to identify potential donors whose interests align with his center's research.

Contract research provides steady revenue streams but requires careful balance. State agencies, nonprofits, and corporations may contract with research centers for evaluation studies, needs assessments, or policy analysis. While these contracts can provide crucial operating funds, they also pose risks: timelines driven by client needs rather than academic calendars, potential constraints on publication, and the challenge of maintaining scholarly independence while meeting client expectations.

Revenue-generating programs offer perhaps the most entrepreneurial pathway to sustainability. Many successful social science research centers develop training programs, workshops, or certificate courses that generate revenue while advancing their research missions. A center studying organizational communication might offer corporate training on crisis messaging. A lab focused on educational equity could develop professional development programs for teachers. These programs require initial investment and ongoing management but can provide stable income streams less dependent on grant cycles. The key is to ensure these programs align with your research mission rather than becoming distractions from scholarly work.

Navigating Commercialization and Intellectual Property

The push toward research commercialization presents both opportunities and unprecedented challenges for social scientists. Universities increasingly expect all researchers—not just those in STEM fields—to explore commercialization potential, yet few social scientists understand what this means for their work or how to navigate the complex landscape of intellectual property, technology transfer, and entrepreneurial ventures.

The federal government has recognized this trend through programs specifically designed to help researchers explore commercialization. The I-Corps (Innovation Corps) program, offered through NSF and other agencies, provides intensive training in customer discovery and market validation. Participants learn to conduct systematic interviews with potential users, analyze market needs, and evaluate whether their research has commercial potential. SBIR (Small Business Innovation Research) and STTR (Small Business Technology Transfer) programs provide funding specifically for commercialization efforts, requiring researchers to form companies or partner with existing businesses.

For social scientists, these programs can feel particularly business-like, unless they have that type of background. Keri attended a regional I-Corps program where they taught her team customer discovery—basically how to cold-call potential users and ask what they need. This program approaches the process like a marketing bootcamp, teaching you to make daily progress reports and conduct market analysis. With her marketing background from before academia, she recognized the techniques, but for many academics, this entrepreneurial mindset feels completely unlike the academic processes they know so well.

The commercialization landscape differs significantly for social scientists compared to our STEM colleagues. We rarely develop patentable technologies or medical devices. Instead, our commercializable assets might include assessment tools, training protocols, intervention programs, or consulting methodologies. These require different approaches to protection and commercialization than traditional patents. Understanding what constitutes intellectual property in social science contexts becomes crucial. A colleague of Kerk's developed a comprehensive assessment tool for measuring student engagement. What started as a research instrument became a commercially valuable product licensed to educational technology companies. Another researcher's community intervention protocol, initially developed through federal grants, eventually became the foundation for a consulting practice serving nonprofit organizations.

However, navigating intellectual property agreements remains one of the most challenging aspects of research commercialization for social scientists. Universities maintain complex policies about IP ownership, and these policies often assume STEM-style innovations rather than social science contributions. Contract negotiations with industry partners can become particularly contentious around IP rights. As Keri has discovered it can be hard to convince a technology transfer office that the project will not generate IP because it is a different type of research. Legal advice is often to include extensive IP clauses in the contract, and that can cause contract negotiations to go on for months. Keri walked away from one situation because it was taking too much of her time, and the legal negotiations were stalling.

The situation becomes even more complex when collaborating across institutions or with international partners. Data sharing agreements that seem straightforward can end up experiencing months of legal negotiations about potential IP rights. One researcher we talked with attempted to share NSF-funded data with a colleague in the Netherlands and found themselves caught in a lengthy legal battle between institutions about hypothetical IP rights that might emerge from collaborative analysis.

Some researchers sidestep university IP complications entirely by carefully separating their commercial activities from their academic work.

One professor, planning to eventually leave academia for consulting, meticulously documented that all commercial development happened on personal equipment, outside university time, without using any university resources. While this approach protected their independent IP rights, it also meant forgoing university support and resources that might have accelerated their commercial success.

The Hidden Challenges No One Discusses

While university administrators enthusiastically promote research leadership opportunities, they rarely acknowledge the unique challenges social scientists face in these roles. Understanding these hidden obstacles—and developing strategies to address them—can mean the difference between success and burnout.

Perhaps the most damaging misconception is that social science research centers can achieve financial sustainability within two to three years. This timeline might work for a well-connected STEM researcher who negotiated a million-dollar startup package and has access to multimillion-dollar federal funding programs, but it's dangerously unrealistic for social scientists operating in different funding ecosystems. Building the relationships, credibility, and diversified funding portfolio necessary for sustainability typically requires five to seven years minimum—a reality rarely acknowledged in initial negotiations. Dr. Shalonda Williams learned this lesson painfully when she accepted directorship of a new Center for Social Innovation with a three-year runway to sustainability. She spent the first year just learning about the landscape including who the funders were, what they wanted, and how to speak their language. By year two, she was starting to build relationships and submit proposals. But grants take time—often a year from submission to funding. By the time her three-year clock ran out, she was just starting to see results from her efforts. Fortunately, she had a sympathetic dean who understood the reality and extended her timeline, but she acknowledges that not everyone is so lucky.

Unlike other administrative roles, such as department chairs, who enjoy established support networks—regular meetings with other chairs, leadership training programs, clear policy guidelines—research center directors often operate in isolation. No handbook explains how or if it is possible to negotiate indirect cost return rates to support their Center activities. No monthly meetings provide peer support for managing difficult personnel situations.

This isolation feels particularly acute during crises. When a major funder suddenly changes priorities, when a key staff member leaves unexpectedly, or when university budget cuts threaten center operations, directors must navigate challenges with limited institutional support available to traditional academic leaders. The very entrepreneurial nature that universities celebrate also leaves research leaders vulnerable and unsupported when difficulties arise. The contrast with traditional administrative roles is stark. Department chairs attend orientation programs, receive policy manuals, and join established communities of practice. Research center directors often discover basic operational requirements through trial and error, sometimes learning about crucial policies only after inadvertently violating them.

Social science research leaders face a peculiar catch-22: universities want them to generate significant external funding, but the broader research community often questions their capacity for such leadership and their funding options can be more limited than STEM colleagues. This skepticism comes not from malice but from unfamiliarity. STEM researchers who dominate university research enterprises simply don't understand social science methods, contributions, or potential for large-scale impact. One urban planning scholar recalls presenting their work on community resilience to a review panel dominated by engineers and computer scientists. He said they kept asking him why his team needed two years for data collection. They couldn't understand that building trust with vulnerable communities takes time, that their methods require deep engagement rather than quick technical fixes. They wanted to fund the project but insisted he complete it in six months.

Breaking through requires patient relationship building and strategic demonstration of value. One successful strategy involves starting with supporting roles on interdisciplinary teams, proving your value through exceptional contributions, and then gradually taking on more leadership responsibility. When an engineer saw how a social scientist's expertise in adoption of innovations transformed their technology transfer grant, they became an advocate, later recommending that social scientist as PI for a major infrastructure grant.

Perhaps the most profound challenge is the ongoing negotiation of professional identity. Research leadership demands skills and mindsets that may feel antithetical to scholarly training: thinking about revenue instead of theory, managing people instead of ideas, selling vision instead of defending arguments. Some days, you feel more like a small business owner than a professor, and reconciling these competing identities requires constant emotional work.

Strategic Approaches for Success

Despite these challenges, many social scientists successfully build thriving research enterprises. Their experiences reveal strategic approaches that can guide others considering similar paths. But before writing a single grant proposal or developing any programs, invest time in building relationships across your institution and beyond. Successful research leaders spend their first months meeting with potential collaborators, understanding institutional resources, and learning the landscape of possible funders. This relationship-building phase may feel unproductive compared to immediately pursuing funding, but it provides the foundation for everything that follows. Pay particular attention to building bridges with STEM colleagues who might become collaborators or champions. Look for those who already value interdisciplinary work or have expressed frustration with purely technical approaches to complex problems. These allies can provide crucial credibility when you're ready to lead interdisciplinary initiatives.

One anthropologist spent her first year as center director having coffee with faculty across campus, learning about their research challenges and looking for connection points. These informal conversations led to three major collaborative grants within two years. She shared that she was genuinely curious about her colleagues' work and where social science perspectives might add value. When opportunities arose, she already had relationships and mutual understanding to pursue funding together.

Relying on any single funding source leaves research enterprises vulnerable to changing priorities or budget cuts. Successful social science research leaders think like portfolio managers, balancing different types of funding with varying risk levels and timelines (see Chapter 18 for ideas on how to do this). A healthy portfolio might include federal grants providing stable multiyear support, foundation grants aligned with specific programs, contract research providing steady operational funds, revenue-generating training programs creating predictable income, and donor support for strategic initiatives and emergency needs. This diversification requires different skills for each funding type, but the security it provides justifies the investment in learning these varied approaches.

Rather than launching immediately into a formal center structure, consider building incrementally. Start with informal research groups or reading circles to identify potential collaborators and test working relationships. Establish a lab structure to formalize growing research programs and learn basic management skills. Only when you've demonstrated success at smaller scales—and understood the true demands of research leadership—should you consider the leap to formal center or institute status. This incremental approach offers multiple advantages: you learn skills progressively rather than all at once, you build credibility through demonstrated success, and you can adjust course based on experience rather than committing to unsustainable structures.

The pressure to become evermore entrepreneurial can distance research leaders from the scholarly work that brought them success. Resist this pressure by maintaining some direct research involvement, even as administrative demands grow. This might mean protecting time for your own writing, staying involved with one key project, or teaching one course annually to stay connected with students and ideas. Maintaining scholarly engagement serves multiple purposes: it preserves your credibility with faculty colleagues, keeps you grounded in the intellectual work that motivated your career, and provides personal satisfaction amid the challenges of administration and fundraising.

Box 10.2 Making the Decision: A Framework for Evaluation

Before accepting or pursuing research leadership opportunities, conduct honest self-assessment about your readiness, motivations, and resources.

- Are you prepared for fundamental changes in your daily work and professional identity?
- Can you tolerate the uncertainty and stress of revenue generation?
- Do you have the emotional resilience to handle isolation and criticism?
- Is your personal life stable enough to support increased professional demands?

Consider the institutional support available.

- What concrete resources will your institution provide?
- Is the timeline for sustainability realistic given your field and funding landscape?
- Will you have access to necessary administrative support?
- How will your institution evaluate success, and are these metrics achievable?

Evaluate strategic alignment with your career goals.

- Does this opportunity advance your research agenda or distract from it?
- Can you maintain scholarly productivity while building the enterprise?
- What happens if the venture fails—is there a graceful exit strategy?

These questions require honest answers, not optimistic assumptions. Understanding both opportunities and risks helps make informed decisions rather than reactive ones.

The Path Forward

Research leadership represents both tremendous opportunity and significant challenge for social scientists willing to expand their professional identities and skill sets. Success requires more than traditional scholarly excellence—it demands entrepreneurial thinking, strategic relationship building, and persistent navigation of institutional cultures that may not fully understand or support social science research enterprises.

For those who successfully make this transition, the rewards extend beyond personal achievement. Research leaders shape scholarly fields through the programs they build and the scholars they support. They create bridges between academic knowledge and real-world impact. They demonstrate the vital contributions social and behavioral scientists make to addressing society's most complex challenges. Most importantly, they create sustainable structures that outlast individual careers, building legacies of discovery and impact.

The path isn't for everyone. The challenges are real, the support structures inadequate, and the learning curve steep. But for social scientists seeking new challenges at mid-career or beyond, research leadership offers opportunities to amplify impact and create lasting institutional change. The key lies in approaching these opportunities with clear eyes, realistic expectations, and strategic preparation for the complex journey ahead. And as you put your plan together to negotiate what you need to have a successful research enterprise, you may find yourself needing to leave your current institution to find one willing and able to see the value in investing to set you up for research success.

As universities continue evolving their research enterprises, social scientists must claim their place at the leadership table. Our expertise in human behavior, social systems, and organizational dynamics positions us uniquely to lead complex interdisciplinary initiatives, but we rarely have received the type of research-specific leadership training needed to be successful. Practical skills like getting institutional buy-in, managing up, supervising a team, and managing competing priorities are important things to learn. Yet the question isn't whether social scientists can succeed as research leaders—many already have. The question is whether we can build better support structures, share hard-won wisdom, and create pathways for the next generation of social science research leaders to thrive.

Checklist: Essential Elements to Negotiate When Considering a Research Leadership Role

Timeline and Operating Expectations

- ☐ Minimum three-to-five-year runway before fully operating
  - ☐ There need to be annual milestones along the way.
- ☐ Clear, written metrics for evaluating success beyond revenue targets
- ☐ Annual review process that accounts for building-phase realities
- ☐ Explicit agreement about options if timelines aren't met
- ☐ Protection from changing expectations due to leadership transitions

Financial Terms and Resources

- ☐ Assess your access to flexible funding (professorships, startup costs)
  - ☐ Multiyear seed funding commitment for operations
  - ☐ Access to bridge funding when waiting on the next award to fund
- ☐ Administrative support (even shared can be very helpful)
- ☐ Negotiation options around indirect cost return rates to support your entity
- ☐ Clear policies on revenue retention and reinvestment

Personnel and Staffing Support

- ☐ Plan to recruit faculty and staff to run their awards through your research entity
- ☐ Determine if more than one director could help support the research entity's growth
- ☐ Administrative support (even shared can be very helpful)
- ☐ Funding for key personnel during establishment phase
- ☐ Access to experienced graduate assistants

- ☐ Clear hiring authority and HR support
- ☐ Succession planning for key positions

Workload and Time Management

- ☐ Course release/specific course assignment formulas to support research time demands
- ☐ Summer salary support
- ☐ Reduced service/committee obligations
- ☐ Protected time for maintaining research activities
- ☐ Clear boundaries on teaching obligations

Infrastructure and Operational Support

- ☐ Appropriate space allocation (shared can work well)
- ☐ Technology infrastructure and software access
- ☐ Website and social media development and maintenance support
- ☐ Communications and marketing assistance
- ☐ Access to college and/or university development officers

Professional Development Resources

- ☐ Funding for leadership development and training programs
- ☐ Support for fundraising skill development
- ☐ Access to mentorship from successful research leaders
- ☐ Conference attendance for networking and learning

Institutional Integration

- ☐ Formal recognition within university structure
- ☐ Representation in relevant leadership committees
- ☐ Access to institutional data and resources
- ☐ Clear reporting lines and authority
- ☐ Protection from competing institutional demands

Risk Management and Exit Strategy

- ☐ Institutional support during funding gaps
- ☐ Graceful exit options if venture doesn't succeed (e.g., return to faculty)
- ☐ Protection of tenure and faculty status
- ☐ Negotiate a sabbatical to get your research program refocused after stepping down

11

Grant Opportunities for Graduate Students

This chapter serves multiple audiences and meshes well with many of the other chapters in the book. If you are faculty, a research staff member, or a graduate program director mentoring graduate students and early-career scholars, this chapter gives you many ideas for how to support your students' journeys. Furthermore, if you are considering a career move to another institution, the Grant-Savvy Job Market List of Questions to Ask in the chapter can help at any stage of your career. If you are a graduate student, especially one who does not have many externally funded faculty around you, this chapter can provide you with much guidance. If you are a research administrator, this chapter can provide insight into why graduate students and early-career scholars in social and behavioral science and humanities fields have limited exposure to seeking and managing awards.

Graduate school represents a critical period for developing your research skills, establishing your scholarly identity, and preparing for your future career. While coursework and comprehensive exams often receive the most attention during graduate training, learning about the funding landscape and developing grant-seeking skills can provide significant advantages during your master's and/or doctoral program and in your postgraduation career. This chapter explores the various funding opportunities available to graduate students, the strategic benefits of early engagement with grant-seeking, and practical steps for building your funding foundation during graduate school.

The Graduate Student Advantage in Grant-Seeking

As a graduate student, you possess several unique advantages in the funding landscape that may not be immediately apparent. Many funding agencies specifically prioritize supporting emerging scholars, recognizing that investments in early-career researchers can yield significant long-term returns for the field. Graduate student grant competitions often have lower application volumes than faculty competitions, potentially improving your odds of success. Additionally, the expectations for preliminary data and extensive track records are typically more modest for graduate student applicants. Here are just a few of those opportunities to get you started:

Table 11 Possible Grant Opportunities for Graduate Students

Dissertation	NSF Doctoral Dissertation Research Grant (vary by directorate)
	NSF Graduate Research Fellowship Program
	American Association of University Women Dissertation Fellowship
	Social Science Research Council (opportunities vary)
	NIH R36 Dissertation/Predoctoral Award
	American Sociological Association Doctoral Dissertation Awards
	Wenner-Gren Foundation Dissertation Awards
	Harry Frank Guggenheim Emerging Scholars Award
	Graham Foundation Carter Manny Award (architecture)
	Your own institution! Ask about every opportunity available early in your graduate career and keep track of these.
Doctoral Student	Horowitz Foundation
	American Scandinavian Foundation

Graduate school also provides an ideal environment for learning about grant seeking without the intense pressure that faculty face. You have access to mentors who can guide you through the process, institutional resources designed to support student development, and time to experiment with different approaches without the career-defining stakes that characterize faculty grant competitions. The mistakes you make as a graduate student grant seeker become valuable learning experiences rather than career setbacks.

Perhaps most importantly, developing grant-seeking skills during graduate school positions you strategically for your postgraduation career, regardless of whether you pursue academic or nonacademic paths. In academic careers, early experience with grant seeking demonstrates initiative and preparation that can distinguish you in competitive job markets. For nonacademic careers, grant-writing skills translate directly to proposal development, project management, and stakeholder communication abilities that employers value across sectors.

Understanding the Graduate Student Funding Landscape

The funding opportunities available to graduate students fall into several distinct categories, each serving different purposes and requiring different approaches. Understanding these categories helps you develop a strategic approach to funding that aligns with your academic goals and career timeline.

Dissertation Support Grants

Dissertation grants represent perhaps the most significant funding opportunity for doctoral students. These grants typically support the final stages of doctoral research, including data collection, analysis, and writing. Major sources include the National Science Foundation's Doctoral Dissertation Research Grants, which support dissertation research across multiple disciplines, and specialized programs like the Social Science Research Council's various fellowship programs.

Dissertation grants serve multiple purposes beyond simply providing financial support. The application process requires you to articulate your research project clearly and persuasively, developing skills that will serve you throughout your career. Successfully competing for dissertation funding demonstrates to potential employers that your research has been evaluated and endorsed by external reviewers, providing third-party validation of your scholarly potential.

The timeline for dissertation grant applications typically requires advance planning. Many programs have annual deadlines occurring months before you might need the funding, requiring you to begin planning your application strategy early in your dissertation development process. This timing provides benefits by forcing you to think through your research design thoroughly and identify potential challenges before you encounter them in the field.

Dissertation grants often have specific requirements about how funds can be used, but these restrictions typically align well with genuine dissertation needs. Common allowable expenses include travel for data collection, participant compensation, research materials and supplies, software and technology costs, and transcription or data processing services. Some programs also allow for limited living stipends during intensive research periods.

Conference Travel and Professional Development Funding

Presenting your research at academic conferences represents a crucial component of professional development, but travel costs can quickly become prohibitive on typical graduate student budgets. Numerous funding sources exist specifically to support graduate student conference participation, ranging from small departmental travel grants to national fellowship programs. Professional associations in most fields offer graduate student travel awards, often tied to conference paper presentations or poster sessions. These awards typically require you to submit your accepted abstract along with budget information and sometimes brief statements about how the conference participation will benefit your professional development. The application process is usually straightforward, but competition can be intense for major conferences.

Your institution likely offers internal travel grants for graduate students, administered through graduate schools, centers and institutes, student government organizations, or academic departments. These grants often have rolling deadlines and may be easier to secure than external funding, making them valuable supplements to other funding sources. Understanding your institution's internal funding landscape requires some investigation, as these opportunities are often poorly publicized.

External fellowship programs sometimes include professional development components that can support conference travel, research visits, or specialized training opportunities. The Social Science Research Council, American Council of Learned Societies, and various foundation programs offer such opportunities, though they typically require more extensive applications than simple travel grants.

Research Support Grants

Many graduate research projects require financial support for participant compensation, research materials, data collection expenses, or other project-related costs. Various funding sources exist to support these needs, though they often require creative approaches to identify and access. Small grants programs, sometimes called seed grants or pilot grants, exist at many institutions to support student research projects. These grants typically range from a few hundred to several thousand dollars and can cover expenses like participant payments, software licenses, research materials, or small equipment purchases. The application process is usually designed as a learning experience, providing students with practice in grant writing while supporting genuine research needs.

Community foundations and local organizations sometimes offer grants for research projects that benefit their constituencies or address local issues. These opportunities require research to identify, but they can provide both funding and community connections that enhance your research impact. Projects involving community engagement, public health, education, or social services may be particularly well positioned for this type of support.

Research-intensive courses or independent study projects sometimes qualify for small grants from academic departments or interdisciplinary programs. These grants can support pilot projects that later develop into dissertation research or provide preliminary data for larger grant applications. The key is that thinking strategically about how small-scale funding can contribute to your larger research agenda.

Fellowship Programs

Graduate fellowships represent some of the most prestigious and valuable funding opportunities available to doctoral students. Major programs like the National Science Foundation Graduate Research Fellowship Program, Ford Foundation Fellowship Programs, and various disciplinary fellowship competitions provide multiyear support that can transform your graduate school experience. These fellowships offer advantages beyond financial support. Fellowship recipients often gain access to exclusive professional development opportunities, networking events, and mentoring programs. The prestige associated with major fellowships can open doors to research collaborations, conference presentations, and job opportunities. Perhaps most importantly, fellowships provide intellectual freedom by reducing dependence on advisor funding and allowing you to pursue your own research interests.

The application process for major fellowships typically requires extensive preparation, including research statements, personal statements, and letters of recommendation. Personal statements in a fellowship proposal are different from the type of statement written to get into graduate school. The framing of this type of statement can be unique, so seek out advisors and mentors to help. Many successful applicants spend months crafting their applications, often working with multiple mentors to refine their materials. This intensive preparation process itself provides valuable experience in articulating your research vision and professional goals.

Fellowship applications often require you to demonstrate broader impacts beyond your immediate research project. This requirement encourages you to think about how your work contributes to societal goals, educational objectives, or diversity and inclusion efforts. Developing this broader perspective enhances your ability to communicate with diverse audiences throughout your career.

Building Your Grant-Seeking Skills Progressively

Successful graduate student grant seekers typically adopt a progressive approach, starting with smaller, more manageable opportunities and gradually building toward larger, more competitive programs. This progression allows you to develop skills, build confidence, and establish a track record of success that strengthens future applications.

Beginning with internal grants provides a low-stakes environment for learning basic grant-writing skills. Most institutions offer small grants for graduate student research, travel, or professional development. While the funding amounts may be modest, these applications allow you to practice articulating research questions, developing budgets, and writing persuasively about your work's significance.

External travel grants represent a natural next step, as they typically require more polished applications but focus on concrete, achievable goals. Successfully securing travel funding demonstrates your ability to compete in external competitions while providing tangible benefits for your professional development.

Dissertation grants require more extensive preparation but offer substantial rewards for successful applicants. The application process typically involves detailed research plans, comprehensive literature reviews, and sophisticated discussions of methodology and broader impacts. Successfully navigating this process provides excellent preparation for faculty grant seeking.

Fellowship applications represent the most intensive graduate student grant-seeking experience, requiring comprehensive self-presentation and long-term vision articulation. Whether successful or not, the fellowship application process typically generates materials and insights that benefit job market preparation and future grant applications.

Practical Strategies for Graduate Student Grant Success

Developing effective grant-seeking skills during graduate school requires strategic planning and consistent effort over time. The most successful graduate student grant-seekers adopt systematic approaches that integrate funding pursuit with their broader academic development.

Start Early and Plan Strategically

Successful grant seeking requires advance planning, as most funding opportunities have specific deadlines, extensive preparation requirements, and a timeline of up to a year before the funding arrives. Create a calendar of relevant deadlines during your first year of graduate school and update it regularly as you discover new opportunities. This forward-looking approach allows you to plan your research timeline around funding opportunities rather than scrambling to find support for projects already underway.

Research the funding landscape in your field systematically, using resources like your institution's research development office, professional association websites, and databases like Pivot or GrantScape. Understanding what funding opportunities exist helps you make strategic decisions about research directions, collaboration opportunities, and skill-development priorities.

Develop relationships with faculty members who have successful grant-seeking experience. These mentors can provide insights about funding opportunities, feedback on application materials, and connections to potential collaborators. Most faculty members are willing to share their expertise with motivated graduate students, but you need to approach these relationships thoughtfully and respectfully.

Align Funding Pursuit with Academic Goals

The most effective graduate student grant-seeking strategies align funding pursuit with broader academic and professional development goals. Rather than pursuing grants simply for financial support, think strategically about how different funding opportunities can advance your research agenda, professional skills, and career positioning.

Dissertation grants should support research projects that genuinely advance your intellectual development and contribute to scholarly knowledge in your field. While funding considerations might influence specific methodological choices or project scope, your fundamental research questions, rather than funding availability, should drive the process.

Professional development funding should support activities that genuinely enhance your skills and career prospects. Conference presentations provide valuable experience in communicating your research to scholarly audiences, but they should represent work that you are proud to share rather than preliminary projects pursued primarily for travel funding.

Develop Your Professional Communication Skills

Grant applications require you to communicate clearly and persuasively about complex research projects to diverse audiences. These communication skills prove valuable throughout your career, regardless of whether you continue pursuing grants after graduation.

Practice writing for nonspecialist audiences by developing multiple versions of your research description tailored to different contexts. A description written for your dissertation committee will differ significantly from one written for a fellowship application, which will differ again from one written for a general audience. Developing facility with these different communication styles enhances your versatility as a scholar and professional.

Seek feedback on your writing from multiple sources, including faculty mentors, peer colleagues, and potentially nonacademic audiences. Different readers will identify different strengths and weaknesses in your applications, helping you develop more effective communication strategies.

Learn from Both Success and Rejection

Grant applications, even unsuccessful ones, provide valuable learning experiences that contribute to your professional development. Rejection is common in grant competitions, even among highly qualified applicants, and learning to handle rejection constructively represents an important professional skill.

When applications are unsuccessful, request feedback from reviewers when possible. Many programs provide detailed reviewer comments that can help you understand how your application was perceived and identify areas for improvement in future submissions.

Successful applications provide learning opportunities as well. Analyze which elements of your successful applications were most effective, and consider how you can apply those lessons to future submissions. Share your successful strategies with peer colleagues, contributing to a culture of mutual support and learning.

Preparing for the Academic Job Market: Grant-Related Questions to Ask

As you advance through graduate school and begin preparing for the academic job market, understanding the grant expectations and support structures at potential institutions becomes crucial for making informed career decisions. During campus visits and interviews, asking strategic questions about grant expectations can help you assess whether an institution will provide the support you need to succeed. **But beware! Some departments and colleges will not be ready to answer these types of questions, so tread carefully, and read your audience.** Back off in asking the more detailed questions if you can tell they do not have an external-funding-seeking culture or readiness.

The questions below provide a systematic framework for gathering information about institutional grant culture, support structures, and expectations. Not every question will be appropriate for every interview situation, but having this comprehensive list helps ensure you gather the information needed to make informed decisions about your career.

Academic Job Market Checklist: Grant-Related Questions for Campus Visits

Institutional Structure & Support

- ☐ What percentage of faculty in your department currently have external funding?
- ☐ Is there an expectation (formal or informal) that I will apply for grants?
- ☐ If so, is there a specific dollar amount or number of applications expected?
- ☐ What pre-award support exists at the department, college, and university levels?
- ☐ What post-award administrative support would I receive if funded?
- ☐ Does the university offer internal seed grants to help junior faculty develop preliminary data?
- ☐ Does the institution have a research development office that assists with finding funding opportunities?

Tenure & Promotion Considerations

- ☐ How is external funding weighted in tenure decisions in this department?
- ☐ Could you share examples of recently tenured faculty members' funding profiles?
- ☐ If I secure grants, would expectations for my publication output change?
- ☐ How does the department view time spent on unsuccessful grant applications?
- ☐ Would interdisciplinary grants be valued the same as disciplinary ones?
- ☐ Who would typically write external letters for my tenure case, and how do they view grants?
- ☐ Can I see the department's written tenure and promotion guidelines?

Teaching & Time Management

- ☐ What is the standard teaching load for tenure-track faculty?
- ☐ Is there a course release policy for new faculty?
- ☐ Can grant funding "buy out" teaching time? If so, at what rate?
- ☐ What are typical service expectations for pre-tenure faculty?
- ☐ How are teaching assignments determined, and how much flexibility would I have?
- ☐ What mentoring requirements exist for graduate students?

Graduate Student Resources

- ☐ How are graduate students typically funded in this department?
- ☐ Are graduate students primarily expected to teach or conduct research?
- ☐ If I bring in funding for a graduate student, would that create conflicts with departmental needs?
- ☐ Can I meet with graduate students to discuss their research experiences?
- ☐ What is the process for recruiting graduate students to work on funded projects?
- ☐ Are there restrictions on summer funding for graduate students?

Departmental Culture

- ☐ Could you describe how collaborative research is viewed in the department?
- ☐ How do faculty typically share resources or equipment?
- ☐ Are there regular forums for sharing grant opportunities or collaborative writing?
- ☐ What has been the experience of recent junior faculty with external funding?
- ☐ How does the department celebrate or recognize grant success?
- ☐ How are indirect cost returns from grants distributed?

Field-Specific Considerations

- ☐ Which funding agencies have faculty in this department had success with?
- ☐ Is there institutional support for attending grant-writing workshops?
- ☐ How does the department view publications in interdisciplinary venues that might result from grant-funded work?
- ☐ Are there particular funding sources that the department especially values?
- ☐ How have recent junior faculty balanced field-specific publication expectations with interdisciplinary grant work?

Final Reflection Questions (for yourself)

- ☐ Based on conversations, does this department seem to have realistic expectations about grants?
- ☐ Did I observe signs of genuine support for junior faculty development?
- ☐ Did answers about grants align with or contradict other tenure expectations they described?
- ☐ Would I have the resources and support needed to be successful with grants here?
- ☐ Did administrators and faculty members give consistent answers about grant expectations?

Remember: Different answers from different people may signal unclear expectations or changing norms. Pay attention to both what is said and what is unsaid, and consider asking the same questions to multiple people to triangulate information.

Preparing for Postgraduation Funding Success

The grant-seeking skills you develop during graduate school provide a foundation for continued funding success throughout your career. However, the transition from graduate student to postdoctoral researcher or faculty member requires adapting your approach to new expectations and opportunities.

Graduate student grant experience demonstrates initiative and preparation that potential employers value. Document your funding successes carefully, including both successful applications and the professional development activities they enabled. This documentation provides concrete evidence of your potential for future funding success. The relationships you develop during graduate school grant seeking often prove valuable throughout your career. Program officers, reviewers, and fellow applicants can become long-term professional contacts who provide opportunities for collaboration, mentorship, and career advancement.

Perhaps most importantly, the confidence and skills you develop through graduate student grant seeking prepare you for the more intense funding pressures of faculty careers. Having successfully navigated grant competitions as a graduate student provides both practical experience and psychological preparation for the ongoing funding challenges that characterize academic careers.

Integrating Grant Seeking with Academic Development

The most successful graduate student grant seekers integrate funding pursuit with their broader academic development rather than treating it as a separate activity. This integration requires thinking strategically about how grant-seeking activities can advance multiple goals simultaneously. Research planning benefits from considering potential funding sources early in the process. Understanding what types of projects different agencies support can help you design research that is both intellectually compelling and strategically positioned for funding success. This does not mean allowing funding considerations to drive your research agenda; rather, it means ensuring that your genuine intellectual interests align with fundable research directions.

Professional networking opportunities often emerge through grant-seeking activities. Review panels, fellowship programs, and funding agency events provide opportunities to meet established scholars in your field and peers who share your research interests. These connections can lead to collaboration opportunities, mentorship relationships, and job market advantages.

Conclusion

Graduateschoolprovidesanidealenvironmentfordevelopinggrant-seeking skills that will serve you throughout your career. The combination of mentorship access, institutional support, and learning-focused environment allows you to experiment with grant-seeking strategies and build expertise without the high-stakes pressure that characterizes faculty funding competition.

The key to successful graduate student grant seeking lies in adopting a strategic, progressive approach that aligns funding pursuit with your broader academic and professional development goals. Start with smaller, more manageable opportunities to build skills and confidence, then gradually progress toward larger and more competitive programs. Remember to check reviewing timeline and requirements to receive the funding to properly set your expectations. Throughout this process, focus on developing the communication skills, professional relationships, and strategic thinking abilities that will serve you regardless of your postgraduation career path.

As you prepare for the academic job market, use the comprehensive checklist provided in this chapter to assess potential institutions' grant expectations and support structures. Understanding these factors will help you make informed decisions about career opportunities and ensure you choose positions where you can thrive.

Remember that grant-seeking success is not just about securing funding but about developing the professional skills and scholarly reputation that will benefit you throughout your career. Whether you ultimately pursue an academic or nonacademic career, the experience of articulating research significance, developing project budgets, and communicating with diverse stakeholders provides valuable preparation for professional success.

As you progress through graduate school, view grant seeking not as an additional burden, but as an integral component of your professional development. The skills you develop, relationships you build, and confidence you gain through graduate student grant seeking will provide a foundation for continued success in whatever career path you choose to pursue.

12

Writing for Your Reviewer Audience

Writing a compelling grant proposal requires more than technical proficiency—it demands a deep understanding of who will read, evaluate, and ultimately decide the fate of your research funding request. This chapter pulls back the curtain on the grant review process, revealing the human dynamics, institutional structures, and practical realities that shape how your proposal will be evaluated. By understanding these behind-the-scenes elements, you can craft proposals that speak directly to reviewer needs and navigate the complex evaluation landscape more effectively.

The Reality of Grant Review: Who Actually Reads Your Proposal

Perhaps the most crucial insight for grant writers is understanding that the people who will review your proposal are almost certainly not the experts you imagine. They are most often actual humans with the typical biases and flaws we see in people. We have observed through extensive panel service that reviewers often know general information about your field and methods but are limited in their specific knowledge. This reality stems from multiple filtering factors that eliminate the most obvious reviewers:

First, your closest collaborators, those who truly understand your work, are conflicted out of the review process. If you've published with someone or worked together on previous projects, they cannot review your proposal. Second, your direct competitors might be listed on your conflicts of interest form, removing another group of subject matter experts. Third, the remaining pool of topic experts may not be available when funding agencies recruit reviewers. Finally, even those who agree to review might not be available for the specific panel dates.

This systematic elimination of subject matter experts means you must write for an educated but potentially unfamiliar audience. In our experience serving on numerous panels, we've rarely received proposals squarely in our areas of expertise. We often feel like we're stretching to review for someone else's field. Kerk was asked to serve on a specialized panel for computer science even though he is not a computer scientist. The program officer wanted to expand the input from reviewers and include people who could carefully evaluate the human-center design aspects of these proposals.

The disciplinary diversity creates both challenges and opportunities. We recall reviewing a proposal where a theory popular in political policy research was presented as novel when communication scholars had been working with a similar line of theorizing for decades and thus did not see the research as novel. The senior scholar presenting the work insisted that people in their field cited this new line of theorizing all the time, which led to a frank discussion about cross-disciplinary awareness. These moments highlight how scholars from different fields can be unaware of each other's contributions, even when studying similar phenomena.

In some types of funding proposals, the person reviewing and deciding whether to fund the work is the program officer, or a designated technical expert within the funding organization. This is a common practice with some foundations, as well as smaller-dollar-amount proposals in some federal or state agencies.

Understanding Review Panel Dynamics

A typical form of external funding peer review involves review panels—groups of scientists and sometimes practitioners with varied backgrounds—who independently evaluate proposals and then come together online or in person to discuss the proposals. Serving on a panel is a great opportunity to lend your expertise and evaluate the highest levels of science being performed. However, this is a labor-intensive service; one that your peers and supervisors may not fully understand. From our experience, the time commitment for serving on a single panel often exceeds forty hours. This includes the time spent reviewing between three and eighteen individual proposals and then attending a one- to three-day meeting where the proposals are individually discussed. Reviewers typically evaluate all aspects of the proposal, not just the narrative or research statement. Many will examine biosketches, budgets, data handling, and sharing protocols, as well as any specialized content such as video pitches. Despite this time commitment, these experiences have positively shaped both Kerk's and Keri's understanding of how to write for a reviewer audience. If you get the opportunity to serve on a review panel, try to say yes. You will learn a lot and do meaningful service.

The Performance Aspect of Panel Review

When serving on a review panel, the lead reviewer for each proposal performs for their peers. This performance pressure significantly influences how proposals are discussed. There is substantial pressure because you're performing for your peers without necessarily knowing their full opinions, so you're making your claims without detailed knowledge of the varied perspectives in the room.

One common panel structure assigns the reviewer who rated the proposal highest to present it first, a practice that creates interesting psychological dynamics. There's unique pressure when you know you rated a proposal the highest while others rated it lower. Sometimes you find yourself advocating really hard because you see something novel that you believe others on the panel need to understand.

This advocacy role becomes particularly challenging when reviewers lack complete expertise in the proposal's methods or theory. It is easy to experience moments of uncertainty and wonder whether someone else in the room might know a particular method or theory better. Early-career or new panel reviewers especially struggle with how much of their lack of expertise to reveal on a given proposal.

Power Dynamics and Interdisciplinary Tensions

Interdisciplinary panels introduce additional layers of complexity through power dynamics between fields. When serving on interdisciplinary panels, certain disciplines may be perceived as more legitimate than others—for instance, communication might be viewed as less rigorous than engineering or medicine. These perceived hierarchies affect how reviewers interact and how seriously different perspectives are taken.

Academic rank creates another dimension of power dynamics. We've observed how assistant professors on their first panels often hesitate and feel they need to justify their positions more when disagreeing with senior colleagues. Junior reviewers tend to be more enthusiastic about proposals and reluctant to criticize, while experienced reviewers feel comfortable pointing out weaknesses directly.

Despite these dynamics, the review process generally maintains professionalism and respect. In our extensive experience, we have never been on a panel where we felt disrespected. The people who volunteer their time for panels are committed to having productive conversations about getting the best research funded.

The First Impression

How proposals are initially presented to the panel can determine their fate. A colleague once shared how, during their first NSF panel, they weren't sure how to balance the conversation and defaulted to the critical mode common in academic settings—emphasizing what needed to be changed rather than what was strong. They set a negative tone for the proposal, and it went downhill fast with no one rescuing it. They felt horrible afterward because the proposal wasn't actually that bad, but they had simply presented it with too much criticism at the start.

This highlights why clear, accessible writing matters so intensely. When reviewers can easily identify and articulate your proposal's strengths, they become more effective advocates. Conversely, proposals that require extensive effort to decode may suffer from lukewarm or negative initial presentations that doom their chances.

The Multiple Review Layers

Most funding agencies employ multiple review mechanisms that create different challenges for proposal writers. Understanding these layers helps explain why consistency and clarity matter so much.

Ad Hoc Reviews: The Isolation Challenge

Before panel meetings, many agencies solicit ad hoc reviews from individual reviewers who evaluate proposals in isolation. This process creates unique dynamics because reviewers don't have a chance to look at other proposals in the pool for comparison.

The variance in ad hoc reviews can be dramatic. You may get lucky with a reviewer who is positive and gentle in their approach, or you may encounter someone who is overly critical of every proposal. Without the calibration that comes from seeing multiple proposals or hearing other perspectives, individual reviewers may apply wildly different standards. This variability matters because initial scores often determine whether proposals receive full panel discussion. If you have three reviews and two rate you low, panels typically won't spend time discussing your proposal. Conversely, if you have two higher ratings and only one negative review, you get to have a discussion on the panel.

The number of ad hoc reviews varies significantly—from as few as three to as many as seven or eight. Each additional reviewer increases the likelihood that someone from a very different field or methodological tradition will evaluate your work, amplifying the importance of writing for diverse audiences.

Agency-Specific Review Processes

Different funding agencies have developed distinct review cultures that affect how proposals should be written. The Patient-Centered Outcomes Research Institute (PCORI), for example, requires extensive multistage reviews. The process can be time consuming because giving a proposal a thorough review using a detailed rubric may take a full day for each proposal. PCORI's process includes multiple rounds before panels meet: reviewers submit initial reviews, program officers review these reviews and ask clarifying questions, reviewers revise their evaluations, and only then do panels convene. While this thoroughness aims to provide better feedback to applicants, it also means reviewers may be more critical of unclear or poorly organized proposals that make their job harder.

The National Science Foundation typically uses a different approach, combining ad hoc reviews with panel discussions. Some NSF programs rely more heavily on panels, while others weight ad hoc reviews more strongly. Understanding these variations—often by talking to program officers or previous applicants—can help you tailor your writing strategy.

Understanding the Soft Pitch Process

Applying for foundation funding often differs significantly from federal agencies. As Amanda Stanley, executive director at COMPASS, a nonprofit organization based in Portland, Oregon, that supports environmental scientists explains in Sohn (2020), private foundations often begin with a "soft pitch" that presents a brief case for the project. These pitches should cover: "'Here's what I'm trying to do. Here's why it's important. Here's a little bit about me and the people I'm collaborating with. Would you like to talk further?'" (p. 2).

This soft pitch approach recognizes that foundations typically operate differently from many federal agencies. While some other funders, including federal agencies, can also utilize soft-pitch formats, foundations often prioritize relationship building and mission alignment over purely scientific merit. Understanding these different cultures helps you adapt your approach appropriately for different funding sources.

Writing Strategies Based on Review Realities

Understanding how reviews actually work should fundamentally reshape how you approach grant writing. Several key strategies emerge from reviewers' behind-the-scenes experiences.

Write for the Tired, Distracted, Nonexpert Reader

Reviewers rarely read proposals under ideal conditions. We often assume reviewers will read proposals on a Sunday afternoon when they have nothing else to do, with a cup of coffee in hand, sitting on a comfortable couch. The reality is starkly different. Reviewers often read proposals between meetings, on flights, or during Uber rides from the airport to the hotel.

This means your proposal must be comprehensible even to someone reading in suboptimal conditions. You have to write so clearly that no matter what challenges reviewers are facing, they can still understand your points and review effectively.

Follow Headers and Guidelines Exactly

One of the most consistent pieces of advice concerns following formatting guidelines precisely. When asked whether applicants need to use exact headers from funding announcements, the answer is emphatically yes—exactly, word for word. It's not questionable.

The reasoning extends beyond mere rule-following. For many proposals, if you don't use the exact language and headings specified, you make it difficult for reviewers to assess your proposal. They may not know which paragraphs contain information for intellectual contributions, theory, and sections discussing implications and impacts.

Reviewers actively look for specific sections. Every panel uses specific headers and criteria that they expect to find in the proposal. These often become additional review criteria. Creative headers might seem more engaging, but they force reviewers to hunt for required information, potentially missing key elements of your proposal.

Address Feasibility Explicitly

Discussions of feasibility dominate many review panels. Project goals or specific aims of the research should be written so that each can be accomplished independent of the success of other phases of the research. We constantly include contingency plans in our proposals. If findings from study one will impact study two, spell out alternatives. We've heard too many panel discussions where reviewers say a project would be great if study one works, but the proposers haven't explained what they'll do if it doesn't. Multiyear or multi-study proposals face particular scrutiny. Even if the research goals do not rely on a particular outcome, reviewers often conclude that proposals are way too ambitious for the dollar amount requested. Even really cool ideas can go unfunded because they're simply not feasible within the proposed budget and timeline.

Demonstrate Broader or Societal Impacts Creatively

Reviewers appreciate proposals that go beyond standard approaches to broader impacts. Constantly be thinking about novel ways to address broader impacts—unique ways to give back to populations that really pull the whole proposal together. Many proposals treat broader impacts as an afterthought, but reviewers notice and appreciate creative, integrated approaches that show genuine thought about how the research will benefit society beyond academic publications.

The Emotional Dimension of Review

As Peña et al. (2023) note, "Sharing your research ideas can be unnerving; a 'rejection' can feel like an attack. This isn't a productive mindset. Instead, try to view feedback as peer suggestions that increase the impact of your research" (p. 2). Understanding that reviewers are human beings who want to fund good science can help reframe the review process from judgment to conversation.

Beyond technical requirements, consistent themes emerge about what makes reviewers' jobs easier and what frustrates them. Understanding these human elements can improve both your proposal's reception and your relationship with the review process. Most reviewers volunteer substantial time because they care about advancing science. The rigorous review process means reviewers often go back and review literature that others have mentioned during discussions.

Red Team Reviews: Learning from Mock Panels

One of the most valuable preparatory exercises involves red team reviews—mock review panels that provide feedback before submission. These exercises reveal how actual panels might respond to your proposal while there's still time to make changes. Red team reviews can range from informal feedback sessions to elaborate multiday mock panels. We've participated in red teams where institutions flew reviewers in and hosted them for two days to simulate an entire review process. This level of investment reflects serious institutional commitment to proposal success.

The value of red team reviews extends beyond catching errors or weak arguments. They help writers understand how their proposals will be discussed, what questions reviewers might raise, and where additional clarity is needed. In our experience, the vast majority of proposals that have had red team reviews have been funded—every penny invested has paid off.

Even informal versions provide valuable perspective. Getting proposals written early enough for individual faculty to run them by more experienced colleagues can make a significant difference. The key is getting outside readers who can simulate the informed-but-not-expert perspective of actual review panels.

Conclusion: Writing for Real Humans in Complex Systems

The grant review process involves real humans making difficult decisions under challenging conditions within complex institutional systems. Your reviewers will likely be accomplished researchers from adjacent fields, reading your proposal between other commitments, trying to fairly evaluate work outside their immediate expertise while managing panel dynamics and institutional requirements.

Understanding these realities should inspire both humility and strategic thinking. Humility because even excellent proposals face substantial challenges in the review process. Strategic thinking because knowing how reviews actually work allows you to craft proposals that navigate these challenges more successfully.

Reviewers genuinely want to fund good science. They volunteer their time, engage seriously with proposals, and often advocate passionately for work they believe deserves support. Your job as a proposal writer is to make their job as easy as possible—to write so clearly that tired reviewers can quickly grasp your ideas, so precisely that nonexperts can evaluate your methods, and so compellingly that someone will champion your work in panel discussions.

By writing for the real conditions of grant review rather than an idealized process, you significantly improve your chances of success. Remember that behind every review is a human reader trying to make fair decisions about distributing limited resources. Respect their time, acknowledge their constraints, and write in ways that enable them to become advocates for your research. This human-centered approach to grant writing, informed by understanding the review process from the inside, provides the foundation for more successful proposals and ultimately, for advancing your research agenda.

13

Grant-Writing Mechanics

While understanding your reviewer audience provides the strategic foundation for grant writing, the mechanical aspects of how you craft your prose can make the difference between a proposal that gets funded and one that gets forgotten. This chapter focuses on the nuts and bolts of grant writing—the specific techniques, structures, and stylistic choices that make proposals clear, persuasive, and memorable. Please note that there are entire courses and books written on how to write grants, and we have a list of resources for you to learn more Appendix B. These mechanics matter because even the most innovative research ideas can be undermined by poor presentation, while well-crafted proposals can elevate good ideas into fundable projects.

The Fundamental Shift: From Academic to Persuasive Writing

Grant writing demands a fundamental departure from the academic writing style that dominates journal articles and scholarly books. Where academic writing often values complexity, nuance, and exhaustive literature reviews, grant writing requires clarity, directness, and strategic selection. This isn't dumbing down your ideas—it's presenting them in ways that enable quick comprehension and evaluation by busy reviewers.

The most important mechanical shift involves moving from passive to active voice. Active voice is a grammatical concept where the subject performs the activity. This type of writing tends to be clearer and more direct. By contrast, academic writing has traditionally favored passive constructions that emphasize objectivity and distance the researcher from the research. In Keri's Grant Writing for Graduate Students course, she passes out worksheets to help her students practice shifting their writing in a more approachable grant-writing style that reverses the academic writing style they have honed in graduate education. The goal is to get your reader excited about your project and not make them struggle to read and comprehend the text. Compare these examples:

- **Academic style:** "It will be determined whether social media usage patterns are associated with community resilience indicators."
- **Grant style:** "We will determine whether social media usage patterns predict community resilience."

The active construction immediately conveys agency, confidence, and clarity. It tells reviewers that you—not some abstract force—will conduct this research. This shift extends throughout your proposal. Instead of "Data will be collected," write "We will collect data." Rather than "It is hypothesized," state "We hypothesize."

A Word About Generative AI

As generative AI tools become more prevalent in research processes, researchers should be aware of institutional guidelines for GenAI use, particularly regarding tools that are freely available but use submitted text for training purposes or retain the text in some form. Many free AI tools include terms of service stating that anything you input can be used to train the model or may be stored in ways you don't control. This creates potential problems for grant-funded research. If you're developing proprietary methods, creating potentially patentable processes, or working with sensitive data, using these tools might constitute disclosure of information in ways that could affect commercialization of intellectual property in the future. Some sponsor agreements explicitly prohibit sharing project information with third parties without prior approval, and uploading grant text to a free AI service could violate these terms.

Before using generative AI tools for any aspect of your grant work, this is what we recommend:

- Check your institution's policies on AI use in research
- Review your sponsor's terms and conditions regarding data sharing and third-party tools
- If you're working with sensitive populations, protected data, or proprietary information, consult with your IRB, research administrator, or technology transfer office
- Consider using AI tools that don't retain or train on user data (typically paid services with specific privacy protections)

The landscape around AI use in research is evolving rapidly, and institutional policies are still catching up with the technology. When in doubt, ask before using AI tools for grant-related work.

Learning from Proposal Libraries

Before diving into the mechanics of writing, successful grant writers often study examples of funded proposals. As Rapaport et al. (2022) explain, "Proposal libraries are collections of proposals, both funded and unfunded, that were previously submitted for consideration by funding agencies" (p. 1). Building and using such a library can provide invaluable insights into what works. Some agencies (including NIH and NEH) have examples of funded proposals on their websites, and some PIs are willing to share at least part of their proposals with new investigators.

The Three-Step Analysis Approach

Rapaport et al. (2022) recommend a systematic three-step approach to analyzing proposals in your library:

1 **Assess structure.** "Start by taking a big-picture view of the proposal. Scan each page but don't read the text (yet). Consider the margins, font size, figure placement, and more. Is it filled to the brim with text, or does it have space to breathe?" (p. 2). This initial assessment helps you understand how successful proposals use visual design to enhance readability.

2. **Assess content.** "Next, give the proposal a quick read to examine the placement of ideas within the sections or subsections of the proposal" (p. 2). Look for patterns in how successful proposals organize information, how much space they dedicate to different components, and where key ideas appear.
3. **Assess word choice.** "Finally, give the text a closer read.... Look closely at word choice, such as the authors' use of jargon and field-specific acronyms: both can make applications unapproachable and difficult to read" (p. 3). Pay attention to how successful proposals balance technical accuracy with accessibility.

To build your own proposal library, Rapaport et al. (2022) suggest: "Ask your peers or mentors whether they would be willing to share their proposals with you. Many funders publish lists of people who've been awarded grants, so reaching out to previous winners is a good way to start" (p. 1).

Word Choice as Strategic Communication

Every word in a grant proposal should earn its place through clarity and impact. Successful grant writers understand that word choice affects not just comprehension but also reviewer confidence in your ability to complete the proposed work.

Conveying Certainty and Capability

Strong proposals use language that conveys competence without overconfidence. As Rapaport et al. (2022) emphasize, "Active verbs convey precision and action, which is important in science" and note that "'I will' is more compelling than 'I plan to' or 'I hope to'" (p. 3). Consider the progression from weak to strong formulations:

- **Weak:** We hope to identify factors that influence community response.
- **Better:** We plan to identify factors that influence community response.
- **Strong:** We will identify factors that influence community response.

The strongest version doesn't hedge—it makes a clear commitment while remaining realistic. This pattern applies throughout your proposal. Replace "we aim to develop" with "we will develop," "we seek to understand" with "we will examine," and "we intend to explore" with "we will investigate."

However, certainty must be balanced with scientific accuracy. When discussing potential outcomes or future implications, acknowledge uncertainty appropriately:

- **Overconfident:** This research will transform how communities prepare for disasters.
- **Appropriate:** This research will provide communities with evidence-based strategies that can enhance disaster preparedness.

Eliminating Jargon While Maintaining Precision

Grant proposals must be technically accurate while remaining accessible to reviewers from adjacent fields. This requires careful attention to terminology and explanation. The goal isn't to eliminate all technical terms—reviewers are accomplished scholars who can handle complexity. Instead, provide brief clarifications that enable nonspecialists to follow your reasoning.

- **Too jargonistic:** We will employ a hermeneutic phenomenological approach to explore participants' lifeworlds.
- **Appropriately accessible:** We will use hermeneutic phenomenology—a qualitative approach that explores how people interpret and make meaning from their lived experiences—to understand how residents experience neighborhood change.

When introducing specialized terminology, follow a simple pattern: use the term, provide a brief explanation in common language, then continue using the term. This respects reviewers' intelligence while ensuring comprehension.

Structural Clarity Through Strategic Organization

How you organize information within sections can dramatically affect comprehension and persuasion. Grant proposals benefit from explicit structural signals that guide readers through your logic.

The Power of Topic Sentences

Each paragraph should begin with a clear topic sentence that announces its main point (Lentz et al., 2025). This isn't elementary writing—it's strategic communication for busy readers who may be skimming to extract key information. Strong topic sentences allow reviewers to follow your argument even if they don't read every word.

Consider this paragraph opening: Three methodological innovations distinguish our approach from previous research. This immediately tells reviewers what to expect and why this paragraph matters. They can choose to read the details or, if pressed for time, move on knowing they understand your claim about methodological innovation.

Using Parallel Structure for Complex Information

When presenting multiple related points, parallel structure enhances both comprehension and retention. This technique proves especially valuable when describing research objectives, methodological steps, or expected outcomes.

- **Without parallel structure:** The project will first identify key stakeholders. Then we want to understand what their main concerns are. Third is developing interventions. Finally, we'll look at whether the interventions worked.
- **With parallel structure:** The project will:
  - Identify key community stakeholders
  - Analyze stakeholder concerns and priorities

- Develop targeted interventions
- Evaluate intervention effectiveness

The parallel structure makes the logical progression clear and memorable while using fewer words.

Visual Design as Communication

Grant proposals are visual documents, and their appearance affects how reviewers perceive and process information. While specific formatting requirements vary by funder, certain design principles enhance readability across all contexts.

Strategic Use of White Space

Dense blocks of text exhaust readers and obscure key points. White space—the empty areas around text—provides visual breathing room that enhances comprehension. For a reviewer, it's exhausting to read large blocks of text.

Create white space through:

- Short paragraphs (three to five sentences maximum in most cases)
- Bulleted or numbered lists for related items (if appropriate for your proposal)
- Section breaks between major topics
- Space between paragraphs (but be sure formatting is consistent to make the proposal easier to read)
- Graphics and tables that clarify and create a visual break
- Margins that frame the text appropriately

Reviewers reading their twentieth proposal will appreciate documents that don't feel overwhelming at first glance.

Headers as Navigation Tools

Headers do more than organize—they create a mental map that helps reviewers understand and remember your proposal's structure. Effective headers are:

- **Descriptive rather than generic:**
    - Weak: Methods
    - Strong: Mixed-Methods Approach to Understanding Community Resilience
- **Parallel in structure:**
    - Identifying Key Stakeholders
    - Analyzing Stakeholder Networks
    - Building Stakeholder Capacity
- **Hierarchical to show relationships:**
    - Main header: Research Design
        - Subheader: Quantitative Component: Survey of Community Organizations
        - Subheader: Qualitative Component: Stakeholder Interviews

Strategic Emphasis Techniques

Bold text, when used sparingly, can highlight crucial information for skimming reviewers. However, overuse diminishes its effectiveness. Reserve bold for:

- Key findings or innovations
- Important deadlines or milestones
- Review criteria
- Critical budget information
- Major section transitions

Italics serve better for introducing new terms or providing subtle emphasis within sentences. Underlining should generally be avoided as it can appear aggressive and is harder to read.

Writing Compelling Openings and Transitions

The opening sentences of your proposal and each major section carry disproportionate weight. They determine whether reviewers engage fully or merely skim through your content. From our experience, it is shocking how many times these first sentences contain typographical errors or are so long that a reader gets lost in the sentence. Don't do this! Double-check and reread these opening sections because they really do matter.

The Hook Principle

Your proposal's opening should immediately establish significance and create intellectual interest. Avoid starting with broad generalizations or extensive background. Instead, lead with the specific problem or opportunity your research addresses.

- **Weak opening:** Urban planning research has long been interested in how communities respond to challenges. Many scholars have examined various aspects of community resilience. This proposal builds on that tradition.
- **Strong opening:** When Hurricane Maria devastated Puerto Rico, some communities were rebuilt within months while others still struggle years later. This dramatic variation in recovery trajectories reveals a critical gap in our understanding of community resilience—we don't know why some communities bounce back while structurally similar communities founder.

The strong opening immediately presents a concrete problem that reviewers can visualize and understand why it matters.

Transitional Bridges

Smooth transitions between sections and paragraphs create coherence and momentum. Each major section should begin by connecting to what came before while previewing what follows. **Effective transition between problem statement and methods:** "Having identified the critical gap in understanding differential community recovery, we propose a mixed-methods study that captures both the structural factors and social processes that enable resilience."

This single sentence reminds reviewers of the problem while setting up the methodological discussion.

Managing Sentence-Level Clarity

At the sentence level, clarity emerges from careful attention to structure, length, and rhythm. Grant writing favors shorter sentences than typical academic prose,.but variation prevents monotony.

The Power of Sentence Variety

Mix simple, compound, and complex sentences to create engaging prose that maintains reader attention. After a complex sentence explaining methodology, follow with a simple statement that reinforces the key point.

> **Example:** We will conduct semi-structured interviews with community leaders, residents, and government officials, using a purposive sampling strategy to ensure representation across demographic groups and geographic areas. This approach captures diverse perspectives on resilience. Interview data will be analyzed using thematic analysis, with two coders independently reviewing transcripts to ensure reliability.

The rhythm—complex, simple, complex—helps readers process information without fatigue.

Avoiding Ambiguous Pronouns

In the interest of brevity, writers sometimes create confusion through unclear pronoun references. Each "it," "they," or "this" should have an unmistakable antecedent.

- **Ambiguous:** We will survey residents and interview leaders. They will provide insights into community dynamics. (Who is "they"—residents, leaders, or both?)
- **Clear:** We will survey residents and interview leaders. These complementary methods will provide insights into community dynamics.

The Art of Being Concise Without Being Dense

Grant proposals must convey substantial information within strict page limits, creating pressure to pack every sentence with content. However, density can defeat comprehension. The goal is to achieve maximum clarity with minimum words. Keri often reminds people who write with her to never use the phrase "the ways in which" because that can be replaced with "how." There are many examples, so let's look at a few of them.

- **Eliminate redundancy:**
  - Wordy: We will collaborate together with community partners
  - Concise: We will collaborate with community partners
- **Choose single words over phrases:**
  - Wordy: in order to understand
  - Concise: to understand
- **Remove unnecessary qualifiers:**
  - Wordy: It is quite possible that participants may perhaps experience some degree of change
  - Concise: Participants may experience change
- **Combine related sentences:**
  - Wordy: We will collect survey data. The data will be analyzed using regression analysis. This analysis will reveal patterns.
  - Concise: We will analyze survey data using regression analysis to reveal patterns.

Maintaining Momentum Through Pacing

Successful proposals maintain forward momentum that carries reviewers through the document. This momentum emerges from careful pacing at multiple levels. Each major section should follow a similar rhythm: establish context quickly, develop the main points with appropriate detail, and conclude with clear takeaways. Avoid sections that start slowly with extensive background before reaching the main point.

Within paragraphs, place the most important information in positions of emphasis—typically the beginning and end. The middle of paragraphs can contain supporting detail, but key claims should appear where reviewers are most likely to notice them.

When technical detail is necessary, consider using a "layered" approach. Provide the essential information in the main text with additional detail in well-labeled appendices or supplementary sections. Appendices are not allowed by some funding agencies, so be sure and read the style guide or proposal writing details before deciding on how you want to approach extra documents. When it is allowed, this approach helps expert reviewers verify your rigor while preventing nonspecialists from getting bogged down.

Common Mechanical Pitfalls and How to Avoid Them

Several mechanical errors appear repeatedly in grant proposals. Recognizing and avoiding these can immediately improve your writing. Many proposals spend too much space on background information before reaching the core research questions. Remember that reviewers are evaluating what you will do, not demonstrating your comprehensive knowledge of the field. Background should be sufficient to establish context and significance—no more.

While you should write for educated readers, don't assume reviewers share your specific theoretical or methodological background. Brief explanations of key concepts ensure all reviewers can evaluate your proposal fairly. As Rapaport et al. (2022) remind us, "top-tier grant writers can explain even complex ideas to non-experts" (p. 3).

Strong proposals tell a coherent story from problem identification through anticipated impact. Each section should clearly connect to this narrative arc. If reviewers can't see how your methods address your research questions or how your timeline enables your objectives, the proposal lacks coherence.

Crucial information—your innovation, your unique qualifications, your key insight—sometimes appears deep within sections rather than upfront where reviewers will notice it. Lead with your strongest material in each section.

Writing as a Regular Practice

Developing strong grant writing mechanics requires consistent practice and intentional skill development. As Peña et al. (2023) emphasize, "To accelerate your impact, you need to commit yourself to writing regularly. For example, you might begin each Monday, Tuesday, and Friday with a cup of tea and at least an hour of distraction-free writing" (p. 2). This regular practice helps develop the writing muscles necessary for clear, compelling proposals. By contrast, some people find that intense writing sessions or cowriting with collaborators work better with their schedule than regularly scheduled writing. Use the approach that works for you.

The Revision Process: From Good to Funded

First drafts of grant proposals are rarely fundable. The revision process transforms competent drafts into compelling proposals through systematic improvement of mechanical elements. Asking a colleague, especially one with an expertise different from your own, is a great way to identify issues. When revising your own work, here are some suggestions:

- **Reading for Flow**
    - Read your proposal aloud to identify awkward constructions, overly long sentences, and unclear transitions. If you stumble while reading, reviewers will stumble while evaluating. Mark these passages for revision.
- **The Reverse Outline Test**
    - After drafting, create a reverse outline by summarizing each paragraph in one sentence. This reveals whether your argument flows logically and whether any paragraphs lack a clear purpose.

Paragraphs that can't be summarized in a single sentence likely need restructuring.

- **The Tired Reviewer Test**
  - Set your proposal aside for at least twenty-four hours, then read it quickly while slightly distracted—perhaps with background music or after a long day. What information do you retain? What sections blur together? This approximates how a tired reviewer might experience your proposal.

Conclusion: Mechanics in Service of Ideas

Excellent grant writing mechanics don't replace innovative ideas or rigorous methodology—they reveal and amplify them. By mastering these mechanical elements, you ensure that reviewers can quickly grasp your vision, understand your approach, and appreciate your capacity to execute the proposed research.

The techniques discussed in this chapter require practice to implement effectively. Start by focusing on one or two elements in each proposal you write. Perhaps begin with activating your voice and clarifying your structure. As these become natural, pay attention to transitions and visual design. Over time, these mechanical considerations will become second nature, freeing you to focus on the intellectual substance of your research.

Remember that every mechanical choice—from word selection to paragraph structure to visual design—should serve a single purpose: making it easier for reviewers to understand and support your research. When mechanics align with content, when clarity reinforces significance, and when structure supports argument, your proposals gain the power not just to inform but to persuade. This is the ultimate goal of grant writing mechanics: creating documents so clear and compelling that reviewers become advocates for your research vision.

14

Writing Research Plans and Broader Impacts

When you are ready to write a grant, we recommend you attend grant-writing workshops and read specifics about writing grants. You can find a list of several options in Appendix B. In this chapter, we focus on two critical components that often suffer in social science grant application: a compelling research plan that demonstrates methodological rigor and feasibility, and a broader impacts section that articulates how your work will benefit society beyond academic publications. These elements require different writing approaches than typical academic prose, demanding both technical precision and accessible communication about real-world relevance. This chapter explores how to craft these essential components while navigating the career implications of different approaches to community engagement and impact.

Writing Effective Research Plans

A compelling research plan must achieve multiple objectives simultaneously. It needs to demonstrate that important research questions can be addressed feasibly by qualified researchers with appropriate support, and sometimes, it is appropriate to justify these research questions using theory. This seemingly simple formula actually demands sophisticated understanding of how to communicate complex ideas accessibly, how to anticipate and address reviewer concerns, and how to present your work as both innovative and executable.

Writing proposals also provides an opportunity to reconnect with your deeper purpose as a researcher. As Peña et al. (2023) note, "Writing proposals provides an opportunity to revisit, revise and reprioritize your goals, think creatively about your strategy and receive feedback from an interdisciplinary community of scientists whose insights can strengthen your research programme and increase its impact" (p. 1). This reframing can transform grant writing from a burdensome task into an intellectually enriching experience.

The Importance of Contingency Planning

One of the most critical elements that distinguishes fundable research plans from those that fall short is explicit attention to contingency planning. Success should not be defined as whether a hypothesis is supported; the results should be worthwhile regardless of whether the hypothesis is confirmed or rejected, and that should be clear to reviewers. Include contingency plans in your proposals, particularly for multi-aim, multiyear, or multi-study projects where findings from one phase impact subsequent phases. If findings from study one will impact study two, spell out alternatives explicitly.

We've heard too many panel discussions where reviewers conclude that a project would be great if study one works, but the proposers haven't explained what they'll do if it doesn't. This lack of foresight can doom otherwise excellent proposals. For example, when one of Keri's teams submitted a no-cost extension request, they literally referred back to the contingency plan in the original proposal, explaining that because the community didn't experience an extremely cold winter (and our project was about extreme cold), they would implement the alternative approach we had outlined.

The key is to think through where reviewers might identify potential failure points and proactively address them. Where might they say, "If that doesn't happen, this isn't feasible"? Find those vulnerabilities and explain your backup plans. This demonstrates the kind of systematic thinking that gives reviewers confidence in your ability to navigate the inevitable challenges of research.

Feasibility as a Central Concern

As discussed in Chapter 12, overall project feasibility dominates many review panels. We've seen excellent proposals fail because reviewers believed the scope was unrealistic given the resources and timeline requested. For example, when working with human subjects, you need to clearly articulate if you already have approval to begin the work and include details about recruitment. The challenge is balancing ambition with realism. You want to propose significant work that justifies the investment, but not so much that reviewers question your judgment or ability to deliver. One effective strategy is to clearly delineate primary objectives that you are confident you can achieve from secondary objectives that represent additional value if everything goes smoothly.

Writing Quantitative Research Plans

When developing quantitative research plans for grant proposals, researchers face unique challenges that differ significantly from writing journal articles. One of the most common struggles is the limited space available to convey all necessary methodological details while still addressing other critical proposal components.

Reviewers need to see that you've thought through every aspect of your research design and can execute it successfully. Unlike journal articles, where you report completed work, proposals require you to anticipate challenges and prove feasibility before beginning the research. This often means providing enough methodological detail to establish credibility without overwhelming the limited space available.

For surveys or experimental designs, it's generally not feasible to include every scale or measure in full. Instead, cite established scales and provide a brief one-sentence description of what each scale measures. This approach gives reviewers enough information to understand your methodology without requiring them to look up citations, which many won't have time to do.

Critical Details for Experimental Designs

With experimental designs, crucial details often get overlooked. Clearly specify whether your design is between-subjects or within-subjects, and importantly, explain why you've made this methodological choice. Different disciplinary traditions have different preferences for experimental designs, and in interdisciplinary panels, these preferences can conflict dramatically. We've witnessed panel discussions where one reviewer stated, "I won't fund it because it's a within-subjects design," while another declared, "I won't fund it because it's a between-subjects design" about the same proposal. This makes explicit justification of methodological decisions essential rather than assuming reviewers will understand your reasoning.

Throughout your methods section, provide justifications for each methodological choice. A compelling proposal constantly explains, justifies, and provides details for the reasons behind choices. Even when you think something is common sense or standard practice in your field, explicitly state your reasoning. This demonstrates your expertise and careful consideration of all aspects of the research design.

Navigating Space Constraints

For shorter proposals (some formats allow only five pages), difficult decisions about what to include become inevitable. This can be frustrating, especially when reviewers later critique elements you intentionally cut due to space limitations. With experience, you'll develop better judgment about what's essential to include, but the process requires difficult trade-offs.

A helpful rule of thumb is to consider your audience (see Chapter 12): Who will review this proposal? What disciplinary background might they have? What can you reasonably assume they know or don't know about your methods? Remember that many reviewers won't be experts in your specific methodological approach. The majority of proposals we've reviewed—perhaps 80 percent—have been outside our immediate expertise. This reality means you should write for educated readers who may be learning about your approach while evaluating it.

Mixed-methods research requires thoughtful integration rather than simply combining qualitative and quantitative components. Funders want to see how each approach contributes uniquely to answering the research questions and how the two strands will be connected, sequenced, or merged to generate more robust insights. Clear justification of the mixed-methods design—whether explanatory, exploratory, or convergent—is essential for demonstrating methodological coherence and feasibility.

Writing Qualitative Research Plans

Qualitative research is highly fundable, and both Keri and Kerk have had repeated success getting their qualitative work funded, even as part of interdisciplinary teams. But presenting it effectively in grant proposals requires special attention to demonstrate methodological rigor and feasibility. Many funding agencies, including the National Science Foundation and even the Department of Defense, fund qualitative studies, but they expect detailed plans that convey systematic approaches and thoughtful design.

The tension between planned structure and responsive flexibility is central to qualitative research. Consider the analogy of planning a vacation to Hawaii. If you were taking a five-day trip to Hawaii for the first time, you wouldn't arrive without an itinerary, hoping to "figure it out" once you get there. While you might adjust your plans based on local recommendations or unexpected opportunities, you would still start with a detailed daily plan to maximize your time.

Funding agencies operate with a similar mindset. They understand that research may adapt as you collect data and make discoveries, but they will not fund researchers who arrive without a plan. A detailed plan, even one that acknowledges potential adjustments, provides assurance that their investment will yield valuable results within the proposed timeframe and budget.

Educating Reviewers About Methodological Rigor

When proposing qualitative research, your first task is often to educate reviewers about how your approach is systematic and rigorous. Many reviewers, particularly those from fields dominated by quantitative methods, may be unfamiliar with qualitative methodologies or may hold misconceptions about their rigor. Your proposal needs to demonstrate that your qualitative study follows established methodological protocols that ensure reliable and valid findings.

Explain clearly how your data collection and analysis procedures ensure systematic investigation. If you're conducting interviews, detail your sampling strategy, interview protocols, and analysis procedures. If you're doing ethnographic research, outline your observation protocols, field note procedures, and analytical approach. The goal is to show that your qualitative research follows established methodological principles.

Providing Detailed Methods and Contingency Plans

The most common mistake in qualitative research proposals is lack of methodological detail. Vague statements about "going into the field" or "conducting interviews" without specific procedures will not inspire confidence. Include specific details about:

- Sampling strategies and recruitment procedures
- Data collection methods with examples of questions or observation protocols
- Analytical approaches with examples of coding strategies
- Quality control measures like member checking or multiple coders
- Timeline for each phase of the research

For instance, Kerk had a successful proposal for ethnographic research that detailed how his team would use maximum variation sampling strategies even while employing snowball sampling techniques. At the end of each interview, Kerk and his team would ask participants to recommend someone demographically and professionally different from themselves to help diversify the sample. This level of detail showed careful planning while allowing for the flexibility inherent in qualitative approaches.

Crafting Compelling Broader Impacts

The broader impacts or societal impacts sections often receive insufficient attention from researchers who view them as an afterthought rather than an integral component of their proposal. Think about novel ways to address broader impacts—unique ways to give back to populations that really pull the whole proposal together. This section can make the difference between a good proposal and a funded one. Many proposals treat broader impacts as a checklist: we'll train graduate students, publish papers, and maybe give a community presentation. While these activities have value, reviewers notice and appreciate creative, integrated approaches that show genuine thought about how the research will benefit society beyond academic circles.

Consider how your research might:

- Address pressing societal challenges in innovative ways
- Create tools or resources that communities can use independently
- Build capacity within underserved populations
- Bridge gaps between research and practice
- Generate insights that inform policy or practice

The key is connecting these impacts directly to your research activities rather than treating them as add-ons. The most compelling broader impacts emerge naturally from the research itself.

Community Partners as Team Members

Increasingly, funding agencies emphasize meaningful community engagement in research projects, creating opportunities for community partners to serve in formal roles beyond traditional advisory positions. These roles can range from Advisory Board membership to full co-PI status, each bringing unique opportunities and challenges.

When community partners join research teams as co-PIs or coinvestigators, the administrative challenges can be substantial. Most community organizations lack the infrastructure that universities have developed for grant management. One emergency management coordinator who joined one of Keri's research teams as a co-PI exemplified both the challenges and rewards of meaningful partnership. As mentioned in detail in Chapter 4, without a strong partnering university research administration team to help him obtain an NSF ID and navigate institutional approvals, his participation would have been impossible.

The process proved so challenging that we maintained a backup plan to shift him to an advisory board role if we couldn't complete his coinvestigator establishment in time. We started months in advance but still weren't certain we would meet the deadline until the day before submission. Yet when the grant was funded, his pride in being a co-PI on an NSF grant was palpable—he told everyone about this achievement. His involvement brought credibility and practical insights that strengthened the project immeasurably.

Ethical Considerations in Community Engagement

This is a good time to review what we discussed in Chapter 4 about including community partners in research. There are many things to consider, and in addition to what is discussed in this book, we encourage anyone engaging the community to review the specific ethical considerations for their type of research. For example, in disaster-related work, the Natural Hazard Center offers training on ethically conducting disaster-related work (Natural Hazards Center), and their researchers have published papers discussing codes of conduct in this context (Gaillard & Peek, 2019).

Career Implications of Grant-Funded Work

While external funding can advance research agendas and provide resources for impactful work, it's crucial to understand how grant-funded projects can affect your academic career trajectory, particularly regarding tenure and promotion decisions.

As we discuss in Chapter 21, there's often a tension between doing innovative interdisciplinary work that funders value and maintaining the disciplinary visibility needed for career advancement. When you spend significant time advocating for your field on interdisciplinary panels or writing grants for diverse funding agencies, you may become less visible within your own discipline.

We've experienced this personally. By writing grants for computer science and engineering programs, serving on interdisciplinary panels, and publishing in venues outside our home field, we've advanced our disciplines' presence in these spaces. However, this advocacy work often goes unrecognized by our own fields. We take pride in working on interdisciplinary teams and serving our institutions through successful grant funding, but we also recognize how this work can impact disciplinary standing.

The challenge lies in balancing multiple professional identities. You need to decide how much of an expert you want to become in your discipline versus how much of an expert you want to become in the topic or area you study. These are different paths with different rewards and recognition structures.

Your institution plays a crucial role in these decisions. At research-intensive universities with strong disciplinary departments, maintaining disciplinary visibility might be essential for tenure. At institutions that value interdisciplinary work or external funding, broader collaborations might be rewarded. The key is understanding your specific context and making deliberate choices rather than accidentally drifting into patterns that don't serve your career goals.

Box 14.1 Learning from Rejection and Building Resilience

An essential but often overlooked aspect of grant writing is developing resilience in the face of rejection. Rejection can become a powerful learning tool. Feedback can be a great learning experience. Many funded researchers keep copies of their harshest reviews to show others that even in the face of criticism, you can pick yourself back up and try again.

When facing rejection, consider these strategies:

- Analyze reviewer comments for patterns
- Revise and resubmit when appropriate
- Use criticism to strengthen future proposals

The key is viewing rejection not as a personal failure but as part of the iterative process of developing fundable ideas. View feedback as peer suggestions that can help increase the impact of your research, much like journal peer reviews. Another way to think of this is as a "protracted conversation between the funder, grant writer, and reviewers" (Peña et al., 2023, p. 2). Shifting your perspective to one that learns from the experience is important.

Building Community Through Grant Writing

One of the most effective ways to improve grant writing skills and maintain motivation is through community building. Writing groups can be a good way to learn from peers. "Once you have a writing group, leverage it to make yourself accountable.... Sharing your goals sets a clear intention; the group can then check in on how everyone's doing at the end of the session" (Peña et al., 2023, p. 2).

Writing groups serve multiple purposes:

- Providing accountability and structure
- Offering peer feedback on drafts
- Creating social support during challenging processes
- Sharing knowledge about funding opportunities
- Celebrating successes together

The social aspect of grant writing can transform what many researchers describe as a "lonely" and "isolating" process into a collaborative and supportive experience. This community approach not only improves the quality of proposals but also helps maintain motivation through the inevitable ups and downs of the funding cycle.

Writing for Success

The research plan and broader impacts sections of your proposal work together to tell a compelling story about why your research matters and how it will succeed. The research plan demonstrates your methodological sophistication and ability to execute complex projects. The broader impacts section shows that you understand and embrace the responsibility that comes with public or foundation funding—to ensure that your research benefits society broadly.

Whether writing quantitative or qualitative research plans, the key principles remain consistent: provide enough detail to inspire confidence, justify your methodological choices explicitly, anticipate potential challenges, and demonstrate feasibility within the proposed timeline and budget. For broader impacts, think creatively about how your research can make a difference, involve community partners meaningfully when appropriate, and connect impacts directly to your research activities.

Remember that reviewers are evaluating not just your ideas but your judgment, planning ability, and understanding of what it takes to conduct successful research. By crafting research plans that balance innovation with feasibility and broader impacts that demonstrate genuine commitment to societal benefit, you create proposals that reviewers want to fund. The investment in developing these sections thoughtfully pays dividends not just in funding success but in conducting research that truly makes a difference.

In the next chapter, we address what is probably the most daunting topic to comprehend about writing grants: Budgets. As you will learn, the problem isn't the math; it is knowing what you can budget, how to budget it, and how to justify your research expenses in ways that support your goals. This is one of the longest chapters in the book, packed with detailed examples. But when you finish reading it, you will have many new strategies to help you elevate your research plans and succeed in the external funding world.

15

Understanding Grant Budgets: From Confusion to Confidence

Dr. María Elena Vásquez had spent months crafting what she believed was the perfect NSF CAREER proposal. As a health psychology professor in her second year on the tenure track, she had worked closely with a mentor to develop a five-year research program that would establish her as a leader in stress and decision-making research. When her mentor examined the program solicitation for CAREER awards, she suggested Maria aim for $475,000 in total funding, María initially panicked. "How am I ever going to spend and budget for a multiyear, grant of that size?" she asked.

Her mentor helped her brainstorm different budget categories and then directed her to work with her institution's pre-award team to finalize the budget template. The pre-award administrator was efficient and helpful, entering all the numbers María had discussed with her mentor. When they finished, the budget totaled exactly $475,000, and María felt confident and excited about her submission.

Seven months later, María received the call she had been hoping for: her CAREER proposal was funded. She was ecstatic, calling her mentor immediately to share the wonderful news. But as they celebrated, María mentioned something that puzzled her. "I have this really weird question," she said. "I got some information from my post-award support team that said I would have $316,000 to work with for my budget. I don't understand how my budget got cut so much, because I put my budget in at $475,000, and now I only have $316,000 to work with."

Her mentor paused. "María, you do realize that your university added the indirect cost rate on top of your direct costs, right?" "What are you talking about?" María replied. "What are indirect costs, and what are direct costs?"

This conversation reveals one of the most fundamental misunderstandings that plague early-career scholars entering the world of external funding: the relationship between direct costs (the money you actually have to spend on research activities) and indirect costs (the institutional overhead charged by universities to support the research enterprise). María had worked through the budget process with her grant administrators, but no one had explained—and she hadn't thought to ask—what portion of her total budget would actually be available for her research activities versus what would go to the university for facilities and administrative costs.

Unfortunately, María's experience isn't unique. It represents a common gap in grant-seeking preparation that can lead to significant misunderstandings about project scope, resource allocation, and research feasibility. This chapter aims to demystify the budgeting process, helping you understand not only what you can budget for but also how to think strategically about resource allocation and institutional requirements.

From Intimidation to Understanding: Learning to Think in Budget Categories

Before diving deeper into the complexities of grant budgeting, several key terms need definition to make the rest of this chapter accessible to newcomers. Remember, there is a full glossary of definitions in Appendix 1. You've already learned about **indirect costs** (also called Facilities & Administration costs, F&A costs, or overhead costs)—the percentage that universities charge on top of direct costs to support research infrastructure. **Fringe benefits** represent the additional costs beyond salary that employers pay for health insurance, retirement contributions, social security, unemployment insurance, and other benefits—typically ranging from 18 to 39 percent of salary depending on employee category and institution.

Direct costs are expenses directly related to your research project that you control and spend. **Sub-awards** are portions of your grant funding that go to collaborating institutions to support their project contributions. **Per diem** refers to daily allowances for meals and incidental expenses during travel, often set at standard rates regardless of actual spending. **Principal Investigator (PI)** is the lead researcher responsible for the scientific and technical direction of the project. **Course buyout** is funding used to release faculty from teaching obligations so they can focus on research. **Summer salary** provides compensation during months not covered by the standard nine-month academic contract. Understanding these terms provides the foundation for comprehending the budget development process and communicating effectively with research administrators.

Both of us remember vividly our early reactions to grant budgeting. Keri's first encounter with external funding involved a $50,000 opportunity that seemed impossibly large. Having grown accustomed to internal grants of $5000 to pay participant compensation or $7000 for a part-time graduate stipend, the idea of responsibly spending $50,000 felt overwhelming. The mental block wasn't about research design or methodology—it was simply not understanding what categories of expenses could be included in a grant budget.

Now, years later, when someone mentions a $100,000 grant opportunity, Keri's immediate reaction is that such funding is "not going to pay for much—that is too low of an amount to be able to do meaningful multiyear research." This dramatic shift in perspective comes from understanding how quickly budget categories consume available funds once you account for salaries, fringe benefits, indirect costs, and tuition for graduate students.

The transformation from viewing $50,000 as overwhelming to seeing $100,000 as insufficient illustrates a crucial learning curve in external funding-thinking development: understanding the true cost of conducting research within institutional frameworks. Until you can wrap your brain around the different categories that budgets include, it's nearly impossible to accurately assess what funding level you actually need to accomplish your research goals.

Kerk's early experiences provide additional insight into common budgeting misunderstandings. His first exposure to externally funded research came through a consulting role on a Gates Foundation grant where he expected to receive the full amount discussed, not understanding that routing payments through the university would result in substantial deductions for indirect costs and taxes. What initially seemed like a windfall turned into a more modest compensation after the university's overhead and tax obligations were met.

Even basic travel concepts proved confusing. As a graduate student accustomed to paying conference expenses out of pocket with minimal departmental support, Kerk initially didn't understand per diem policies when told to "just claim per diem" rather than submit individual meal receipts. Having trained himself to survive on minimal expenses—buying food from CVS near conference hotels rather than eating at restaurants—he continued submitting actual receipts for small purchases instead of claiming the full per diem allowance he was entitled to receive.

Perhaps most tellingly, when Kerk's first grant included two months of summer salary, he had no idea what this meant until the paycheck arrived. The concept that academic salaries typically cover nine months and that some grants could provide additional compensation for summer research work was completely foreign, despite being fundamental to how much of the academic research funding operates. Clarifying if and how different researchers and staff on projects are paid is important. Some people, including some faculty, have twelve-month appointments, and calculating how each is to be paid, often requires some conversations with budget experts. Not all faculty are on nine-month academic appointments; some have twelve-month contracts that structure salary very differently. Calendar-year appointments typically do not allow for additional summer salary, which means budgeting for personnel on these grants must account for full-year compensation rather than supplemental summer support. Clarifying appointment type early helps avoid budgeting errors and ensures accurate communication with research administrators.

Understanding the broad categories that comprise typical social science research budgets helps in developing comprehensive and realistic funding requests. While every institution's budget, and sometimes every department or college budget template can differ, a helpful way to understand primary budget categories is using the Uniform Guidance cost principles language. These categories are what are called "allowable costs," which are costs that are reasonable, allocatable to the grant, consistently treated the same across the institution, and in conformance to the terms and conditions of the agency. Table 15.1 outlines the primary budget categories and their typical components:

Table 15.1 Budget Categories

Budget Category	Components	Key Considerations
Personnel	PI salary, collaborator compensation, graduate students, postdocs, undergraduate researchers, administrative support	Includes salary + fringe benefits; varies by appointment type and institution
Travel	Conference presentations, community site visits, research collaboration meetings	Requires detailed justification including specific conferences, estimated costs, and research relevance
Equipment & Supplies	Computers, software licenses, research materials, office supplies	Must align with institutional procurement policies and sponsor guidelines
Participant Costs	Compensation, incentives, recruitment expenses	Subject to IRB approval and tax reporting requirements above certain thresholds
Services	Transcription, translation, statistical consultation, data management	May require competitive bidding or approved vendor lists
Other Direct Costs	Communication, publication fees, consultant fees, sub-awards	Varies significantly by sponsor and institutional policies
Indirect Costs	University overhead (F&A costs)	Calculated as percentage of direct costs; rates negotiated between institution and federal government

This categorization provides a framework for systematic budget development while ensuring comprehensive coverage of project needs. Each category requires detailed planning and institutional coordination to ensure accuracy and compliance.

Kerk and Keri Learning First as a Consultant

Both of our early exposures to grant budgeting came through serving as consultants on other researchers' projects, an experience that provided valuable but incomplete understanding of the budget development process. Keri's first funded research involvement came through a Texas Department of Transportation project where the principal investigator assigned her specific interview tasks and provided explicit CV language describing her role and funding amount. While this gave her exposure to funded research, it didn't provide insight into how budgets were constructed or what decisions went into allocating resources across different project components.

The consultant experience proved valuable for understanding project execution but limited for comprehending budget development. Seeing only one piece of a larger budget puzzle, neither of us initially understood how individual consultant fees fit into overall project financing or what other expenses were required to support the research enterprise.

This partial exposure highlights why many social scientists and humanities scholars struggle with budget development: their graduate programs typically provide limited exposure to the financial realities of research funding. The skills needed for budget development—understanding institutional overhead, calculating true personnel costs, estimating equipment and supply needs—are rarely part of social science doctoral training.

Our early budget development experiences were transformed when we began working with skilled pre-award administrators who could translate research ideas into feasible financial plans. Keri's first comprehensive budgeting experience involved sitting in a research administrator's office (Julie Campos, see Chapter 8 for her insight into faculty getting external funding), watching over her shoulder as questions about staffing needs and project requirements were translated into spreadsheet entries with appropriate cost categories, fringe benefit calculations, and indirect cost applications.

This collaborative approach proved essential because budget templates contain hidden formulas and institution-specific requirements that faculty cannot reasonably be expected to navigate independently. Julie, the pre-award administrator, asked strategic questions: "How many people do you feel like you need to help you do the work? What kind of positions do you want to hire?" As Keri answered these questions, numbers appeared in the spreadsheet, providing real-time education about the relationship between research plans and financial requirements.

The learning curve for budget spreadsheet management remains steep even after several grant cycles. Hidden formulas, automatically calculated indirect costs, and institution-specific requirements mean that even experienced researchers benefit from administrative oversight to avoid errors that could prove costly during project implementation.

Quality research administration support transforms the budgeting process from intimidating technical exercise to strategic planning conversation. Rather than struggling with spreadsheet mechanics, faculty can focus on articulating their research needs and understanding how financial constraints might affect project design. The administrator's expertise ensures that budgets comply with institutional policies while accurately reflecting project requirements.

Understanding Direct Costs vs. Indirect Costs: The Foundation of Grant Budgeting

Let's start by understanding the fundamental distinction between direct and indirect costs that confused María in our opening story. This distinction affects every aspect of budget planning and determines how much money you actually have available for research activities.

Direct costs represent the funds you control and spend directly on research activities: salaries, equipment, travel, participant compensation, and other project-specific expenses. These are the costs you typically think about when planning research activities.

Indirect costs (also called overhead, facilities and administration costs, or F&A costs) represent the university's charge for supporting the research enterprise. This institutional overhead covers office space, utilities, library resources, research administration support, compliance oversight, and other infrastructure costs that enable research to occur. These rates are often negotiated between a university and external funders (e.g., 50%). However, some funders cap the rate at which they will allow a university or research institute to charge for their indirect costs (e.g., 15%).

Understanding indirect cost calculations is essential for realistic budget planning. If your institution has a 50 percent indirect cost rate, this means the university adds 50 percent to your direct costs, not that you receive only 50 percent of the total grant amount. For example, if you need $100,000 in direct costs for your research, your total grant request would be $150,000 ($100,000 direct costs + $50,000 indirect costs).

The confusion in our opening story arose because María thought her $475,000 budget represented money available for research activities, when in fact approximately $159,000 of that total was designated for indirect costs, leaving roughly $316,000 for direct expenses. This fundamental misunderstanding could have led to serious problems if she had planned research activities requiring the full $475,000 in direct funding.

Some budget categories are exempt from indirect cost calculations, most commonly tuition payments for graduate students. Budget spreadsheets typically handle these exemptions automatically, but understanding which expenses are indirect-eligible versus indirect-exempt helps in strategic budget planning.

The rationale behind indirect costs deserves explanation to help new researchers understand why universities charge these fees. Indirect costs support the research enterprise infrastructure that enables your work to occur. For STEM researchers, this might include specialized laboratory facilities, safety equipment, and technical support staff. For social scientists, indirect costs cover office space, research administration support, library resources, IT infrastructure, and compliance oversight. The university typically retains the majority of indirect cost recovery, while distributing smaller percentages to colleges, departments, or research centers to support local research activities.

Indirect cost rates are negotiated between individual universities and the federal government, typically ranging from 20 percent to over 60 percent depending on institutional infrastructure and research intensity. These rates undergo periodic renegotiation based on detailed financial analyses of institutional research support costs. However, not all awards generate indirect cost recovery for the institution. Some sponsors—particularly private foundations, professional associations, fellowship programs, and small seed-grant mechanisms—either prohibit F&A entirely or set rates so low that the institution recovers little to nothing.

Personnel Costs: The Heart of Most Social Science Budgets

Personnel costs typically represent the largest category in social science research budgets, encompassing compensation for principal investigators, collaborators, students, and staff. Understanding the true cost of personnel—including salary, fringe benefits, and associated institutional requirements—is essential for realistic budget development.

Principal Investigator (PI) Compensation

PIs can include their own compensation in grant budgets through several mechanisms, each with different institutional requirements and implications. **Summer salary** provides additional compensation during months not covered by your academic year contract, typically enabling you to focus on research without seeking other summer employment or teaching overload courses. When budgeting summer salary, it's important to understand that some funding agencies impose salary caps regardless of your actual institutional salary. The National Institutes of Health, for example, sets annual salary caps that limit the amount that can be charged to grants. For fiscal year 2024, the NIH salary cap was $221,900, meaning that regardless of your actual salary, grant budgets cannot exceed this amount for annual compensation.

Course buyouts represent another common PI compensation mechanism, allowing you to reduce teaching obligations to focus on grant-funded research. However, the true cost of course buyouts often surprises new grant writers. While hiring an adjunct to teach your course might cost $7000, your institution may charge $25,000 or more for a course buyout because you're not just covering replacement teaching costs—you're compensating for your full salary, fringe benefits, and institutional overhead associated with your employment.

Course buyout policies vary significantly across institutions and often change over time. Some universities offer different buyout rates based on whether you're simultaneously funding graduate students or meeting other institutional criteria. Understanding your institution's specific policies and current rates is essential before including course buyouts in grant proposals.

The economics of course buyouts create interesting strategic decisions. Spending $25,000 on a course buyout might provide limited research time compared to hiring a graduate student for a full year. Alternatively, you might negotiate to teach a course you've previously prepared, use teaching assistant support, or focus on time management strategies rather than seeking course buyouts.

Interdisciplinary collaboration can create particular tensions around course buyouts. When working with engineering colleagues who typically teach one course per semester while you teach two or three, requesting $25,000 for course buyout can seem unreasonable to collaborators who don't understand the structural differences in teaching loads across disciplines. These conversations require diplomatic explanation of disciplinary differences while advocating for equitable resource allocation.

Graduate Student Funding

Graduate student support represents one of the most common and valuable uses of grant funding, but calculating true costs requires understanding multiple interconnected factors. Graduate students can be funded through various mechanisms, each with different cost implications and institutional requirements.

Many institutions bring graduate students in social sciences and humanities primarily to support teaching missions through twenty-hour-per-week teaching assistantships. Grant funding can buy students out of teaching obligations, converting their time to research activities. This typically requires paying their full twenty-hour salary plus fringe benefits plus tuition costs.

Alternatively, some institutions allow "split appointments" where students maintain partial teaching responsibilities while adding grant-funded research hours. For example, students might teach ten hours while working ten hours on grant-funded research, up to the typical maximum of twenty hours per week total employment.

The mechanics of exceeding twenty-hour limits often involve enrolling students in "career development" or research credit hours that enable additional work hours beyond standard employment limits. Rules governing these arrangements vary significantly across institutions and student categories. International students face additional restrictions, and first-semester students often have different limitations than continuing students.

Summer employment creates additional complications because standard employment rules may be temporarily suspended during breaks. Students might be able to work up to forty hours per week between semesters when they don't have competing teaching obligations, though visa requirements and other factors can limit these opportunities.

Calculating graduate student costs requires budgeting for salary (varying by student level at some institutions), fringe benefits (typically 18–39 percent of salary), and tuition (which can dramatically exceed salary costs at some institutions). The total cost of a graduate student—particularly at private institutions with high tuition rates—can exceed the cost of hiring postdoctoral researchers, creating strategic decisions about staffing models.

Faculty Collaborator Compensation

Funding other faculty follows principles similar to PI compensation, with additional complexities around salary transparency and collaborative expectations. Budget development requires navigating potentially sensitive conversations about compensation differences and resource allocation. Some collaborators may not understand grant budgeting conventions, potentially viewing minimal summer salary allocations (such as 0.5 months) as inadequate recognition for their contributions. Educating collaborators about budget constraints and funding norms helps manage expectations and maintain productive relationships.

Fringe benefit rates for faculty can vary based on benefit elections, creating awkward situations where PIs must ask collaborators about family health insurance status to calculate accurate budget amounts. Some institutions have moved to flat-rate fringe calculations to avoid these uncomfortable conversations, but practices vary significantly across universities.

Postdoctoral Researchers and Research Scientists

Postdoctoral positions require funding salary plus fringe benefits without tuition costs, potentially making them more cost-effective than graduate students at institutions with high tuition rates. However, postdocs require additional infrastructure support: office space, computers, software licenses, professional development funding, and vacation accrual that must be paid out upon departure.

Research scientist positions offer similar cost structures but different career expectations. Unlike postdocs who anticipate transitioning to faculty positions, research scientists may build longer-term careers in these roles, requiring different approaches to professional development and retention.

Full-time staff positions require comprehensive support planning that extends beyond basic salary and benefits. Equipment needs, professional development opportunities, and workplace infrastructure all require budget consideration for successful staff integration.

Professional development expenses for staff members, including conference attendance, training programs, and continuing education, represent legitimate budget categories that support project quality and staff retention. These might include software training, methodological workshops, or professional certification programs relevant to project needs.

Undergraduate Researchers and Administrative Support

Undergraduate research support typically involves lower hourly wages and minimal fringe benefits, making these positions cost-effective for appropriate tasks. However, training requirements and supervision needs must be factored into cost-benefit calculations.

Many professional associations offer undergraduate research presentation opportunities with reduced registration fees or special sessions designed for student presenters. Building these opportunities into project planning creates multiple benefits from single budget investments.

This strategy provides valuable professional development while advancing project dissemination goals.

Administrative support, when allowable by sponsors, can dramatically improve project efficiency and principal investigator productivity. Even partial administrative support—perhaps eight hours per week—can free up substantial PI time for research activities while ensuring that routine administrative tasks are handled efficiently and correctly.

Travel: Strategic Investment in Research Dissemination

Travel represents a crucial but complex budget category that requires detailed planning and institutional knowledge. Effective travel budgeting involves understanding per diem policies, reimbursement procedures, and sponsor-specific requirements that vary significantly across funding sources.

Conference Travel Planning and Budget Justifications

Conference travel budgets should include comprehensive cost estimates: airfare, ground transportation, hotel accommodations, meals per diem, conference registration fees, and incidental expenses. For multiyear grants, this means researching typical costs for conferences you plan to attend over the entire project period.

Budget justifications for travel require specificity that often surprises new grant writers. Rather than general statements about "conference travel," effective justifications identify specific conferences, estimate costs for each travel component, and explain how presentations relate to project goals. For a five-year grant, this might involve identifying specific conferences for each year, researching typical airfare costs to those cities, and calculating total travel expenses for each trip.

A well-developed travel budget justification might read:

> Year 1: Dr. Vásquez will present preliminary findings at the American Psychological Association Annual Convention in Washington, D.C. (August 2025). Estimated costs include: roundtrip airfare Austin–Washington, D.C. ($450), hotel accommodation three nights at conference

rate ($180/night = $540), ground transportation ($75), meals per diem three days at federal rate ($69/day = $207), conference registration ($395). Total Year 1 conference travel: $1,667.

This level of detail demonstrates thorough planning while providing reviewers with confidence that travel budgets are realistic and well-considered. For community-engaged research, similar detail should be provided for site visits, stakeholder meetings, and community partner collaborations.

Community-engaged research adds additional travel complexity, requiring budgets for site visits, community partner meetings, and stakeholder engagement activities. These trips require similar detailed planning but may involve different cost structures and reimbursement policies than academic conference travel. Budget justifications should specify the number of site visits planned, duration of stays, number of travelers, and relationship between travel and research objectives.

Per Diem and Reimbursement Policies

Per diem policies vary dramatically across funding sources and institutions, requiring careful attention to specific requirements. Some sponsors provide comprehensive per diem, covering meals, hotels, and incidental expenses. Others separate meals from lodging allowances. Understanding these distinctions affects both budget planning and post-travel reimbursement processes.

Federal grants often impose additional travel restrictions, such as requiring American carriers for international travel regardless of cost considerations. International travel on federal grants typically requires advance approval and justification in original budget submissions, with some agencies requiring specific forms or preapproval processes. Federal agencies are increasingly implementing research security requirements that affect international travel, including pre-travel disclosures, restricted-entity checks, and export-control review. Many universities now require travelers to complete security briefings and, in some cases, use loaner devices rather than personal or university laptops when traveling abroad. These policies are designed to safeguard researchers and federally funded work from unintended disclosure and to ensure compliance with evolving federal research security standards.

Many institutions now require principal investigators to complete federally mandated research security and responsible conduct of research (RCR) training before funds can be released. These requirements, driven by related federal initiatives, cover topics such as disclosure of foreign affiliations, handling of sensitive data, cybersecurity expectations, and export-control awareness. PIs should check their institution's training schedule early, as missing these requirements can delay award activation or block hiring and expenditures.

State funding may impose particularly restrictive travel policies, limiting hotel reimbursement amounts, excluding tip reimbursement, and requiring tax-exempt purchasing procedures. Failure to follow these specific requirements can result in personal financial responsibility for noncompliant expenses. Some state funders will not reimburse state taxes if tax-exempt forms are not used during purchase, and tips for meals are considered discretionary and non-reimbursable.

Conference-provided meals create additional complexity, as many institutions will not allow per diem claims for meals if meals are provided by conference organizers, even if the traveler has dietary restrictions or chooses not to consume the food provided by the conferences. This requires careful tracking of conference schedules and meal provisions when calculating per diem claims.

Cash Flow Considerations

Many institutions require any traveler to pay travel expenses personally and seek reimbursement afterward, creating significant cash flow challenges. Booking international airfare months in advance while waiting for post-travel reimbursement can create substantial financial burdens, particularly for graduate students and early-career faculty.

Some institutions offer cash advance procedures or institutional credit cards that minimize out-of-pocket expenses, but these often require additional paperwork and administrative oversight. Understanding your institution's financial procedures helps identify ways to minimize personal financial impacts of grant-funded travel.

The reimbursement timeline can extend several months, particularly when international travel involves complex documentation requirements or when institutional processing faces delays. Planning for these extended reimbursement periods helps prevent financial strain on research team members.

Equipment and Supplies: Supporting Research Infrastructure

Computer equipment and software represent common budget categories that require institutional coordination to ensure compliance and avoid duplication. Universities often maintain standard computer configurations for grant-funded positions, requiring specific budget amounts rather than general estimates.

Technology and Equipment Budget Justifications

Comprehensive computer budgets might include desktop or laptop computers, external monitors, docking stations for flexible work arrangements, external cameras for video conferencing, and specialized software licenses. Understanding what your institution provides automatically (such as Microsoft Office) versus what requires separate procurement helps avoid over-budgeting or under-budgeting for technology needs.

Budget justifications for equipment should specify exact configurations and explain research-related needs. For example:

> One laptop computer for postdoctoral researcher ($1,800): MacBook Pro with sufficient processing power for qualitative data analysis software (NVivo) and statistical computing (R/RStudio). Includes external monitor ($300) and webcam ($150) for video conference interviews with community partners. Microsoft Office provided by institution; specialized software licenses for NVivo ($1,200) and Zoom Pro account for secure video interviews ($150/year).

Software licensing can be particularly complex, with institutional, compliance, and security requirements affecting what platforms are permissible for research use. AI transcription and analysis tools, for example, may require specific security protections when working with confidential human subjects' data. Some institutions maintain approved vendor lists or require competitive bidding for software purchases above certain thresholds.

Professional development expenses for staff members, including conference attendance, training programs, and continuing education, represent legitimate budget categories that support project quality and staff retention. These might include software training, methodological workshops, or professional certification programs relevant to project needs.

Research Materials and Supplies

Beyond technology, social science research often requires various materials and supplies: recording equipment for interviews, transcription software, survey platform subscriptions, printing and copying costs, postage for mail surveys, office supplies, and communication costs.

Budget justifications should connect these items clearly to research activities:

> Digital audio recorders (2 units at $200 each = $400) for conducting semi-structured interviews with community leaders. Transcription software subscription ($50/month × 36 months = $1,800) for processing interview data while maintaining HIPAA compliance through a secure, encrypted platform.

Participant Support: The Ethics and Logistics of Compensation

Participant compensation represents one of the most ethically important and logistically complex budget categories in social science research. Effective budgeting requires understanding institutional review board policies, payment processing procedures, and tax reporting requirements.

Determining Appropriate Compensation and Budget Justifications

Participant compensation rates require coordination with institutional review boards to ensure appropriate levels that provide fair compensation without constituting coercion. IRB policies may set maximum compensation rates regardless of project needs or researcher preferences.

Compensation planning requires statistical considerations such as power analyses to determine necessary sample sizes, which directly affect total compensation costs. Understanding your research design requirements before budgeting helps ensure adequate resources for participant recruitment and retention.

A thorough participant compensation budget justification might read:

> Based on power analysis for detecting medium effect sizes (d = 0.5) with 80% power and $\alpha = 0.05$, we require 64 participants per condition (128 total). Allowing for 20% attrition, we will recruit 160 participants. Each participant will complete a 90-minute interview session. Compensation of $45 per participant ($0.50 per minute) aligns with IRB guidelines for time-based compensation and community standards for research participation in this population. Total participant compensation: 160 participants × $45 = $7,200."

This justification demonstrates statistical planning, ethical consideration, and alignment with institutional policies while providing clear cost calculations that reviewers can evaluate for reasonableness.

Payment Processing Challenges

The logistics of participant payment prove more complex than simply purchasing gift cards and seeking reimbursement. Universities often require specialized procedures for participant payments, potentially involving dedicated staff members, approval processes, and documentation requirements.

Some institutions charge administrative fees for participant payment processing even if it is an external grant, requiring budget planning that accounts for these additional costs. One researcher encountered a 40 percent administrative fee charged by their institution's research center for processing participant gift cards—a substantial expense that transformed participant compensation budgeting.

> Budget justifications should account for these administrative costs: "Participant gift card processing fee (40% of participant compensation): $7,200 × 0.40 = $2,880. Total participant support costs: $10,080."

While such fees may seem excessive, they reflect the administrative burden and compliance requirements associated with participant payment processing.

Payments above certain thresholds (typically $600 per participant per year) require tax reporting and participant social security number collection, creating additional administrative burdens and potential participation barriers. Understanding these thresholds helps in developing compensation strategies that balance fair payment with administrative feasibility.

International participants create additional complications, with some institutions unable to provide compensation to non-U.S. residents regardless of study location. Tax withholding requirements for international participants can reduce the actual compensation received, potentially affecting participation rates and research feasibility.

Specialized Services and Consultation

Statistical Support and Data Management

Some funding agencies, particularly NIH, expect or require statistical consultation even for researchers with strong quantitative backgrounds. Budgeting for statistical support, data management services, and specialized analysis assistance ensures compliance with sponsor expectations while supporting research quality.

Budget justifications should specify the type and extent of statistical support needed:

> Biostatistician consultation (Dr. Jane Smith, 20 hours at $150/hour = $3,000): Power analysis refinement, analysis plan development, and review of statistical procedures for longitudinal data analysis. Data management specialist (40 hours at $75/hour = $3,000): Database design, data cleaning protocols, and preparation of analysis files for complex survey data."

Transcription and Translation Services

Translation and transcription services represent significant budget categories for research involving multiple languages or extensive qualitative data. AI-based services may offer cost savings but require careful evaluation of security and compliance requirements, particularly when working with confidential human subjects data.

Budget justifications should account for data volume and turnaround requirements:

> Professional transcription services for 160 interviews averaging 60 minutes each (160 hours of audio). Rate of $1.50 per audio minute for verbatim transcription with 7-day turnaround = $14,400. Spanish-English translation for interviews conducted in Spanish (estimated 50% of sample): 80 interviews requiring translation at $0.05 per word, averaging 7,500 words per interview = $30,000.

Before assuming AI transcription will reduce costs, verify that your institution permits use of specific AI platforms for confidential research data. Many AI services cannot guarantee data security required for human subjects research, potentially necessitating more expensive but compliant professional services.

Community Engagement and Collaborative Support

Community Partnership Development

Community-engaged research may require budgeting for community partner training, organizational capacity building, or collaborative research infrastructure. These expenses support equitable partnership development while enhancing research quality and community benefit.

Budget justifications might include:

> Community partner training workshop ($5,000): Facilitation costs, materials, refreshments, and modest honoraria ($100 × 25 partners = $2,500) for community advisory board members attending full-day

> research methods training. Venue rental and catering for partnership meetings throughout project period ($500 × 8 meetings = $4,000).

Payment to community organizations for participant recruitment assistance or cultural competency training represents legitimate research expenses that strengthen study validity while supporting community partnerships. These arrangements require careful documentation and may need IRB approval as part of recruitment procedures.

Subawards and Institutional Collaborations

Collaborative research often requires subawards to partner institutions or consultant agreements with external experts. Subawards to other universities typically require paying indirect costs both at your institution and the receiving institution, though there can be caps on a certain amount (e.g., the first $25,000) of subaward funding. A $100,000 subaward might incur indirect costs only on the first $25,000 at your institution, with the receiving institution adding its indirect costs to the full amount.

Budget justifications for subawards should specify the collaborating institution's role and deliverables:

> Subaward to University of California, Davis (Dr. Robert Johnson, coinvestigator): $75,000 over three years to conduct focus groups with agricultural workers (n = 12 groups, 8–10 participants each). Includes salary support for co-I (0.5-month summer salary × 3 years), graduate student (0.25 FTE × 2 years), participant compensation, travel for site visits, and UC Davis indirect costs.

Publication and Dissemination Costs

Open Access and Publication Fees

Academic publishing costs have increased dramatically, with open access fees ranging from $3000 to $15,000 or more per article. Many funding agencies now require or encourage open access publication, making these costs legitimate budget items.

Budget justifications should estimate publication output and associated costs:

> Open access publication fees: Based on projected output of 6 peer-reviewed articles over project period, budget $8,000 per article average for open access fees in target journals (*Journal of Health Psychology*: $3,500; *Health Psychology*: $4,200; *American Journal of Community Psychology*: $3,800). Total publication costs: $48,000.

Conference and Workshop Organization

Some grants support conference organization, symposium development, or workshop facilitation as part of dissemination activities. These events require comprehensive budget planning including venue costs, speaker honoraria, travel support for participants, catering, and materials.

Budget justifications should provide detailed event planning:

> Annual research symposium (Years 2, 3, 4): Venue rental ($2,000), keynote speaker honorarium and travel ($3,000), refreshments for 100 attendees ($1,500), printed materials and signage ($500). Total per symposium: $7,000 × 3 events = $21,000.

Strategic Opportunities and Flexibility

Many funding agencies offer supplement opportunities that can address budget shortfalls or expand project scope. NSF supplements, for example, can support undergraduate research experiences, international collaboration, or equipment upgrades not included in original proposals.

Understanding supplement opportunities during initial budget planning provides strategic options for project enhancement while offering potential solutions for unforeseen needs or exciting new directions that emerge during project implementation. Budget narratives might note: "We will explore NSF Research Experiences for Undergraduates (REU) supplements to provide summer research opportunities for undergraduate students interested in health psychology research."

Some funding opportunities require institutional cost sharing or matching funds, where your university contributes resources to the project. Understanding your institution's policies about cost sharing helps determine feasibility of different funding opportunities. Cost sharing might include waived indirect costs, contributed salary time, or provided equipment and facilities. These contributions must be documented and tracked throughout the project period, requiring coordination with institutional research administration.

Making Peace with Budget Uncertainty

Despite detailed planning, grant budgets inevitably involve uncertainty that can frustrate researchers accustomed to precise calculations. Salary increases, tuition changes, fringe benefit adjustments, and institutional policy modifications all affect budget accuracy over multiyear projects.

Graduate student credit hour enrollment during summer sessions can vary based on individual academic needs, with researchers having limited ability to dictate enrollment levels. As noted in Chapter 6, a student choosing six credits instead of three credits can substantially affect tuition expenses, requiring flexible budget planning that accommodates reasonable variations.

Faculty colleague salary increases beyond anticipated levels can affect collaborative budgets, particularly when working with institutions that have different salary structures or promotion timelines. Market adjustments, retention raises, and promotion increases all introduce budget uncertainty that requires adaptive management.

The unpredictability that characterizes budget execution reinforces the importance of working with experienced research administrators who understand these challenges and can provide guidance for managing budget variations while maintaining compliance with sponsor requirements.

Annual escalation factors built into multiyear budgets help account for predictable increases, but unexpected changes still might require budget modifications and sponsor approval through formal amendment processes.

Building Budget Confidence Through Institutional Support

After presenting this extensive catalog of budget considerations, we want to emphasize that you don't need to master all these details immediately or independently. Most research institutions provide pre-award support specifically designed to help faculty navigate budget development effectively. Take advantage of institutional workshops, individual consultations, and collaborative budget development sessions. Research administrators bring years of experience with institutional policies, sponsor requirements, and strategic budget planning that complement your research expertise.

The goal of understanding budget categories isn't to become a budget expert overnight, but to be a more informed collaborator in the budget development process. Knowing what questions to ask, what factors to consider, and what resources you need helps you work more effectively with institutional support while ensuring your budget accurately reflects your research plans.

Creative Funding Strategies and Cost-Saving Approaches

Beyond traditional budget categories, experienced grant writers develop creative approaches to maximize resources and minimize costs through strategic partnerships and institutional collaborations.

Many universities provide undergraduate research programs, honors college funding, or specialized research experience offices that can support project staffing without direct grant expenses. These partnerships create win-win situations where institutional funds support student development while your grant resources focus on other project needs. Work-study programs can provide cost-effective undergraduate research support, with federal work-study funds covering substantial portions of student wages. However, work-study positions may have restrictions on the types of activities students can perform, requiring coordination with financial aid offices to ensure compliance.

Some institutions maintain shared core facilities for specialized equipment, data analysis services, or technical support that can reduce individual grant equipment costs. Understanding these shared resources helps avoid over-budgeting for services that are already available through institutional infrastructure.

Multi-institutional collaborations can achieve economies of scale for expensive services like large-scale data collection, specialized software licenses, or equipment purchases. Rather than each institution purchasing individual licenses for expensive analysis software, collaborative arrangements can share costs while providing broader access.

International collaboration supplements available through some funding agencies can support research exchanges, collaborative workshops, or joint data collection efforts that would be prohibitively expensive through standard grant mechanisms.

Advanced Budget Considerations for Complex Projects

Multiyear Budget Planning and Escalation

Complex, multiyear projects require sophisticated budget planning that accounts for predictable cost increases while maintaining sponsor spending limits. Annual escalation factors typically range from 3 to 5 percent for salary and fringe increases, though actual increases may vary significantly based on institutional policies and market conditions.

Some sponsors prefer level funding across project years, requiring researchers to build escalation into early years to accommodate higher costs in later project periods. This approach requires careful cash flow planning to ensure adequate resources are available when needed.

Budget narratives should explain escalation assumptions and demonstrate understanding of multiyear cost management:

> Personnel costs include 3% annual escalation for salary increases and 4% escalation for fringe benefit rate adjustments based on institutional historical averages. Total personnel costs by year: Year 1: $85,000; Year 2: $88,400; Year 3: $91,900.

Complex Institutional Arrangements

Some research projects involve partnerships with multiple institution types—universities, community colleges, nonprofit organizations, and government agencies—each with different overhead rates, procurement policies, and administrative requirements. These complex arrangements require careful coordination during budget development to ensure all partners understand cost allocation, reporting requirements, and administrative responsibilities. Statement of Work should specify financial arrangements and resource commitments to avoid misunderstandings during project implementation.

Nonprofit organization partnerships may involve different cost structures than university collaborations, potentially requiring different approaches to personnel classification, equipment ownership, and intellectual property arrangements.

International Research Considerations

International research components add layers of complexity including currency exchange considerations, international travel requirements, and cross-border payment processing challenges. Some funding agencies require special approval for international activities, even when involving U.S. researchers traveling abroad. Budget justifications should address these requirements explicitly and demonstrate understanding of sponsor policies regarding international research.

Currency fluctuation protection strategies might be necessary for projects involving substantial international expenses over extended time periods. Some institutions offer financial instruments to hedge against exchange rate changes for large international commitments.

Technology and Data Management Budgeting

Modern research involving human subjects data faces increasingly complex security and compliance requirements that affect technology budgeting. HIPAA-compliant data storage, encrypted communication platforms, and secure data analysis environments may require specialized software subscriptions or cloud services.

Budget justifications should address data security requirements:

> Secure cloud storage for confidential research data (Box Business Plus): $15/user/month × 4 users × 36 months = $2,160. HIPAA-compliant video conferencing platform for remote interviews (Zoom Healthcare): $200/month × 24 months = $4,800.

Post-Award Budget Modifications

While detailed post-award budget management is covered in subsequent chapters, initial budget development should consider the administrative infrastructure needed for successful project implementation.

Most sponsors allow budget modifications within certain parameters—for example, 25 percent between major budget categories without formal approval. Understanding these policies during budget development helps create flexibility for adapting to changing project needs. Some budget categories may have stricter modification limits. Equipment purchases often require specific justification and pre-approval, while travel budget modifications might be more flexible depending on sponsor policies.

Financial Risk Management

Experienced grant writers build modest contingencies into budgets to protect against cost overruns while maintaining sponsor cost-effectiveness expectations. These contingencies might take the form of conservative cost estimates, alternative service providers, or flexible resource allocation across budget categories.

Understanding which budget categories typically experience cost overruns—participant recruitment often exceeds projections, while equipment costs may be lower than anticipated—helps inform strategic budget allocation decisions.

Clear agreements with institutional administrators about cost-sharing, resource provision, and support during budget shortfalls help protect projects from unexpected financial pressures.

Some institutions provide bridge funding or internal cost sharing when projects experience budget challenges due to circumstances beyond PI control. Understanding these support mechanisms helps inform risk management planning.

Building Budget Confidence Through Practice and Mentorship

Serving on grant review panels provides invaluable education about budget evaluation from the reviewer perspective. Understanding how reviewers assess budget reasonableness, cost-effectiveness, and resource allocation helps improve your own budget development skills.

Many funding agencies actively seek social science reviewers for interdisciplinary panels, providing opportunities to gain insider knowledge about budget evaluation while contributing professional service to your field.

Seeking mentorship from experienced grant writers in your field provides personalized guidance about budget development strategies, institutional navigation, and sponsor-specific requirements. Collaborative budget development with experienced colleagues—serving as co-PI or collaborator on others' grants before leading your own—provides hands-on learning opportunities that complement formal training.

Embracing the Learning Process

We've shared this level of detail because we've made virtually every mistake described in this chapter. The confusion about indirect costs, the surprise at personnel expenses, the underestimation of travel costs, the complexity of participant payment—we've encountered all these challenges and many others. Our hope is that by sharing these experiences and the lessons we've learned, you can avoid some of the pitfalls that caused us stress, frustration, and unnecessary complications.

Remember that budget development is an iterative process that improves with experience. Your first budget will likely contain errors or omissions that require revision. Your tenth budget will reflect knowledge and strategic thinking that wasn't possible initially. The learning curve is steep but manageable, particularly when you work with institutional support and maintain realistic expectations about the complexity involved.

The transformation from viewing $50,000 as overwhelming to understanding how to strategically allocate $250,000 or more represents more than just learning budget mechanics—it reflects developing the strategic mindset necessary for successful research leadership. Budget development forces you to think systematically about resource requirements, timeline coordination, and project management in ways that strengthen overall research planning.

Don't expect to memorize every detail presented in this chapter. Instead, use this information as a reference guide for asking informed questions, identifying potential budget categories, and working effectively with research administrators who bring specialized expertise to the budget development process.

Moving Forward with Confidence

Take a deep breath. We've thrown an enormous amount of detail at you in this chapter—we know it can feel overwhelming. But here's the thing: you don't have to master this alone, and you don't need to become a budget expert overnight.

Budget development represents a crucial component of grant seeking that thousands of social scientists successfully navigate every year. The key is understanding that this is a collaborative process. Your institution's pre-award support team exists specifically to help you translate your research vision into realistic financial plans. They've seen many budget challenges and can guide you through the technical requirements while you focus on what you do best—designing meaningful research.

Start by building relationships with your research administrators and understanding what institutional support is available. Rather than working backward from available funding amounts, identify what you actually need to accomplish your research goals, then work with your support team to create budgets that reflect those requirements honestly and strategically.

View budget development as an opportunity to think systematically about resource allocation and project management. The process of calculating personnel costs, estimating travel expenses, and planning for research infrastructure actually helps clarify project scope, identify potential challenges, and develop realistic timelines—all of which strengthen your research planning.

Every experienced grant seeker started exactly where you are now, learning through experience, mistakes, and institutional support. As we mentioned in the introductory chapter, the complexity we've described shouldn't discourage you from pursuing external funding—it should prepare you to approach budget development thoughtfully and strategically. The investment you make in understanding these fundamentals will pay dividends throughout your research career, enabling you to pursue increasingly ambitious projects while maintaining the fiscal responsibility that funders expect.

The goal is simple: become an informed and strategic researcher who can articulate resource needs clearly, work effectively with administrative support, and develop budgets that truly support your research objectives. With patience, institutional collaboration, and systematic attention to the factors we've outlined, you can develop the budget confidence necessary to pursue the funding your research deserves.

Unlike María in our opening story, the next time a colleague expresses confusion about indirect costs or wonders how they could possibly spend $100,000 on research, you'll be able to provide some insight. You'll understand that their $475,000 grant doesn't mean $475,000 in research funds, and you'll know to ask the right questions about fringe benefits, course buyout costs, and participant payment procedures. Most importantly, you'll know that budget confusion is normal and that institutional support exists to help navigate these complexities. That understanding—and your willingness to share it—contributes to building a more grant-literate community of social science researchers.

16

You Got the Grant: Communicating Your Success

Your heart races as you read the subject line: "Notice of Award." After months of waiting, rewriting, and wondering, the news is official, and your grant has been recommended for funding. The euphoria washes over you in waves. All those late nights crafting the perfect narrative, the countless revisions, the budget calculations that made your eyes cross—it all paid off. You did it!

Take a moment to savor this victory. Seriously, pause and celebrate. Getting external funding as a social scientist is no small feat. You've joined an elite group of scholars who have successfully navigated the complex world of grant seeking.

Even as the initial excitement settles, a new reality emerges: your work has just begun. In fact, some would argue the real work starts now. Before diving into the logistics of account numbers, hiring processes, and compliance requirements, let's talk about something more fundamental.

During this celebration period, while the joy is fresh and the possibilities feel endless, write down what this grant will enable you to accomplish that you couldn't have done without it. Be specific. Maybe it's recruiting a nationally representative sample for your study on political polarization. Perhaps it's hiring that statistician whose expertise will unlock new analytical approaches to your data. Possibly, it's the ability to compensate community partners fairly for their time and knowledge, ensuring more equitable research practices.

Box 16.1 Imagining the Possibilities

Imagine you have received the funding for the main project this book has made you think about. Set this book down, walk away from the computer, and feel the excitement of achieving such an accomplishment. Then, come back to the book and take five minutes to create a bulleted list of what the funding will help you accomplish. Think about the monetary size of the award, and stay focused on the positive outcomes you can now achieve. Celebration and dreaming are an important part of being successful when seeking funding. Write those things here:

____

____

____

____

____

This list becomes your North Star, a guiding light for the challenging days ahead. There will be challenging days when you're drowning in paperwork, navigating institutional bureaucracy, or managing personnel conflicts. When those moments arrive (and they will), return to this list. Remind yourself why you pursued this funding. Remember the research questions that kept you up at night, the communities you want to serve, the knowledge gaps you're determined to fill. This North Star will sustain you through the inevitable frustrations of grant management.

Sharing the Good News: Strategic Communication

Once you've had your private celebration, it's time to share the news strategically. Start with your immediate team—coinvestigators, research partners, community collaborators. These are the people who helped make your grant possible, and they deserve to hear directly from you. But here's a detail many new PIs miss: include a gentle reminder that while the award has been announced, the funds haven't arrived yet. Say something like, "I'm thrilled to share that it looks like our grant has been recommended for funding! The official start date is October 1, but it may take several weeks for the funds to be available and accounts to be set up. I'll keep everyone updated as we move forward."

This early communication manages expectations and prevents awkward conversations later when eager team members wonder why they can't start spending money immediately. The gap between award notification and fund availability often surprises new PIs. It might take a month or more for your institution to process the award, set up accounts, and make funds accessible. Some institutions even require specific documentation—like IRB approvals—before they'll process the award. For example, a "118 determination" (as stated in 45 CFR 46.118) might be needed, formally documenting that no work with human subjects will begin until IRB approval is obtained.

Don't forget to notify your institutional support team. Your pre-award administrator, the person who helped you prepare and submit the proposal, deserves special recognition. As mentioned in Chapter 8, learning about successful awards is one of the most rewarding aspects of a research administrator's job. They take pride in your success because they contributed to it. A simple email saying "We got it! Thank you for all your help" can brighten their entire week and strengthen a relationship you'll need for future proposals. Similarly, be sure to alert your post-award administrator immediately. They may not have received institutional notification yet, and early communication helps them prepare for the work ahead. The sooner they know, the sooner they can begin setting up accounts and explaining the specific rules governing your funds.

Crafting Your Message for Multiple Audiences

As news of your award spreads, you'll need to communicate about your project to various audiences, each requiring a different approach. This is where many academics struggle. We're trained to write for peer reviewers and disciplinary colleagues, not journalists, administrators, or the public. Yet these audiences matter tremendously for your project's visibility.

Start by creating multiple versions of your project description. First, write a one-sentence version: "This project examines how rural communities adapt to climate change through innovative social networks." This version becomes invaluable when your dean needs to mention your work at a board meeting or when someone asks about your research at a conference reception. Keep it simple, jargon-free, and focused on impact.

Next, develop a two-paragraph version for university communications and press releases. This version requires translating academic language into accessible prose. Instead of "This project employs mixed-methods approaches to investigate the intersection of social capital theory and climate adaptation strategies in non-metropolitan contexts," try "This project studies how people in rural areas work together to handle climate challenges like droughts and floods. By understanding these community connections, we can help other rural areas prepare for climate change."

The importance of these brief descriptions becomes clear when you provide them to department chairs and deans. They don't have time to read your full proposal, but when given clear, simple language, they become champions for your work. Your preparation literally pays dividends when administrators need to highlight faculty achievements or justify resource allocations. Your university's marketing and communications team might want to feature your award. Be prepared to work with them on press releases, website features, or social media posts. They'll need photos, quotations, and simplified explanations of complex concepts. Having these materials ready accelerates the communication process and ensures an accurate representation of your work.

Generative AI tools have revolutionized this translation process. You can input your technical project summary and ask for versions suitable for different audiences—policymakers, community members, and journalists. These tools provide excellent starting points, but always review and refine messages to ensure accuracy and maintain your authentic voice. Be sure to also check your institutional rules for how to use these AI tools in allowable ways.

Gaining Internal Visibility

Internal publications at your institution may be valuable low-effort opportunities for gaining visibility and practice communicating about your work. These include departmental newsletters often featuring faculty research highlights, college or university-wide research magazines or publications, institutional social media features about faculty accomplishments, campus newspaper stories about research projects, and internal blogs or research communication platforms. These internal venues offer several advantages: They require less formal writing than external publications, typically have short turnaround times, and reach key audiences including your department chair, dean, and provost—people who make decisions about your tenure, promotion, and merit raises. Being featured in internal publications also provides material you can reference on your CV (under "public engagement" or "research communication" sections) and demonstrates your commitment to making research accessible.

When you receive grant funding, proactively reach out to your institution's communications or public relations office. Many institutions actively seek faculty research stories but don't always know what's happening in every department. Offering to be featured makes their job easier and ensures your work gets visibility.

Navigating Press Attention: Lessons from the Field

The Texas floods of 2025 thrust Keri into an unexpected media spotlight that illuminated both the opportunities and challenges of press engagement for funded researchers. She had many prior experiences being interviewed by the media, and some very high-profile interviews on major U.S. networks (e.g., CBS, National Public Radio), but this experience was by far the most extensive. Keri also had taught students how to handle on-the-spot questions in multiple classes, and she had taken multiple media trainings at her university. That would come in handy during this experience.

When flooding devastated communities across the Hill Country, media outlets suddenly sought expertise on crisis communication and disaster response—precisely Keri's research area. She was heavily funded by the State of Texas to conduct flood communication research and had recent projects funded by the National Science Foundation that the media easily found with a quick Google search. What started with local TV news appearances (Austin TV, KXAN) and audio interviews (e.g., San Antonio affiliate with National Public Radio, NPR, Austin American Statesman) quickly escalated to national and international coverage (e.g., CNN, British Broadcasting Center (BBC), an NBC extended segment, National NPR, Marketplace, The Hill, and others), providing valuable lessons about managing press attention as a grant-funded researcher.

The Value of Starting Local

The initial local interviews served as important warm-ups. Keri was able to watch herself on the first few local news segments and critique her own performance. She realized she was talking too slowly, didn't have the energy level she wanted while speaking through an online web link, and had made the mistake of writing out bullet points and almost reading them—something she knew not to do because it sounds scripted. This self-assessment proved invaluable as media requests multiplied and the stakes increased with national outlets.

The most effective preparation involves developing clear talking points organized into three categories. What is your lane of expertise? What can you confidently comment on? What are you unwilling to discuss? Perhaps most importantly, what are your "dreaded questions"—the ones that make you think, "Oh gosh, I don't want to answer that." For Keri, the dreaded questions during the flood coverage centered on blame and accountability. She didn't want people asking who was to blame or whether officials had made wrong decisions, because that was not her area of expertise. Almost everybody tried to get her to engage in exactly what she dreaded most. Her solution was proactive communication that set clear boundaries.

Setting Boundaries Through Strategic Communication

When media outlets reached out, Keri developed a standard response that filtered requests effectively. She would respond: "I'd love to participate. This is my area of expertise.... However, I am not on the ground and don't know anything about the unfolding operations. If you're looking for somebody who knows that, I'm not the right person for you."

This approach filtered out outlets seeking sensational blame narratives. NBC's Morning Joe passed when she sent that message. CNN, however, responded positively: "No problem. We know what you're an expert on." They even scheduled a practice session with sample questions aligned with her expertise, demonstrating the value of working with outlets that understand your actual area of knowledge.

The CNN Experience: When Preparation Meets Reality

Despite thorough preparation—studying the host's interview style, practicing responses, testing technology—Keri's CNN appearance demonstrated how quickly situations can change in live media. Minutes before going on air, she learned her interviewer had been switched. The carefully researched preparation for one host's style suddenly became less relevant.

The very first question deviated completely from what they had practiced: "So, it sounds like a lot of things went wrong." The interviewer started taking her down a path of questions that weren't even remotely close to what they had practiced the day before. Keri believed they had deliberately bait-and-switched her on the questions. Her response strategy proved crucial: she decided to answer the question she wanted to answer, not their question. When pressed about timelines and accountability, she pivoted to educate viewers about the emergency response process, saying, "Quite often, there is a lot going on in response, and it is very likely that officials do not know exactly what was said when. That is the reason why there are after-action reviews, because after things settle down, they go back and reconstruct these timelines."

This technique of "going broad" when faced with blame-focused questions became her standard approach. Rather than engaging with specific accusations, she would explain systems and processes, maintaining her role as an educator rather than a pundit.

Different Interview Formats, Different Strategies

Through multiple media engagements in which both Keri and Kerk have been involved, clear patterns emerge about how different interview formats require different approaches:

- **Video Interviews:** Live or recorded video interviews demand particular attention to visual presentation. Natural lighting proves crucial. For example, Keri's 6:15 a.m. CNN interview suffered from a lack of natural light she typically relied upon, so she scrambled to set up additional lighting before going on air. In addition, the technical setup for remote, live interviews often involves logging into platforms where you cannot see the interviewer or their reactions, requiring you to maintain eye contact with the camera rather than your screen. A helpful tip is to put a sticky note right by your camera because you need to remember you're maintaining eye contact with that camera, not your screen.
- **Audio-Only Interviews:** Phone or podcast interviews allow more physical freedom but require different energy management. For audio-only interviews, Keri stands up, walks around, and uses her hands to gesture because she's trying to get energy into her voice. She knows they're going to take a snippet, and that's what's going to appear on outlets like NPR. The challenge with audio interviews lies in their unpredictability—despite hour-long conversations, only a sentence or two might make the final cut.
- **Background Interviews:** Sometimes media outlets send junior reporters to gather background information about complex topics. These interviews can result in direct quotes, but they also consume significant time. You can really spend a whole lot of time giving background information, and nothing actually makes it on the air because they're learning. For new academics, these can serve as low-stakes practice opportunities. For experienced researchers, they require strategic decisions about time investment.

Box 16.2 How Do You Get Media Opportunities?

University Connections: Sometimes university marketing and press offices get called asking for experts on specific topics and will funnel requests to appropriate faculty. This is the source of many press opportunities.

Published Summaries of Research Projects: While some funders will require a public-facing summary of your work, posting information on a website indexed in search engines can also alert the media to your work.

Network Referrals: Many press conversations come through professional networks—that is, other people being interviewed who recommend you as the real expert in a particular area.

Conscious Decision-Making: Some colleagues refuse to talk on the record to the press but will refer appropriate requests to others. Referrals create networks of trust, where colleagues pass along opportunities that align with your expertise.

Learning from Media Missteps

Both Keri and Kerk learned valuable lessons through less successful media encounters. Kerk's early experience with an NPR affiliate about water conservation research highlighted common mistakes: he gave academic, jargony answers that were not of interest to the outlet. Keri also learned this lesson because such interviews often never air. A subsequent television appearance taught Kerk about pacing: media outlets want soundbites, not long answers. They ask a question, and you give them a ten- to fifteen-second response and move on. They want the conversation to keep going. It's not a panel discussion like academics are used to at conferences.

These experiences underscore a fundamental challenge: *academics are trained to provide comprehensive, nuanced answers. Media outlets want concise, accessible soundbites.* The cognitive shift required can be jarring, especially under the pressure of live interviews.

Strategic Communication Techniques

Several strategies can help researchers manage press interactions more effectively:

- **Build Relationships When Possible**: Taking time to understand what story the journalist is trying to tell can improve outcomes. Keri often asks during interviews, "Is this helpful for your story? Should I go into more depth on this?" This collaborative approach helps ensure your expertise aligns with their narrative needs.
- **Control What You Can**: While you can't control which soundbites journalists select, you can influence the options available. Speak in complete, quotable sentences. Avoid starting thoughts you don't want to finish on air. If you realize you're heading toward problematic territory, pause and redirect rather than completing a potentially damaging statement.
- **Use "Off the Record" Strategically**: When providing context that helps journalists understand complex issues but isn't within your expertise, clearly state, "I'll fill you in on this, but this is off the record, and I don't want you quoting me on this because I'm not an expert in that area."
- **Prepare for the Unexpected**: Even with promised question previews, be ready for surprises. As noted earlier, last-minute changes in interviewers or editorial direction can completely shift an interview's focus. Having broad talking points rather than scripted responses provides necessary flexibility.
- **Graduate Student Considerations**: For graduate students, media engagement can be very stressful, and you have no control over what they're going to pull out of what you say. If that prospect scares you, it might not be the right time for media engagement.

The pressure to respond immediately to media requests can lead to poor performance. When someone emails saying they need to talk before 2:30 p.m. and it's 10 a.m., resist the urge to take the call immediately. Instead, give yourself time to prepare—ideally thirty minutes so you can get in the right mindset and review your talking points. This preparation time isn't optional; it's essential for managing the adrenaline rush that media appearances cause. The level of uncertainty in press interviews is much higher than in other kinds of talk academics typically give, with the possible exception of an academic job talk Q&A session.

Institutional Support and Training

Universities increasingly recognize that faculty media engagement benefits institutional reputation and research impact. Many offer resources that faculty should utilize before their first media encounter. For instance, press training workshops can teach fundamental skills such as bridging techniques, message control, and managing hostile questions. Communications offices often provide talking points assistance and can help translate complex research for public audiences.

The Long-Term Benefits and Responsibilities

Despite the challenges, strategic media engagement can yield significant benefits for funded researchers. It can give you visibility in ways that no other academic output can. The Texas flood coverage led to NBC booking a special segment on disaster preparedness, directly advancing Keri's research agenda's impact. The iterative nature of media engagement also clarifies researchers' own expertise. The more interviews you do, the more you realize what you know and the story you want to tell. You sense-make throughout the process and learn how to connect with a new type of public audience. Such clarity benefits not just media appearances but all research communication.

The skills developed in translating complex ideas for journalists transfer directly to writing public-facing grant reports, community presentations, and policy briefs—all increasingly important aspects of demonstrating research impact. For funded researchers, learning to engage effectively with media represents an opportunity for visibility; it also can increase the societal impact of their work.

Box 16.3 A Readiness Checklist for Press Engagement

Before accepting any media invitation, researchers should assess their preparedness:

Pre-Interview Preparation:

- Have you identified three to five key talking points?
- Can you explain your research in one sentence? Two paragraphs?
- Have you brainstormed questions you're willing and unwilling to answer?
- Have you done research to know the outlet's audience and typical coverage style?
- Have you practiced your responses out loud?
- For TV appearances, have you tested your lighting, background, and sound?
- Have you allocated preparation time before the interview?

During the Interview:

- Are you speaking in complete, quotable sentences?
- Are you maintaining appropriate energy for the format?
- Can you pivot from uncomfortable questions to your key messages?
- Are you avoiding academic jargon and unnecessary complexity?
- For video: Are you maintaining eye contact with the camera?
- For video: Is your environment professional? Is your technology reliable?
- For audio: Can you stand or move to maintain vocal energy?
- For background briefings: Have you decided how much time to invest?

Post-Interview Reflection:

- Did you stay within your expertise boundaries?
- What worked well that you should repeat?
- Should you follow up with clarifications or additional resources?
- Were there moments you wish you'd handled differently? The answer is almost always, yes, so learn from this instead of dwelling on what you wish you had done.

17

The Nuts and Bolts of Setting Up Your New Award

The prior chapter discussed how to navigate the initial excitement of receiving an award and how to begin to communicate about that award. At the same time, you are reviewing your budgets, deciding who you might hire, and getting ready to execute when you get that final notice to proceed.

Before we discuss setting up the new award, let's take a step back and consider an important intermediate step that can happen between submission and the notice of award. This is called a Just-in-Time (JIT) request. This request comes after initial peer review, typically when your proposal has been favorably reviewed and the agency needs additional information before making a final funding decision.

JIT requests ask for updated or additional information, which might include current other support information (what other grants you or key personnel currently have), updated biosketches with recent publications or accomplishments, proof of institutional approvals (IRB, IACUC), or letters stating approval will be obtained, certifications regarding various compliance matters, and human subjects training documentation. Here's what makes JIT requests challenging: they typically come with very short turnaround times, often three to five business days. You'll need to mobilize quickly to gather information from collaborators, obtain documentation from your institution, and submit everything through the required systems.

If you receive a JIT request, treat it as very positive news because it means your proposal survived initial review and is under serious consideration for funding. However, don't let the excitement make you careless. Respond thoroughly and on time. Missing a JIT deadline or submitting incomplete information can remove your proposal from funding consideration.

Prepare for potential JIT requests by keeping your biosketch/CV updated throughout the review period, maintaining good records of when IRB and other approvals were obtained, staying in touch with collaborators so you can reach them quickly if needed, and having your research administrator's contact information readily available. When the JIT request arrives, immediately notify your research administrator—they'll help you understand what's required and ensure you meet all institutional requirements for the response.

While proposals are under review, faculty can often make meaningful progress by preparing elements that do not require funding approval. Drafting IRB protocols, developing recruitment materials or data collection instruments, outlining hiring plans, and organizing early project logistics can significantly accelerate project launch if the award is funded. These preparatory steps help ensure that PIs are ready to move quickly when decisions arrive, particularly for agencies with tight post-award timelines.

When Agencies Cut Your Budget

One reality that surprises many first-time award recipients: agencies often fund proposals at levels below what was requested. The award letter might indicate you're receiving $400,000 when you requested $500,000. This isn't necessarily because reviewers thought your budget was unjustified, but sometimes agencies fund excellent proposals at reduced levels due to limited available funds.

Before you celebrate the award and begin setting up accounts, carefully review what was proposed versus what was awarded. If there is a significant budget reduction, you need to determine whether you can accomplish the proposed scope of work with reduced funding, or whether you need to negotiate a reduced scope with the program officer. This conversation should happen quickly, before finalizing the award agreement. Contact your program officer to discuss: "We proposed 500 interviews but the budget now supports approximately 350. Should we reduce the sample size, or are there other ways to adjust the project scope that would better serve the research goals?" Most program officers appreciate proactive communication about these questions rather than discovering mid-project that you can't deliver what was proposed.

Your research administrator should be part of these conversations, as they can help you understand what budget flexibility you have and what changes require formal sponsor approval. Don't just accept a reduced budget and figure you'll make it work somehow. That path can lead to either a compromised project or cost overruns that your institution won't cover.

The Reality of Account Setup and Budget Management

Moving beyond sharing the good news and the potential publicity is where the real work begins. Your first shock might come when you see how your carefully crafted budget has been translated into institutional accounting categories. That detailed budget you spent hours perfecting—with separate lines for two graduate students, a postdoc, specific equipment, and carefully calculated travel estimates—gets collapsed into broad categories like "Salaries," "Fringe," "Travel," and "Other Direct Costs."

For those who budget meticulously, this transformation can be jarring. Everything carefully detailed gets lumped into huge categories, and it takes time to accept that this is simply how institutional accounting works. The key is to maintain your own detailed budget while understanding how it maps to institutional categories.

Your institution will assign account numbers that seem like random strings of digits, but they do encode important information. A number like "14-264977-12" might indicate a federal grant (14) with specific spending restrictions, administered through a particular department (264977), with a sub-account for travel (12). Your administrators fluently speak this numerical language because they work with these codes daily. You, managing grants as one part of your multifaceted academic role, will likely never achieve such fluency, and that's OK.

The complexity becomes overwhelming when managing multiple grants. With one grant, tracking is manageable. But if you find yourself juggling six grants plus internal funding across multiple accounts, you'll constantly be asking your research administrator, "Which account are you talking about?" Creating your own translation guide is essential because there's rarely a handbook explaining what all the numbers mean. Here's a helpful tip: always keep your submitted budget handy as your "detailed" budget. When administrators reference account numbers, pull up your detailed version to understand what funds they're discussing. Don't hesitate to ask questions such as, "Is that the account for graduate student salaries?" or "Which project does that number refer to?" Your post-award administrators expect these questions from faculty who are still learning about funding budgets and learning to read detailed budget spreadsheets.

A word of warning: things will have changed in the time between submission and award. Salary rates increase, benefit percentages adjust, and tuition rises, something we discussed more in Chapter 15. Your perfectly balanced budget might now be short several thousand dollars. This is completely normal and totally manageable, though many new PIs waste energy stressing about these inevitable adjustments. Rebudgeting and potential rescoping provide the needed solution.

Navigating the Hiring Timeline Challenge

Perhaps no aspect of grant management frustrates social science PIs more than the misalignment of funding cycles and academic hiring calendars. Federal agencies don't coordinate their award announcements with your semester schedule. State contracts arrive when they arrive. Foundations follow their own timelines. Meanwhile, your institution runs on predictable semester rhythms, with graduate student appointments made months in advance.

Consider a common scenario. You receive notification in October that your NSF grant is funded. This is wonderful news, except that all the graduate students are already assigned for the fall semester. The promising student you had in mind is teaching Introduction to Sociology. Another potential candidate just accepted a research assistantship with a colleague. Your carefully planned project timeline assumed you'd have a full team in place by now, but instead you're scrambling to find anyone available for even a few hours per week.

The challenges multiply with different funding types. Federal grants often provide flexibility on start dates, allowing you to delay officially beginning the project until you can properly staff it. But state contracts come with deliverables and deadlines without regard to your academic calendar. Some PIs have received state contracts in which the deliverables were already overdue by the time the funding arrived at their institution, forcing the PI to scramble to hire people while simultaneously trying to meet deadlines that assume they have been working for months already.

The solution requires both strategic planning (remember Chapter 6 is a full chapter about Begin with the Hiring End in Mind?) and political navigation. If you have flexible funding—startup funds, a professorship, discretionary accounts—you might begin supporting students before the grant officially arrives. This assumes you have such resources, which many social scientists don't. More commonly, you'll need to work within existing constraints while building relationships that enable future flexibility.

The Politics of Graduate Student Appointments

The complexity of hiring graduate students on grants deserves special attention, as it often involves navigating delicate departmental politics that nobody warns you about. In many social science departments, graduate student funding is a carefully orchestrated dance. The graduate director (or whoever manages assistantship assignments) must balance teaching needs, student funding packages, and various faculty requests. When you arrive with grant funding wanting to hire specific students, you're disrupting this careful balance.

For example, here is what a colleague heard when she asked to hire a specific graduate student: "We have two unfunded students—why can't you just hire one of those?" The administrator assumed she did not need to hire for specific skills required for project success. And when she explained her need for someone with qualitative methods training and Geographic Information Systems (GIS) expertise, not just any available student, she quickly realized the administrator viewed her as being difficult.

The situation becomes even more complex when considering the student's perspective. A graduate student currently teaching might lose that stable, multiyear position if they join your one-year grant project. Having frank conversations with students about these trade-offs is essential. Yes, research experience is valuable, but if taking your grant means losing guaranteed teaching support for subsequent years, is it worth it? These are hard choices, and no PI should jeopardize a student's long-term funding security.

Some institutions have developed supportive approaches. At Texas Tech, Kerk's associate dean for graduate studies explicitly states, "Whoever has funding gets first pick of graduate students." This policy creates a positive culture around grant seeking. When other faculty receive "free" assistantships because Kerk's grant funding covers multiple students, the administrator explains to the colleagues, "You have a free RA this semester because Kerk is funding six other students with his grants."

This supportive approach remains rare in social science departments, where grant funding often seems to complicate rather than simplify resource allocation. Colleagues report being told that hiring a grant-funded student would "upset the balance" and "create inequities" among graduate students. Others hear that pulling students from teaching means "someone won't get a TA," as if the grant funding itself didn't represent a net gain for the department.

The summer months present particular challenges. Students want to travel, visit family, or return home. International students may face visa restrictions on work hours. Even when students commit to summer work, institutional rules create complications. Some universities require minimum credit hour enrollment during summer if students have a university appointment, forcing PIs to supervise (and sometimes pay for) independent study courses just to meet bureaucratic requirements.

Understanding the Hidden Costs of Success

Becoming a PI transforms your professional life in ways that extend far beyond managing budgets and hiring staff. Think of it as a situation where you wanted to get a new job to improve your income and have more discretionary money. But now that you have a new job, you find out you do not have the professional wardrobe needed to succeed. So, you start shopping, buying clothes to help you look professional, and end up spending more money because you need to dress differently now that you hold this new job.

This analogy perfectly captures the hidden investment required when becoming a PI. You've secured funding to advance your research, but suddenly you need resources for activities the grant won't cover—networking, relationship building, and opportunity development that make future grants possible. The networking imperative becomes clear quickly. Once you become a PI, people start paying attention. You enter a different league where successful PIs look for collaborators. Networking activities have no guarantee of leading to the next grant, but without networking, the likelihood of securing collaborative funding diminishes significantly.

Networking requires resources, particularly travel funding, that your current grants won't cover. One stark example is when Keri was invited to join a multi-institutional team developing a $30 million proposal. She faced the immediate problem of funding travel to the mandatory two-day, in-person proposal-writing meeting. Everyone else on the team advised Keri, "Use your professorship funds." But because Keri was the only co-PI on the team without a professorship at that time (or flexible funds), she had to scramble, "begging around" for someone to cover the flight and another to pay for the hotel.

This incident highlights a central reality: successful grant-seeking often requires flexible funding for activities that can't be charged to specific projects. Meeting with potential collaborators, attending specialized workshops, and presenting at agency-specific conferences—these career-building activities fall outside most grant budgets. Yet without them, sustaining and growing your funding portfolio becomes nearly impossible. Institutions that provide discretionary funding through professorships, research accounts, or other mechanisms enable faculty to seize opportunities. Those without such support leave faculty choosing between personal expenditure and missed opportunities.

The Rules, Regulations, and Compliance Maze

Every funding source comes with its own rules, and keeping them straight becomes a major challenge. The fundamental principle that many new PIs (and quite a few experienced ones as well) don't fully grasp is that funds from one project cannot support work on another project. This seems obvious in theory but proves complex in practice.

Let's say you manage three accounts: startup funds, a state grant, and a federal grant. Your startup funds might offer complete flexibility—so, use them for any legitimate research expense. But if you hire a student on your federal grant, the student cannot spend even an hour working on your state-funded project without proper cost-sharing agreements in place. If that same student travels to a conference, their travel must be paid from the same account that pays their salary, even if another account has more travel funds available.

These restrictions make logical sense from a compliance perspective but create practical headaches. For example, you might have abundant travel money in one account while another runs short, yet you cannot simply shift resources. Your administrators understand these restrictions intimately; when they reference "a 14-type account" versus "discretionary funds," they're not just citing numbers, but invoking entire regulatory frameworks.

The complexity multiplies when collaborating across institutions. Each university interprets federal guidelines slightly differently. What's permissible at one institution might be forbidden at another. Your perfectly reasonable request might induce weeks of negotiation between institutional legal teams, all while project deadlines loom.

Post-award administrators focus primarily on compliance. Their job is ensuring you follow all rules and survive audits. They're protecting the institution from liability, not helping brainstorm creative solutions within constraints. Most institutional rules exist for this reason—either to protect the institution from legal or financial risk or to ensure compliance with external regulations that govern sponsored research. This realization often frustrates PIs who expected the same creative partnership they enjoyed with pre-award staff.

The solution involves developing alternative support networks. Regular calls to colleagues at other institutions provide ideas: "How do you handle this at your university?" While their solutions might not work exactly at your institution, they provide starting points for conversations with administrators: "Will this approach work here?" is more productive than "How should I handle this?" when talking with administrators.

When Colleagues Don't Meet Funder's Deadlines

One of the most uncomfortable aspects of grant management involves dealing with colleagues who view deadlines as suggestions rather than requirements. Federal agencies take reporting seriously—very seriously. If you or any co-PI has overdue reports, new awards can be delayed or even withdrawn. The entire institution might face sanctions for one investigator's delinquency.

These experiences teach hard lessons about accountability in the grant world. As a PI, you're often responsible not just for your own compliance, but also for ensuring your entire team meets obligations. This might mean sending gentle reminders, then firm ones, then potentially difficult conversations about professional responsibility. It definitely means building buffer time into your own deadline management, assuming someone on the team will need extra prompting.

The stakes extend beyond individual projects. The weight of knowing that your mistakes could impact the funding of every colleague at your institution adds pressure, and it also explains why administrators seem so focused on compliance details that might appear trivial.

Building Systems for Long-Term Success

Given the complexities of grant management, building robust systems from the start prevents later chaos. This begins with data management—an unglamorous but critical aspect of project success. Too many PIs learn this lesson through painful experience: the graduate student who maintained all project files in their personal Google Drive that disappeared after graduation; the postdoc who created elaborate file structures accessible only through their login; the research assistant who used creative naming conventions that made sense only to them.

Effective data management requires proactive planning. Establish file structures owned by the PI, not staff members. Create comprehensive documentation for all procedures. Implement consistent naming conventions. Use institutional platforms rather than personal accounts. Set up regular reviews to ensure compliance. Most importantly, budget time for this work. It's not glamorous, but it's essential for long-term success.

The PI must maintain ownership of all root directories, granting team members "editor" access but retaining ultimate control. When someone leaves the project, conduct exit procedures weeks in advance, discussing which files they'll need access to after departure and ensuring all confidential data remain secure. A hard lesson occurs when a full-time employee sets up your entire file structure and then leaves; you might find yourself chasing down university IT administrators and begging for access to your own project data! Separation planning should begin as soon as someone gives notice, with clear checklists covering equipment return, file access, and knowledge transfer.

The challenge of multi-institutional collaboration adds layers of complexity. Document sharing across institutions becomes a nightmare of incompatible systems and security protocols. For example, computer scientists might insist on using Overleaf for collaborative writing, leaving social scientists struggling with unfamiliar platforms. One solution is to have graduate students learn these platforms to serve as intermediaries, though this adds yet another training burden to already overwhelming project management demands.

Travel, Recognition, and Playing by the Rules

Grant-funded travel operates under strict regulations that often surprise new PIs. Every trip must directly support the funded project's aims. Conference presentations must acknowledge the grant. Receipts must be meticulously maintained. Some institutions require pre-approval for any travel, while others have complex reimbursement procedures that can take months to complete.

Some PIs take unusual but valuable steps to understand these systems. Kerk enrolled in his university's travel workshop designed for administrative staff. He wanted to learn the behind-the-scenes travel stuff, and now he makes his own travel arrangements and submits his own travel reimbursements through the university system. This proactive approach eliminated a major source of frustration and delays. Understanding how the system works transforms it from a black box into a manageable process.

The travel challenge extends beyond logistics. As a PI, you'll likely need to travel more than your grants cover. Advisory board meetings, planning sessions for future proposals, and conferences where you're building relationships rather than presenting are essential activities that often fall outside specific project budgets. Without flexible funding from professorships or other sources, PIs can face challenging choices between personal expenditure and missed opportunities.

Foundation funding often includes unique requirements that catch academic researchers off guard. Some foundations expect regular in-person visits to present progress updates. They view grantees as partners in advancing their mission, expecting a level of engagement that goes beyond submitting annual reports. These relationships can be rewarding, but they require time and resources that many academics don't anticipate.

Learning from Mistakes with Grace

Throughout your grant management journey, you will make mistakes. It's not a possibility—it's a certainty. The question is how you learn from them and move forward. The mistakes might be small—forgetting to acknowledge the funder in a conference presentation—or significant—discovering you've been charging expenses to the wrong account for months. Some will be amusing in retrospect, like attempting to submit a proposal six months after the program has ended because of misreading the solicitation. Others might feel catastrophic in the moment but prove manageable with proper communication and corrective action.

What matters is maintaining perspective. Return to your North Star—that list of what this grant enables. Yes, you're dealing with bureaucratic hassles, challenging politics, and systems that seem designed to frustrate rather than facilitate research. But you're also providing opportunities for students who couldn't otherwise afford graduate school. You're compensating community partners fairly for their expertise. And you're generating knowledge that can shape policy and improve lives.

Keep in mind the ripple effects of your success. Students who work on your projects gain invaluable experience. Community partners benefit from fairly compensated collaboration. The knowledge generated can influence decisions affecting thousands. A graduating student recently shared with Keri: "Thank you for all you do for the students. You single-handedly hire more students than our entire department does for summer employment. Most of us could not even get jobs if it were not for the research opportunities you provide us." That feedback makes all the politics and challenges worthwhile.

Moving Forward with Wisdom and Resilience

As you settle into your role as a PI, certain truths become clear. Managing grants will consume more time than you anticipated—plan accordingly. Institutional rules will complicate every decision—learn them rather than fighting them. Press opportunities can be positive—prepare and realize they are almost always stressful. Turnover will create constant challenges—develop systems to manage it rather than hoping it won't happen. Politics and professional jealousies may emerge—navigate carefully rather than ignoring them.

But also remember the tremendous privilege of this position. In a landscape where social scientists increasingly face pressure to secure external funding, you've succeeded. You've joined a community of scholars who understand both the challenges and rewards of grant-funded research. Draw on others' wisdom, share your own experiences, and remember that everyone struggles with these same challenges.

Build relationships with your research administrators, even when their focus on compliance frustrates your desire for innovation. They're protecting both you and the institution from serious consequences. Develop networks of peer PIs who can offer advice and commiseration.

Most importantly, maintain connections to why you pursued this path—the research questions that fascinate you, the communities you serve, and the knowledge you're privileged to create.

The journey from "You got the grant!" to successful project completion is long and sometimes difficult. But armed with realistic expectations, robust systems, and a clear sense of purpose, you can navigate the challenges while maintaining focus on what matters most: conducting research that makes a difference. Your North Star will guide you through the bureaucratic maze, the political challenges, and the inevitable setbacks. Trust in its light, and you'll find your way to meaningful research outcomes that justify every moment of struggle along the path.

18

Managing Your Grant: From Vision to Impact

The euphoria of receiving your grant award has settled. You've navigated the complex setup process, established accounts, begun hiring staff, and started implementing systems. Now comes the real work: managing your grant effectively while maintaining your research vision and maximizing impact. This chapter moves beyond the logistics of getting started to explore the deeper dimensions of grant management: transforming your research from identifying problems to creating solutions, building meaningful community partnerships, and leveraging success for future opportunities.

Managing a grant involves far more than administrative compliance. It requires strategic thinking about how to achieve your research goals while building toward future success. It can be useful to think through your long-term research strategy even before writing that first proposal since that practice situates the proposed project within the longer-term research goals. Successfully managing a grant demands a shift in mindset from simply conducting research to creating a lasting impact—a transition that many social scientists find both challenging and deeply rewarding.

Moving Beyond Problem Identification

For decades, social science training has emphasized identifying and analyzing problems. We're taught to recognize gaps, critique systems, and theorize about dysfunctions. This critical lens serves important scholarly purposes, but external funding opens doors to something more: the opportunity to develop and test solutions. This shift from problem identification to solution development represents one of the most profound transformations that funded research enables.

Consider the traditional arc of unfunded social science research. A scholar identifies an interesting problem, collects data (often limited by personal resources), analyzes findings, writes papers highlighting issues and gaps, and then moves on to the next project. The communities studied rarely benefit directly from this work. As Kerk experienced during an interview, participants often ask pointed questions: "Are you going to tell me just the problems I already know I have, or are you going to tell me solutions to the problems?"

This question cuts to the heart of what's often called "extractive" research—the practice of taking data from communities without giving back meaningful insights or interventions (Gaudry, 2011; Tuck & Yang, 2014), a concept more extensively discussed in Chapter 4. External funding fundamentally changes this dynamic by providing resources to engage more deeply, test interventions, and return to communities with actionable solutions.

The Iterative Journey from Problems to Solutions

The path from identifying problems to developing solutions requires different research approaches and timelines than traditional academic work. A multiyear funded project provides the luxury of iterative research—the ability to identify issues in year one, develop potential solutions in year two, and test those solutions in year three. This extended engagement enables the kind of deep, meaningful research that creates real impact.

Keri's flood safety research in Texas provides a compelling example. She knew that the final deliverable required developing messages to help various groups of Texans decrease their flood risk. Initial research identified that young adult males were most likely to drive through floodwaters—not surprising given their sense of invincibility and the prevalence of large trucks in Texas. The existing public safety message,

"Turn Around Don't Drown," proved ineffective with this demographic. Focus group participants dismissed it: "That's stupid! I'm not gonna die. I have a big truck. I can drive through this water."

Rather than stop at identifying this problem, the funded research allowed Keri to pursue iterative solution development. Through multiple rounds of focus groups, she discovered that these young men's most prized possession was their vehicle—more valuable to them than anything else they owned. When asked what worried them most about their vehicles, the unanimous response was car insurance costs. This insight led to developing new messages that resonated with their actual concerns: "Insurance is high. Keep your car dry" and the more publicly palatable "Keep your car high and dry."

Testing showed these messages immediately connected with the target audience in ways the death-focused messaging never could. Young men who scoffed at warnings about drowning readily acknowledged they didn't want to damage their vehicles or face higher insurance premiums. The multiyear funding made this iterative process possible, moving from problem identification through solution development to tested interventions that the State of Texas could implement.

Building Lasting Community Relationships

One of the most rewarding aspects of funded research involves developing sustained relationships with the communities you study. Unlike traditional research that often involves brief engagements followed by academic publications, funded projects enable ongoing partnerships that transform the research, the researcher, and the participants.

Kerk's work with the cyberinfrastructure community provides a powerful example of how funded research can create meaningful, lasting partnerships. This emerging community sits at the intersection of computer science and scientific research support—professionals who aren't quite computer scientists, aren't traditional IT staff, and aren't domain scientists, but whose work creating complex computational infrastructure enables cutting-edge scientific discovery.

Over more than a decade of funded research with this community, what began as Kerk's anthropological observation evolved into a deep partnership. Kerk attended their conferences regularly, served on organizing committees, and developed genuine friendships within the community. This sustained engagement enabled research contributions that went far beyond traditional academic outputs. His work helped the community understand their emerging professional identity, develop strategies for promoting technology adoption, and navigate the complex organizational dynamics surrounding cyberinfrastructure innovations.

This deep engagement also transformed the research itself. Funded research expectations, particularly around broader impacts and community engagement, push researchers toward more ethical and impactful approaches. When you know you'll face the same community members at next year's conference, when they have access to your publications and will call out inaccuracies, when you've committed to helping solve their problems rather than just studying them, the quality and validity of your research improves dramatically because you more closely consider the outcomes of your work, including how others will respond to it.

Member checking (Birt et al., 2016), the practice of sharing findings with research participants for validation, becomes not only a methodological choice but also an ethical imperative when you maintain ongoing relationships. This accountability produces more rigorous research. As Kerk notes, "I believe in my findings. I believe in the value of my work as a result of doing funded work" because the community engagement ensures accuracy in ways that traditional peer review alone cannot.

Strategic Report Management: Beginning with the End in Mind

One of the most valuable pieces of advice for managing grants comes from a simple practice: obtain a blank copy of your required annual report template on day one of your project. This seemingly minor step can fundamentally reshape how you approach your entire research program. Too many researchers discover report requirements only when the deadline looms. They suddenly face questions about what was proposed versus what was accomplished, requests for specific metrics they didn't track, or emphasis on outcomes they didn't prioritize. The report template serves as more than a bureaucratic requirement—it's a roadmap for project success.

When you understand from day one that you'll need to demonstrate progress on specific dimensions, you can make strategic decisions about student training, data collection timing, and project pacing that align with these expectations. Every major decision throughout the year can be evaluated against the question: "How will this contribute to what I need to report?"

This approach extends beyond federal grants to state contracts and foundation awards, where report requirements often prove even more elaborate and specific. State-funded projects frequently require detailed reports (often hundreds of pages long) written for policy audiences, using exact contract language to demonstrate deliverable completion. Keri's strategy involves outlining the contract requirements at the project's start and using that outline as the beginning of the final report. As she completes each component, she's simultaneously building the final deliverable. This strategy helps the researcher track details and not have to remember them later, when it is time to write the report.

Adapting to Different Reporting Cultures

Different funders maintain distinct reporting cultures that shape project management approaches. Federal agencies typically expect annual reports focusing on research progress, publications, and student training. State agencies often demand more immediate, policy-relevant findings with clear recommendations for future funding or program development. Foundations may request narrative reports emphasizing community impact and alignment with organizational mission. Some funders expect updates within months of project start, asking "What are your findings already?" when traditional academic timelines would barely have data collection underway.

Understanding these different expectations from the outset allows you to structure your project accordingly. If you know your state funder will want preliminary findings at six months, you can design a phased approach with early data collection yielding initial insights. If your foundation program officer expects regular engagement beyond written reports, you can budget time for relationship maintenance alongside research activities.

The Publication Paradox: Navigating Multiple Audiences

One of the most complex challenges in managing funded research involves satisfying multiple audiences with different definitions of productivity and success. Your funder may value conference presentations, technical reports, and rapid dissemination of findings. Your tenure committee likely prioritizes peer-reviewed journal articles in specific venues. Your community partners want accessible, actionable insights they can implement immediately. Balancing these competing demands requires strategic thinking and often considerably more work.

The interdisciplinary nature of many funded projects compounds this challenge. Different academic communities have evolved distinct publication cultures, each with its own logic and value system. Computer science collaborators, for instance, consider peer-reviewed conference papers their gold standard—conferences with acceptance rates below 20 percent that undergo rigorous review. These papers receive digital object identifiers (DOIs) and "count" as major publications in their field. The publishing norm for many branches of social and behavioral sciences as well as humanities scholarship is to present work at a disciplinary conference before submitting it to a journal. The journal publication is the only one that has a DOI.

Keri experienced this cultural clash firsthand when her interdisciplinary team won a top paper award at a communication conference. Her engineering colleagues emailed repeatedly asking, "Where's the DOI? Why are you not giving me a DOI? How do we even report this on our annual report?" She had to explain that requesting a DOI would prevent her and her students from publishing the work in a journal, where it would count for their careers. This wasn't stubbornness; rather, it reflected fundamentally different publication ecosystems that team members hadn't previously understood.

The volume expectations between fields also reflect different research cultures rather than different quality standards. Computer scientists on large teams might collectively publish thirty papers annually, a pace that seems impossible to scholars accustomed to single or dual authorship. But this isn't about cutting corners; it's about different models of knowledge production. Large technical teams can genuinely produce numerous high-quality outputs through distributed effort, with each team member contributing specialized expertise to multiple projects simultaneously.

Speed of publication represents another significant difference. Kerk discovered that his STEM colleagues valued extended abstracts published in conference proceedings specifically because they could report them as products with DOIs within the same year—crucial for annual reports. These extended abstracts undergo peer review and contribute to the STEM field's knowledge base. However, when Kerk reported these same products in his departmental annual report, senior colleagues were genuinely puzzled. They weren't dismissing his work—they simply operated in a system where extended abstracts didn't exist as a recognized category of scholarship.

Such a disconnect in publication cultures creates real challenges for career advancement across disciplines. Time spent producing white papers, technical guides, and infographics that funders value may not align with departmental expectations for tenure. Yet these products often create substantial real-world impact. Kerk's team produced a white paper for the Robert Wood Johnson Foundation that became the key document launching the foundation's new program in its research area. The foundation used its white paper to define an entire funding initiative—clear evidence of research impact. However, as Kerk notes, "to my colleagues in my department, it was not considered a peer-reviewed journal publication, even though the work that went into it was substantial." The team of five coauthors each contributed the equivalent of a full journal article, creating a comprehensive document that shaped foundation funding priorities for years.

Similarly, Keri has produced final reports for state agencies that run hundreds of pages, single-spaced, representing months of analysis and writing. These reports undergo multiple rounds of review by agency staff, who send back detailed critiques requiring substantive revisions—sometimes three or four rounds. The scrutiny rivals peer review, and the reports are often made public, requiring the same attention to quality as any academic publication. Yet these substantial intellectual products typically don't count as research productivity in social science departments.

The solution isn't to choose one audience over another; it is to develop strategies to serve multiple communities from the same research effort. For example, a single data collection effort might yield:

- Technical reports for funders emphasizing practical findings and recommendations
- Peer-reviewed articles for disciplinary advancement focusing on theoretical contributions
- Policy briefs for government audiences highlighting actionable insights
- Community-facing materials presenting findings in accessible formats
- Conference presentations that generate feedback while building reputation (with or without DOIs, depending on the field)
- White papers that influence funding agency priorities

Box 18.1 Strategies for Managing Multiple Outputs

The key to managing these multiple audiences lies in planning diverse outputs from the beginning rather than treating them as afterthoughts. When you know you'll need both a journal article and a state report, you can structure data collection to serve both purposes. When you understand that community partners expect accessible summaries while academic colleagues value theoretical sophistication, you can build translation time into your project timeline.

Several strategies help manage these competing demands:

- **Build writing timelines that account for different venues.** If your funder wants findings within a year but journals take two years to publish, plan for conference presentations or technical reports that satisfy funders while working toward journal publications.
- **Educate collaborators about disciplinary differences.** Take time early in projects to explain publication norms in your field. Your computer science colleague genuinely

may not know that social science conferences don't generate proceedings. Your humanities partner may not understand why engineers need DOIs for annual reports.

- **Track impact beyond traditional metrics.** Start documenting how your work influences policy, shapes funding priorities, or changes practice—even if these impacts don't appear in tenure files. As Keri and Kerk both note, they wish they had been more savvy with tracking impact throughout their careers. These alternative impact metrics increasingly matter to funders and may eventually influence academic evaluation.
- **Negotiate recognition within your department.** Help colleagues understand the value of diverse outputs by explaining their role in building sustained research programs. The white paper that launches a foundation initiative may enable future funded research that does produce traditional publications.

Training materials that extend project impact beyond the funding period

Keri worked on an engineering project in which the team conducted extensive interviews with a utility company to inform major policy decisions in a city. The work required rigorous interview protocols and careful analysis using constant comparative methods, with findings referenced to academic literature. (It was the type of project that makes a researcher feel proud because the work was very thorough.) However, Keri had to sign an agreement at the project's start that she couldn't publish anything from the work—a common requirement in applied research that serves immediate practical needs rather than academic knowledge production.

The reality is that funded research often requires producing twice as much as unfunded work: outputs for funders and outputs for academic advancement. You are essentially doing two jobs because that's two sets of expectations. Rather than viewing this as an unfair burden, successful researchers recognize it as the price of resources that enable more ambitious research than would otherwise be possible. The key is being strategic about how you manage these multiple obligations while maintaining both research quality and personal sustainability.

Financial Management: Confronting Money Mindsets

Perhaps no aspect of grant management activates more anxiety than the responsibility for spending substantial sums of money. For many academics, particularly those from working-class backgrounds and those who have experienced financial instability, managing large budgets can surface deep-seated anxieties about money that affect project implementation.

The challenge goes beyond simple budgeting mechanics. It involves confronting personal relationships with money that may create barriers to effective grant management. Researchers who grew up in financially insecure households often struggle with the mindset shift required to spend grant funds strategically rather than hoarding them against imagined future catastrophes.

Keri's childhood experiences have shaped her grant management approaches. She grew up in a family that lost its home due to a flood when she was in third grade. They lived paycheck to paycheck. She remembers having very little money to spend growing up, and that has impacted the way she spends money on grants. She is always looking for a buffer, for back-up funds. This cautious approach, while understandable, can create problems when funders and administrators expect steady spending that demonstrates project progress.

Kerk has a similar perspective from having grown up in Malaysia and being a first-generation college student. His parents didn't have the education to hold high-paying jobs, and when he was a child they traveled to the city for work while his grandmother raised him in a small town. He grew up being extremely frugal, thinking that resources were limited: even though there is food on the table today, there is no guarantee there will be food on the table tomorrow. This mindset, though valuable for personal financial management, can hinder effective grant administration when applied to research funds that must be spent within specific timeframes for designated purposes.

Developing New Financial Habits

The key insight many researchers discover is that grant money isn't personal money—rather, it is institutional money designated for specific research purposes. This distinction seems obvious intellectually but can be difficult to internalize emotionally. The shift requires developing new habits around financial decision-making, often with the support of mentors who can provide perspective on appropriate spending patterns.

Several strategies help researchers develop healthier relationships with grant spending:

- **Purchase equipment early** in the project period when funds are available and timelines allow for procurement delays.
- **Commit to regular spending reviews** with administrators who can flag underspending concerns before they become problems.
- **Budget for contingencies explicitly** rather than hoarding funds informally, building appropriate buffers into project plans.
- **Seek mentorship** from experienced PIs who can model appropriate spending patterns and provide reassurance about financial decisions.
- **Track spending patterns** from successful projects to understand normal expenditure rhythms and identify when your caution might be excessive.

The irony is that excessive frugality actually can harm future funding prospects. Review panels and program officers do notice when researchers consistently return large portions of their grants unspent. This spending pattern suggests either poor project planning or an inability to execute proposed work. Neither interpretation supports future funding decisions.

Leveraging Success: The Continuous Funding Cycle

Perhaps the most counterintuitive aspect of grant management is that your best opportunity to secure additional funding comes when you're already funded. Success builds upon success in the funding world, creating expanding opportunities for those who effectively manage current grants.

This reality makes strategic planning for future funding an essential component of current grant management.

In addition, the visibility that comes with funding creates networking opportunities that wouldn't otherwise exist. Program officers notice successful projects and may invite participation in new initiatives. Collaborators seek out researchers with proven funding track records. Conference invitations multiply, creating platforms to share work and build relationships that enable future proposals.

The most successful researchers maintain active proposal pipelines even while managing current awards. This might seem overwhelming given existing project demands, but it reflects funding realities. Review cycles mean months or even years between submission and award notification. Gaps between projects can disrupt research teams, lose momentum, and force difficult personnel decisions.

The key to managing continuous proposal development lies in seeing connections between current work and future possibilities. Preliminary findings from one project might seed the next proposal. Methodological innovations developed for current research could anchor applications to different funders. Community partnerships established through one grant might enable new collaborative opportunities.

Understanding Funding Flexibility and Constraints

Every funding source comes with unique rules about how money can be spent, when activities must be completed, and what kinds of changes are permissible. Understanding these constraints—and the flexibility that exists within them—proves crucial for successful grant management.

No-Cost Extensions: Buying Time Without Additional Funds

Most researchers will eventually need more time to complete their projects than originally anticipated. Data collection takes longer than expected, key personnel leave unexpectedly, or global pandemics disrupt carefully laid plans. No-cost extensions (NCEs) provide additional time to complete project activities without additional funding.

Different funders maintain dramatically different policies around NCEs. Some federal agencies routinely approve extensions with minimal justification. Others require extensive documentation of why additional time is needed and what will be accomplished. State agencies using federal pass-through funds may face hard deadlines that cannot be extended regardless of circumstances. If your state funder explains that their federal funding expires on a specific date with no possibility of extension, then you know to build more conservative timelines. If your foundation typically approves one six-month extension, but nothing longer, you can plan accordingly. On the other hand, some funders limit extensions to six-month increments but allow multiple extensions, requiring new requests as each deadline approaches. Understanding these policies early on prevents last-minute scrambles.

Supplemental Funding: Expanding Successful Projects

When projects yield exciting preliminary findings or reveal unexpected opportunities, supplemental funding requests can support expanded work. These supplements typically require demonstrating how additional funds would enhance ongoing research rather than supporting entirely new directions.

The availability of supplemental funding varies across agencies and even across programs within agencies. Some NSF directorates routinely consider supplement requests for promising projects, while others firmly state that no additional funds are available. Program officers often serve as the best source of intelligence about supplement possibilities within their specific programs. The key lies in maintaining communication with program officers who can guide you toward opportunities and away from wasted effort on impossible requests.

The Human Side of Grant Management

Beyond budgets and reports, managing grants fundamentally involves managing your relationships with funders, collaborators, staff, and communities. These relationships often determine project success more than technical execution of research plans.

Program Officer Relationships

Program officers serve multiple roles: funding gatekeepers, serving as technical advisors, and advocating for successful projects. Building positive relationships with program officers requires understanding their perspectives and constraints. They manage portfolios of projects, report to supervisors about program success, and constantly balance competing demands for limited funds. Regular communication from you helps program officers support your success. Brief email updates about project milestones, invitations to attend virtual presentations, and early alerts about potential challenges all build goodwill. When you need guidance about supplements, extensions, or future funding opportunities, established relationships facilitate productive conversations.

Managing Team Dynamics

Funded projects often involve complex teams with diverse perspectives and competing priorities. Principal investigators suddenly find themselves managing personalities, mediating conflicts, and motivating team members—skills rarely taught in graduate school. The time demands of people management often surprise new PIs who budgeted time for research activities but not for the hours spent on personnel issues.

Creating structures for regular communication helps prevent small issues from becoming major problems. Weekly team meetings, clear documentation of decisions, and explicit discussion of authorship and credit early in projects all contribute to smoother collaboration. When conflicts arise—and they will—addressing them promptly prevents poisonous dynamics from undermining project success.

Community Accountability

Perhaps the most rewarding yet challenging relationships involve community partners who contribute to and benefit from research. These partnerships require different engagement strategies than academic collaborations. Community partners often operate on different timelines, have different definitions of success, and expect different types of communication than academic colleagues.

As a reminder of the details discussed in Chapter 4, building genuine partnerships requires:

- **compensating community members fairly** for their time and expertise,
- **sharing findings in accessible formats** that community members can use,
- **involving partners in decision-making** rather than treating them as data sources,
- **maintaining relationships** beyond specific project timelines, and
- **acknowledging expertise** that comes from lived experience alongside academic credentials.

Researcher-community partnerships often produce the most meaningful research outcomes while requiring the most intensive relationship management.

Learning from Challenges and Failures

Every experienced grant manager accumulates stories of challenges overcome and mistakes survived. Such experiences become not failures, but learning opportunities that improve future practice. The key lies in building systems that prevent repeated mistakes while maintaining perspective about inevitable imperfections.

Common challenges include:

- **Hiring delays** that disrupt project timelines when key personnel aren't available as planned.
  - Building buffer time into project schedules and maintaining contingency plans helps manage these disruptions.
- **Budget shortfalls** when costs increase between proposal submission and project implementation.
  - Maintaining communication with your research administrators helps you navigate these challenges.
- **Collaboration conflicts** when team members have different expectations or working styles.
  - Creating explicit team agreements early in projects prevents many conflicts while providing frameworks for resolution when they arise.
- **Community disruptions** when planned research sites become unavailable or community priorities shift.
  - Maintaining multiple community relationships and building flexibility into research designs enables pivoting when necessary.
- **Publication delays** that affect tenure timelines or subsequent funding applications.
  - Starting to write early, involving multiple team members in manuscript development, and maintaining realistic expectations about academic publishing timelines all help manage this challenge.

Looking Ahead: From Single Grants to Research Programs

As you develop comfort with managing individual grants, new possibilities emerge. The skills developed through single project management—financial oversight, team leadership, stakeholder engagement, strategic planning—scale to support larger ambitions. As you learned in Chapter 10, some researchers build formal lab structures housing multiple related projects; others develop research centers that become institutional fixtures; and still others maintain loose confederations of projects united by common themes or methods.

In the next chapter, Chapter 19, we cover the specific challenges and opportunities of managing multiple concurrent awards. The complexity multiplies when juggling different funders with different requirements, managing larger teams with intersecting responsibilities, and maintaining coherent research programs while pursuing diverse funding opportunities.

For those interested in formalizing their research infrastructure, Chapter 10's exploration of leadership in centers, labs, and institutes provides frameworks for thinking about institutional structures that support sustained research programs. These formal structures can provide administrative support, institutional recognition, and platforms for larger initiatives while requiring additional management responsibilities.

The international dimensions of funded research, explored in Chapter 20, become increasingly relevant as research questions transcend national boundaries and funders emphasize global collaboration. Managing grants that involve international partners adds layers of complexity around regulatory compliance, cultural differences, and logistical challenges, while also opening possibilities for transformative research. Throughout these advanced topics, core principles of effective grant management remain constant: maintain focus on research goals while adapting to funder requirements; build genuine partnerships that create mutual benefit; document decisions and learn from challenges; and always remember that grants are means to research ends, not ends in themselves.

Conclusion: Impact Beyond Metrics

Managing grants successfully requires mastering administrative details while maintaining a vision for transformative research. The journey from problem identification to solution development, from extractive research to community partnership, from individual projects to sustained programs, transforms both researchers and research fields.

The metrics captured in annual reports—publications produced, students trained, conferences attended—tell only part of the story. The deeper impacts often resist easy quantification: communities empowered with new tools, partnerships that outlast funding cycles, students inspired to pursue research careers, and knowledge that shapes policy and practice.

These outcomes justify the administrative burden, the stressful deadlines, and the constant juggling that grant management requires.

As you navigate your own grant management journey, remember that perfection isn't the goal—impact is. Every funded project offers opportunities to refine your approach, strengthen your skills, and expand your vision for what research can accomplish. The communities you serve, the students you mentor, and the knowledge you create all benefit from your willingness to embrace both the challenges and opportunities of funded research.

19

Managing Multiple External Funding Awards

Imagine a small, family-owned bakery tucked away in a quiet Chicago neighborhood. For years, they've been perfecting their recipes, serving loyal customers who stop by for their morning coffee and pastries. Then one day, Oprah features their signature cinnamon rolls on her show. The next morning, there's a line wrapped around the block. The phone rings nonstop with orders from across the country. What seemed like a dream come true quickly becomes a nightmare—they have two ovens, three employees, and suddenly thousands of orders they cannot possibly fill. The very success they'd dreamed of threatens to destroy their reputation and their business.

This phenomenon—what media theorist Clay Shirky (2008) calls "success crisis"—happens when demand catastrophically outpaces capacity. Restaurants featured in popular food shows often experience similar crises. Their websites crash under the traffic. Wait times stretch from minutes to hours. Quality suffers as they scramble to meet impossible demands. Customers who once raved about the establishment leave angry reviews: "This place used to be great, but we don't go there anymore. You can never get a table, and when you do, the service is terrible."

In the digital age, this pattern repeats across industries. A small app goes viral overnight, and its servers crash under millions of unexpected users. An Etsy shop gets featured on a popular blog, and the sole craftsperson suddenly faces six months of backorders. In each case, what appears to be success—recognition, demand, opportunity—transforms into an operational crisis that threatens to undo everything the business has built.

When Four Grants Come Calling

This same dynamic plays out in academia, though few outside the system recognize it. Consider what happened to Keri during the last week of July in 2021, when she experienced her own version of the Oprah effect. After years of methodically building her research program and submitting numerous proposals, Keri had developed a steady rhythm of grant applications. Like most researchers, she expected a success rate of perhaps one in three or four submissions. She'd learned to cast a wide net, knowing that most proposals would be rejected despite months of preparation. This is simply the reality of competitive federal funding, where success rates often hover well below 20 percent.

At the time, Keri was already managing several state contracts, which kept her busy, but not overwhelmed. She had found a manageable rhythm, balancing the demands of these existing projects with her teaching responsibilities and ongoing research. Then, in a single week in late July, everything changed.

- Monday brought the first email: one of her National Science Foundation (NSF) proposals had been recommended for funding. She felt the familiar mix of elation and mild panic—there would be graduate students to hire, research protocols to finalize, budgets to manage. But this was manageable. She had trained for this.
- Wednesday's notification arrived with news of a second NSF approval, a project she had submitted months earlier focusing on a different aspect of her research. Her stomach tightened. Two major NSF projects starting simultaneously, on top of her existing state contracts, meant double the startup complexity, double the hiring, double the reporting requirements.
- Thursday delivered the third success: another NSF grant, this time an interdisciplinary team project for which she served as co-PI. Her role was smaller on this grant project, but the coordination requirements were massive—multiple institutions, numerous researchers, monthly meetings, integrated data systems.

- By Friday, when the fourth NSF approval arrived—a proposal she'd submitted almost a year prior—Keri found herself sitting in her office, tears streaming down her face. With four NSF grants approved in one week, on top of her existing state contracts, the very success she'd worked toward for years now felt like a crushing weight.

The Hidden Crisis

Colleagues who noticed Keri's distress that week responded with bewilderment and, sometimes, mockery. "Oh, poor Keri," one said with obvious sarcasm. "Four NSF grants in a week! I wish I had your problems." Another added, "Must be nice to have too much money!" They saw only the surface, the prestige, the funding success rate that would look impressive on her annual review, the apparent validation of her research.

What they couldn't see was the operational nightmare unfolding. Unlike the bakery owner who could potentially hire more bakers or buy more ovens, academic grants come with rigid constraints. Each grant specified exactly how its funds could be used, which personnel could be paid, and what equipment could be purchased. The money that seemed so abundant was already spoken for, committed to specific deliverables with legally binding timelines.

The mathematics were brutal. Keri had budgeted for graduate students on all the grants, not thinking she'd get them all at once. Now she faced the impossible task of hiring that many graduate students in a short period of time. The infrastructure she needed—project managers, administrative support, specialized software systems—couldn't be purchased with grant funds earmarked for research activities. The very rules designed to ensure proper use of federal funds now handcuffed her ability to manage them effectively.

When crisis hits, the first instinct is often to resist the reality of the predicament. Keri spent those first few days after the fourth notification in a state of denial, hoping somehow the situation would resolve itself, that maybe one of the grants would be delayed or that magical administrative support would appear. But resistance only prolonged the agony. It wasn't until she accepted the reality—yes, she had four new NSF grants plus existing state contracts, and yes, she had to find a way to manage them all—that she could begin finding solutions.

Keri contacted the associate dean for research in her college and asked to meet to help her strategize. During the meeting, her associate dean took a practical approach and helped Keri see possibilities rather than just problems. Together, they discovered that some grants would allow pooling money between multiple projects to hire a postdoc or research scientist instead of multiple graduate students. Since Keri had budgeted for tuition in those graduate student roles, that money could be redirected to support a research scientist position. It was complicated—some costs aren't subject to federal indirect cost returns, and they had to navigate the entire system carefully—but having someone who understood these intricacies made all the difference.

This rebudgeting allowed Keri to hire a research scientist, giving her a full-time person who wasn't also required to take classes. Instead of managing seven graduate students across four different projects, she could work with a single experienced researcher who could help coordinate work across multiple grants. The college also provided some flexible funding that allowed Keri to purchase a laptop for her research scientist, an expense that wasn't tied to just one grant, a practical necessity when someone is working across multiple projects.

Reading about these challenges might make you wonder whether pursuing grants is worth the complexity. Here's the honest truth: Keri and Kerk didn't share their stories to discourage you; we shared them so you could learn from our experiences and develop better strategies from the start. Ultimately, we succeeded, built thriving research programs, and we would do it again despite the challenges. The key is entering the grant world with realistic expectations and a strategic approach. You won't avoid all complications, but you can navigate them much more effectively when you understand what to expect and how to respond. That's exactly what this book prepares you to do. This case study reveals the importance of preliminary project management before the notice of award (NOA) occurs. If Keri had thought through a one-year work plan before receiving all the awards, she could have used that as a compass to help her figure out these challenges before the cognitive load was simply too much.

Understanding the True Nature of Soft Money

The term "soft money" takes on new meaning when managing multiple grants. While Keri's solution of hiring a research scientist helped her manage the immediate crisis of four simultaneous grants, it also introduced her to the harsh realities of soft-money positions. Unlike tenure-track faculty who have guaranteed salary support, research scientists and postdocs depend entirely on continued grant funding.

This creates a dilemma that many PIs don't anticipate. You hire talented researchers who reorganize their lives to work on your projects. They might relocate their families, sign apartment leases, or turn down other opportunities. But grant funding is inherently temporary. When Keri's research scientist became fully trained and maximally productive after two years, Keri faced the reality that she couldn't afford to keep her because it is quite expensive to fully fund these types of positions paying not only their salary but also the benefits that can cost an additional 25–40 percent on top of salary.

This situation illustrates why the term "soft money" carries such weight in academic circles. It's not just about funding uncertainty—it's about the human cost of building research programs on temporary foundations. Every PI managing multiple grants must grapple with this reality: the more successful you are at securing grants, the more people become dependent on your continued funding success.

The Portfolio Challenge: Managing Multiple Awards at the Same Time

While Keri's experience of receiving four grants in one week represents an extreme case, the more typical scenario involves managing multiple grants that hit at different times throughout the year. Each grant operates on its own timeline—one might start in January, another in July, a third in October. This staggered approach might seem easier to manage than simultaneous awards, but it creates its own unique challenges.

When grants operate on different timelines, researchers find themselves constantly and simultaneously in different phases. For example, while wrapping up Year 1 reporting for one grant, they might be in the midst of data collection for another project and just beginning to hire staff for a third. This means never getting to focus exclusively on one phase of the research process. The perpetual switching between startup mode, execution mode, and closeout mode—often multiple times within a single day—creates a cognitive burden that many researchers underestimate. The solution lies in planning and being aware that there will be different portfolio management issues when you receive multiple grants.

Kerk's Insight on Managing Multiple Awards

Kerk's journey reveals the chronic challenges of managing multiple grants over extended periods. At one of the universities where Kerk worked, he faced a unique structural challenge that compounded the usual difficulties of multi-grant management. The university's model splits PhD student appointments into ten hours of teaching and ten hours of research. This meant that even when Kerk had grant funding, students were juggling multiple responsibilities and couldn't focus exclusively on research.

The coordination challenges of managing multiple graduate students can become overwhelming when managing six externally funded projects simultaneously. Kerk found himself needing to meet a deadline for one project, so he'd focus intensely on it, but that meant other projects were essentially put on hold. Students on the non-deadline-dependent projects were not necessarily up to speed enough to be proactive and move forward without considerable direction. The challenge intensified because Kerk's projects were often topically distinct and methodologically diverse—a qualitative study here, a quantitative analysis there, a mixed-methods project in between. Students trained in one approach couldn't easily shift to help with another project when deadlines converged. The specialized skills required for each project created silos that prevented the kind of flexible resource allocation that might have eased the pressure.

The Personnel Management Crisis

Both Keri and Kerk's experiences highlight a fundamental challenge in academic grant management: the mismatch between funding structures and personnel needs. Grants assume you can hire qualified researchers quickly, but the reality is far more complex. As Kerk noted, the first semester with any new graduate student is essentially training time when they cannot be relied upon to produce meaningful research output.

This creates a cascade of problems. If you have multiple grants starting simultaneously, you need multiple new students. But training multiple students at once is exponentially more difficult than training them sequentially because you repeat the same basic training multiple times, often in rushed, less effective ways. Meanwhile, the grants' timelines are ticking, and deliverables are coming due before your team is fully functional.

Kerk's solution evolved over several years of trial and error. Rather than keeping projects siloed, he began creating opportunities for cross-project learning. He started holding monthly lab meetings where students from different projects would share what they were working on. This served multiple purposes: students learned about other projects, making it easier to shift them between projects when needed; students developed peer mentoring relationships that reduced the burden on Kerk to train everyone individually; and the meeting conversations created a sense of shared enterprise rather than isolated work.

He also became strategic about hiring, focusing on identifying motivated master's students who were interested in pursuing PhDs. By bringing them on early and training them in specific skills—interviewing techniques, qualitative analysis software, statistical methods—he could create continuity across projects. When one project needed someone with interviewing skills, for example, he could shift a trained student from another project temporarily.

The Critical Challenge of Budget Tracking Across Multiple Awards

One of the most overlooked aspects of managing multiple grants is the sheer complexity of tracking budgets across different funding sources.

As Keri discovered, this is not a problem that technology has adequately solved. Most universities lack automated tools that allow PIs to see their budget status across multiple grants in real time.

The challenge goes beyond simply knowing how much money remains in each grant. Researchers need to track specific budget categories across all their grants. For instance, do you have funds for equipment in Grant A, but not Grant B? Can you hire a student on Grant C, or have you already committed all the personnel funds? Is there travel money available for an upcoming conference, and if so, from which grant should it come?

Keri's solution—creating multiple Excel spreadsheets that she literally prints out for manual review—might seem antiquated, but it's surprisingly common. Even faculty managing seven or more externally funded projects often resort to these manual processes because institutional systems have not been designed for this level of complexity. Although the time spent maintaining these tracking systems is time not spent on research, it is absolutely essential for staying compliant with funding requirements.

The Institutional Politics of Success

An underappreciated aspect of managing multiple grants is navigating the institutional politics that success can induce. When you have multiple grants, you might need more office space for your team, priority access to shared equipment, or additional administrative support. These requests, however reasonable given your funding levels, can be seen as preferential treatment by colleagues who are struggling to secure any external funding. Concern about internal perception adds another layer of stress to an already complex situation. Managing multiple grants means not just managing the projects, but also managing how your success is perceived within your institution.

One final thought about institutional politics and interpersonal complications: these challenges are real, but they are not universal, are manageable, and they shouldn't discourage you from seeking funding. Both of us have been fortunate to have highly supportive deans, colleagues, and collaborators, and they have shared advice with us. Furthermore, the vast majority of grant-funded researchers navigate these dynamics successfully throughout their careers. Most find that the benefits of external funding, specifically, the ability to pursue research questions that matter to them, the resources to do high-quality work, and the career advancement opportunities, far outweigh the political complications. You're not entering a battlefield; you're entering a complex professional landscape where success requires both technical skills and emotional intelligence. You already have the human-centered awareness that is part of your training as a social scientist. This book provides the technical knowledge and strategic framework. Together, these capabilities position you to thrive in the grant world, politics, and all.

The Complexity of Multiple Awards with Multiple Institutions

Managing multiple grants, while challenging, can pale in comparison to the complexity of multi-institutional collaborations. When working with co-PIs and senior personnel across different institutions, you have to recognize that each institution has its own administrative processes, its own indirect cost rates, and its own hiring procedures. Therefore, what seems straightforward in a proposal—"Institution A will handle X while Institution B manages Y"—becomes a maze of inter-institutional agreements, budget transfers, and communication challenges.

The money tensions in these multi-institutional projects can be particularly acute. During the proposal stage, when everyone is optimistic about winning the grant, co-PIs often agree to budget allocations without fully knowing the nuances of how they will actually accomplish the work. They might not realize how insufficient their allocation is until they're deep into project execution. Money issues can quickly become relationship issues, especially when institutions have different cost structures, or when some partners feel they're doing more work than their budget reflects.

Kerk experienced this firsthand on a six-university collaboration where the PI wanted detailed documentation of everyone's effort. This PI expected all compensated collaborators to report their actual effort monthly, including breaking out the percentage of time spent on each task and budget category. This level of scrutiny, while understandable for such a complex project, created an enormous administrative burden and occasional tensions when some institutions appeared to be underperforming relative to their budget allocation.

The Exponential Nature of Complexity

Take a breath because we have introduced much complexity in this chapter, and the goal is not to overwhelm you. Embedded throughout this chapter are the solutions Keri and Kerk found that helped them manage the situations. By reading this book, you are already in a better position to handle the cognitive overload if you experience anything like this in your future. Keep in mind that one of the most vital insights from both Keri and Kerk's experiences is that managing multiple grants doesn't scale linearly. As Kerk discovered when managing five or six concurrent projects, the complexity increases exponentially. It's not simply that each grant adds its own set of requirements; rather, each additional grant multiplies the complexity of managing all the others.

To illustrate this point, consider meeting schedules alone. With one grant, you might have a weekly team meeting. With two grants, you have two meetings, but you also need to ensure they don't conflict. With three grants, you're not just scheduling three meetings—you're managing the conflicts among all three, plus dealing with team members who might be on multiple projects and have limited availability to meet. By the time you reach five or six grants, simply scheduling meetings can consume hours each week. Keri recalls one project where a co-PI's availability was limited to the times her team members taught: an impossible meeting scheduling challenge.

This exponential complexity extends to every aspect of grant management. Budget tracking becomes not just twice as hard with two grants but also requires managing the interactions between budgets. Personnel management involves not just hiring more people, but also coordinating their efforts across projects while maintaining strict separation of funding sources. Reporting requirements don't simply double; they also create conflicts as different agencies require different information at different times.

Strategic Solutions for Multiple Grant Management

Through years of experience, including mistakes, near-disasters, and eventual successes, we've developed strategies for managing multiple grants that go beyond simple time management and organizational tips. These approaches address the fundamental challenges of scaling research operations while maintaining quality and sanity.

Accept Reality and Seek Strategic Help

The most crucial first step when facing multiple grant awards is accepting the reality of the situation. Denial or resistance only delays the inevitable and often makes the situation worse. Once you accept that you have multiple grants to manage, you can begin developing realistic strategies rather than hoping the problem will somehow resolve itself.

Keri's experience with her associate dean for research demonstrates the value of seeking help from those who understand the system. Many faculty members try to handle everything alone, not realizing that experienced administrators have seen these situations before and can offer practical solutions. The key is finding administrators who view their role as enabling research success rather than simply enforcing rules.

Develop a Portfolio Mindset

Both of our experiences point to the importance of thinking beyond individual projects to develop what we call a "portfolio approach." Just as financial advisors recommend diversifying investments, successful grant management often means diversifying across funding sources, project timelines, and staffing models. This portfolio thinking extends to budgeting strategies. Kerk learned to work closely with his college's finance director to plan budgets a year in advance, looking across all projects to identify where he could strategically allocate resources. By seeing the big picture—knowing he'd need five graduate students across three projects in the fall, for instance—he could work with his associate dean in the prior spring to plan hiring more effectively.

Create Transparency and Shared Systems

One of Kerk's most successful innovations has been creating transparency across projects. He developed a master schedule accessible to all his students, showing each project's deadlines and milestones. Students could see when he was overwhelmed with one project's deadline and adjust their expectations accordingly. This practice also helped students understand they were part of something larger than just their individual project.

This transparency extended to resource sharing. When everything was siloed, each project suffered from inefficiencies. By creating shared resources—document templates, analysis protocols, coding schemes—that could be adapted across projects, Kerk reduced redundant work and helped students learn from each other's experiences.

A persistent challenge in managing multiple grants is the constant turnover inherent in academic research teams. Undergraduates graduate after a year or two. Graduate students complete their degrees. Postdocs move on to faculty positions. This turnover means that just as team members become fully productive, they leave, taking their institutional knowledge with them. Establishing systems can provide stabilizing forces.

Build Strong PI Relationships

When working on multi-PI grants, the quality of relationships among the leadership team often determines project success or failure. Regular, honest communication about resource needs, project challenges, and potential reallocations can prevent small issues from becoming major conflicts. We've found that the most successful multi-PI projects are those where the team culture emphasizes collaboration over territory protection. This doesn't mean avoiding difficult conversations about money or effort; rather, it means having those conversations early and constructively, focused on project success and not individual advantage.

When we have a great relationship with our teams, and we are constantly working together on a project, conversations about money are easier to initiate. You might ask a colleague if they are going to need the money allocated to them, and if not, if you can use some of it for another needed purpose in the project. However, Kerk has found that this ideal scenario doesn't always materialize. Because it's money, it can be tricky for some projects. Collaborators may enter into grant proposals thinking they won't get funded, or they may agree to budget allocations without fully understanding the implications. When projects are funded and work begins, these initial agreements can become sources of conflict.

Acknowledging and Overcoming the Hidden Challenges No One Discusses

Through our experiences, we've identified several challenges rarely discussed in grant writing workshops or institutional training sessions. Understanding these hidden difficulties can help researchers more effectively prepare for the realities of multiple-grant management. The psychological toll of juggling multiple projects with different stakeholders, each believing their project should be your top priority, creates constant tension. You're perpetually feeling like you're letting someone down, even when you're working nights and weekends to keep everything moving forward.

The equity challenges in multi-PI projects extend beyond simple budget allocations. Social scientists often have higher teaching loads than STEM colleagues, meaning more funding is needed to buy out courses so the social scientists' teaching/research load can shift giving them more time to do the research. Yet these disparities are rarely acknowledged in budget negotiations, leading to situations in which social science partners are expected to do equivalent work with fewer resources.

As we've learned, equity is complex, and effort is complex. You just need to realize when you walk into this that there are going to be times you have to advocate for yourself because other people are not going to understand what you need to be able to do your part of a project. Managing multiple grants successfully requires more than just good project management skills. It demands a fundamental shift in how we think about our research programs. We must move from thinking about individual projects to integrated portfolios, from solo endeavors to team enterprises, from reactive management to proactive system building.

Most importantly, remember that behind every successful multiple-grant researcher is a network of support: understanding administrators, flexible colleagues, dedicated students, and institutional structures that enable rather than constrain your work. Building and maintaining these relationships and learning to work within the institutional structures is just as important as writing the next winning proposal. In the end, sustainable success comes not from individual heroics but from creating systems and communities that can thrive even under the wonderful (terrible!) pressure of too much success.

Box 19.1 Tips When Feeling Overwhelmed

For those facing their own "four grants in one week" moment, we offer this perspective: the initial panic is normal, the challenges are real, but solutions exist. Accept the reality of your situation quickly, seek help from those who understand the systems, and focus on building sustainable structures rather than just surviving the immediate crisis. The skills developed managing multiple grants—strategic thinking, systematic planning, team building, and graceful juggling of competing demands—will serve throughout your career.

The compounding nature of multiple grant management—where money tensions, deadlines, hiring challenges, and accountability pressures interact to create complexity far beyond the sum of their parts—means that preparation and systematic thinking aren't just helpful; they're essential. Whether you're celebrating your first major award or managing your tenth concurrent project, understanding these dynamics can mean the difference between thriving and merely surviving in the world of externally funded research.

20

International Grant Seeking and Partnering

While we have both worked on awards funded outside the United States, we want to begin this chapter by acknowledging that pursuing grants across national boundaries introduces a level of complexity that can be daunting even for experienced researchers. If international collaboration is something you aspire to pursue, you need to understand that you're entering territory where multiple countries' politics, legal requirements, and administrative rules intersect in ways that can create unexpected challenges. Before even considering an international collaboration, you must check with your institution to determine if such partnerships are allowed and under what conditions they can proceed. The complexity isn't just administrative—it's fundamentally about navigating different academic cultures, funding structures, and research expectations while maintaining the rigor and integrity of your work.

Despite these challenges, international collaborations can offer extraordinary opportunities for intellectual growth, cultural exchange, and research impact that simply cannot be achieved through domestic partnerships alone. It provides opportunities for researchers to learn and access research populations often unobtainable without collaboration.

Understanding the International Funding Landscape

One of the most practical challenges in international collaboration involves understanding how different countries conceptualize and label research roles because differences can create confusion during proposal development and project management. For example, an associate investigator (AI), a role common in Australia, New Zealand, and England, is the same as a principal investigator (PI) in the United States. In Sweden and Scandinavia, they say project leaders, project managers, work package leaders, or named researchers—not PI. Understanding these distinctions becomes necessary when building international teams, as the titles carry different implications for responsibility, authority, and resource allocation. American researchers should invest time in learning the hierarchy and expectations associated with different role designations in their collaborators' systems to avoid misunderstandings about project leadership and decision-making authority.

In addition, researchers working in many countries have different employment structures from those found in most U.S. academic systems. Unlike the American model, where university positions are typically guaranteed and paid for by institutions, many international academic systems operate with substantial soft money components that directly affect researchers' job security. As Shiv Ganesh, an organization communication scholar who has experience working with Swedish funding explains, "In Scandinavia around 40 percent of the faculty and research job lines are guaranteed by the university. The rest of it is soft money, so they are bringing in their own salary." Collaborators outside the United States may be far more dependent on external funding than their U.S. counterparts realize; their grant may be required for their continued employment. This reality creates different pressures and expectations around funding timelines, success rates, and the urgency of proposal development that American researchers, with their guaranteed nine-month salaries, may not fully appreciate.

One of the most significant differences between the U.S. funding landscape and international opportunities lies in the breadth of research that different funding systems in different countries support. Shiv Ganesh has successfully navigated funding systems across multiple countries, including New Zealand, Sweden, and the United States. He explains, "If you look at foundations like the Royal Society of New Zealand, the Australian Research Council Grants, the Swedish Research Council Grants, or even the Canadian Research grants, they explicitly support 'blue skies research'—work that is primarily focused on knowledge development rather than immediate practical applications." Even though these countries increasingly emphasize impact and application, they often provide opportunities to advance fundamental knowledge.

International funding opportunities for social scientists can also emerge through U.S.-affiliated pathways. Some federal agencies in the United States, such as the National Science Foundation (NSF), have established partnerships with equivalent organizations in other countries. For example, the NSF has collaborated with Japan's Science and Technology Agency (JST) on joint funding initiatives: American researchers submit proposals to NSF, while their Japanese collaborators submit parallel proposals to JST. Both agencies then collaborate on the review process, creating opportunities for truly integrated international research teams.

Another pathway involves U.S. funding agencies with explicitly international missions. For example, when the Department of Defense's Minerva program was available, it exemplified an approach that funded research with global implications for U.S. military interests. These proposals, while led by U.S.-based principal investigators, often required research to be conducted in other countries with local partners serving as co-PIs or senior personnel. The execution of such projects demanded not just international collaboration but also deep cultural understanding and on-the-ground partnerships.

Cultural Bridges and Communication Challenges

The importance of cultural bridges in international collaborations cannot be overstated. Keri's work with Japanese researchers on disaster communication revealed how fundamental cultural differences shape both research practices and the very phenomena being studied. For instance, when the Japanese government issues a tsunami warning and instructs people to move to high ground, citizens comply without question. This automatic trust in governmental authority, cultivated through systematic disaster preparedness education from elementary school onward, stands in stark contrast to the skepticism and questioning of authority common in the United States and many other countries.

Hamilton Bean, an American researcher who is an expert on wireless emergency alerts, received funding to spend time in Japan. He built research relationships that served as a cultural and logistical bridge for introducing Keri to his colleagues. Six months later, there was a call for proposals issued by the JST that required the Japanese team to work with a currently funded NSF team. They contacted Keri because she had a current NSF grant, and together, they began working on a proposal. The entire proposal was written in Japanese, a language Keri couldn't read. This created a dynamic in which she had to rely entirely on colleagues to translate sections and explain commitments made in the proposal. The team received the funding, and they began successfully working together on the joint research.

However, the international research team did experience miscommunications about funding flows. While the team included funding in the proposed budget for Keri's graduate student and for Keri's travel to Japan to present their joint work, later the Japanese government couldn't support Keri's travel to Japan. The Japanese team asked Keri if NSF could support her travel, and she inquired and requested funds for her $7000 trip. But the NSF's response was clear: they hadn't reviewed or funded the proposal, so why would they provide supplementary funding?

These experiences underscore some of the communication challenges that can accompany international research projects. They can be incredibly valuable in terms of joint research, but navigating across languages, cultures, and countries adds additional layers to an already-complex external funding world. International research funding has tightened in recent years, with many countries reducing support for foreign collaborators or restricting outgoing funds for work conducted abroad. These shifts can affect travel budgets, student exchanges, and the feasibility of multi-country fieldwork, even when proposed collaboratively. Faculty pursuing international projects should monitor agency announcements closely and verify whether international components remain eligible in each new funding cycle.

Mastering Fulbright Applications: Beyond Cultural Exchange

Fellowship opportunities like the Fulbright represent a distinct category of international funding that requires a fundamentally different approach than traditional research grants. Based on his experience mentoring multiple successful Fulbright recipients—with six out of seven mentees securing awards—Shiv Ganesh has identified key elements that distinguish successful applications. First, he says, "the critical thing is, what will you do there that you cannot do otherwise?" An application needs to show how working abroad is essential to the project goals.

Researchers also need to look both ways to articulate the value of the exchange for both the United States and the country where the Fulbright work will occur. Shiv explains, "How will the exchange of knowledge or practice benefit the United States? And how will being in the other country serve as a catalyst for what's happening in that country?" Bilateral benefit—how your presence abroad will advance knowledge in the United States while simultaneously contributing to the host country's research landscape—is key. This requires moving beyond superficial statements about learning about other cultures to articulating specific, unique contributions that justify the substantial investment in your international experience.

Learning Through International Service

Serving as a reviewer for international funding agencies provides one with valuable insights into global research standards and practices. Both Keri and Kerk have reviewed proposals for various international agencies, including research chair competitions in Canada, the PRIME program in Germany, EU funding opportunities, and individual institutional reviews across multiple countries. These experiences consistently reveal that high-quality research transcends national boundaries. Good research in one country is good research in another, at least based on the research proposals in countries we've reviewed.

What varies are the processes and structures surrounding that research. For instance, European and Nordic countries often have dramatically different doctoral training models than the United States, with fewer required courses and more emphasis on independent research. Graduate students in these systems may be funded at levels comparable to U.S. assistant professors. Yet despite these structural differences, the fundamental standards for rigorous, impactful research remain remarkably consistent.

Keri's experience serving as an external dissertation referee in Norway exemplifies the richness of international academic exchange. Presenting her perspective on a dissertation's theoretical framework before an audience of seventy-five people, participating in multi-day events with dinners and extensive discussions about research quality—these experiences highlight how international engagement helps us understand that differences in process don't equate to differences in quality. They're simply variations in how different academic cultures approach the common goal of advancing knowledge.

The Reality of Volunteer Contributions

An important lesson learned from our collective experiences is that international collaborations often require volunteer contributions from one or more partners. Kerk's involvement in a proposal to the Hong Kong Research Grants Council illustrates this reality: he served as a co-PI with full knowledge that no funding would flow directly to him. What made this arrangement feel equitable was that the bulk of the funding went to data collection and participant compensation rather than to personnel support. When funding primarily supports the research itself rather than individual researchers, volunteer contributions feel more justified.

However, not all volunteer arrangements are created equal. The perception of fairness shifts dramatically if foreign collaborators are being paid while others work as volunteers. Clear communication about funding structures and expectations from the outset can prevent resentment and misunderstandings later in the collaboration.

Please realize that voluntarily committing time and resources to a project for which there is no monetary value can also constitute what some U.S. organizations consider a cost share. Cost-sharing arrangements are sometimes not allowed according to a specific funder, and in other situations, they are almost mandated. This is complicated, and before agreeing to commit any resources for no compensation, be sure to contact your institution and verify that the practice is allowable.

Legal and Administrative Complexities

International collaborations introduce legal complexities that can derail even well-intentioned partnerships. Kerk's collaboration with researchers in the Netherlands provides a cautionary tale about institutional barriers. When he attempted to share NSF-funded data with Dutch colleagues who had internal university funding to hire graduate students for analysis, both universities' legal teams engaged in months of back-and-forth negotiations about data ownership and intellectual property rights. For a social science study with no clear intellectual property implications, this legalistic wrangling represented a frustrating waste of time that delayed the actual research.

Legal complexities multiply when crossing international boundaries. Export controls, data sharing agreements, and institutional review board approvals that must satisfy multiple countries' requirements add layers of administrative burden that can exhaust research teams before they even begin collecting data. The key to pushing through these complexities is anticipating the challenges and building extra time into project timelines to accommodate institutional negotiations.

Building Sustainable International Partnerships

The timeline for international collaborations stretches far beyond domestic partnerships. While you might need a year to develop good collaborative relationships within your own country, international partnerships often require three or more years of relationship building before attempting major grant proposals. This extended timeline reflects not just logistical challenges but also the deeper work of building trust across cultural and institutional differences.

Keri's long-term collaboration with researchers at the University of Nordland (formerly Bodø University) in Norway demonstrates the benefits of sustained partnership. Beginning when she was still a graduate student, this collaboration was supported by Norwegian government funding that brought U.S. graduate students to Norway for summer research. The partnership produced multiple books and numerous papers by faculty and students in both countries while providing deep insights into cultural differences in how societies approach fundamental issues like power structures and policing.

A strategic approach that emerges from international funding landscapes involves demonstrating co-funding or in-kind contributions from multiple institutions. Drawing from his successful experience with the Mistra Environmental Communication program, a $16 million initiative over eight years, Shiv Ganesh emphasizes the importance of showing institutional investment. He was able to cobble together several smaller funding streams and in-kind time commitments from his own U.S.-based university to show the funder that broad support existed for their joint work. This approach of combining funding sources can significantly strengthen international proposals. Even when you cannot directly access funding from a foreign agency, demonstrating that your institution is investing in the collaboration through internal grants, course releases, or other support mechanisms can make your partnership more attractive to international funders; it also shows genuine institutional commitment to the collaborative relationship.

Strategic Considerations for Funding Sources

When pursuing international funding, researchers must carefully consider which funding sources align with their goals and constraints. Some opportunities, like joint NSF-JST calls, require parallel submissions and review processes but keep funding within respective national boundaries. Others, like certain European Union programs, may require partnerships from multiple EU countries—a requirement that became problematic for Kerk when Brexit removed potential UK collaborators from eligibility for Horizon 2020 funding. This type of funding requires collaborators from two EU countries (at the time this was experienced). Nurturing relationships across international borders can be challenging.

Private foundations and foreign government agencies often have their own unique requirements. The Swedish government funding that supported Shiv Ganesh's research in India while he was based in the United States represents one model. The Norwegian funding that supported long-term exchanges between U.S. and Norwegian researchers represents another. Each funding source comes with its own application procedures, eligibility requirements, and restrictions on how funds can be used.

Insights from International Funded Researchers

At the International Communication Association Conference, we convened a panel of nine distinguished scholars from Europe, Asia, and North America who had successfully secured various forms of external funding. In addition to Kerk and Keri's contributions, we would like to acknowledge their contributions to this section of the chapter: Christian Burgers, Vivian Hsueh Hua Chen, Shiv Ganesh, Kirstie McAllum, Amanda Porter, Jack Linchuan, Tien Ee Dominic Yeo. Their collective wisdom for social scientists pursuing grants revealed several universal principles that transcend national boundaries.

The panelists unanimously emphasized that grant writing requires a fundamentally different approach than academic paper writing. Rather than thinking of a grant proposal as a research paper, successful applicants must conceptualize it as a vision and a promise. This shift in perspective is key because grant reviewers are not merely evaluating past research; they also are assessing a proposal's potential for future impact and the applicant's ability to deliver on ambitious goals.

Building from existing strengths emerged as a central theme in the panel's advice. Rather than venturing into completely unfamiliar territory, successful grant writers should focus on areas where they already have established expertise and credibility. This approach allows researchers to leverage their existing knowledge base while demonstrating to reviewers that they possess the necessary background to execute the proposed work successfully.

The panel stressed the importance of building credibility throughout the entire application. This means highlighting not only your own expertise, but also that of your collaborators, citing relevant qualifications, and demonstrating how team members bring complementary skills to the project. Clear communication emerged as another critical factor—writing with clear structure, incorporating visuals, and crafting prose for an intelligent audience that may not be familiar with field-specific jargon.

Perhaps most importantly, the panelists emphasized clearly explaining why a particular funding agency should support your specific project. What makes this work urgent? Why is it a top priority? Why should they fund it now rather than later? These questions should guide the entire narrative structure of the proposal. In addition, when presenting one's methodology, specificity is essential, but it must be accompanied by clear explanations accessible to reviewers who may not be experts in your particular methodological approach.

The panel advocated for creating personalized strategies for grant writing rather than relying on generic approaches. This involves carefully analyzing evaluation criteria, highlighting key requirements, and creating organized checklists to ensure compliance with all specifications. Several panelists stressed the importance of balancing preparation with responsiveness to specific calls for proposals—having research ideas ready while remaining willing to adapt to funding agency priorities.

When reflecting on their early careers, panelists identified several key changes they would make if starting over. They universally wished they had invested more time in seeking out and reviewing successful proposals from colleagues; they wished they had finished proposals much earlier to allow time for feedback, and they wished they had better understood the critical importance of demonstrating feasibility. They also emphasized not taking rejections too personally while warning about the possibility of too much success—when researchers receive multiple grants simultaneously and struggle to manage the resulting workload.

Despite the complexity of international collaborations, certain principles remain constant across funding contexts. Whether writing for NSF, JST, the European Research Council, or a private foundation, successful proposals demonstrate rigorous research design, clear communication, and alignment between research goals and funder priorities. The rhetorical structures may vary, the specific requirements differ, but the fundamental need to balance intellectual merit with broader societal impacts appears consistently across national boundaries.

This universality suggests that the skills developed throughout this book—understanding institutional contexts, building strategic partnerships, communicating research significance to diverse audiences—transfer across international boundaries. An international graduate student in the United States who plans to return home can take these principles with them. A U.S.-based scholar moving abroad will find that while nuances differ, the fundamental questions remain the same: What is the funding landscape here? What are the rules of the game? How can I align my research interests with available opportunities?

Political Landscapes and Shifting Priorities

The political landscapes in many countries are always changing, and what gains favor in one place might lose support in another. Funding priorities shift with changes in government, economic conditions, and social concerns. These shifts aren't unique to any one country—they're a global phenomenon that all researchers must navigate. Being aware of global funding trends helps researchers identify opportunities and adapt their work to changing priorities while maintaining their core research interests.

Some developing countries may place greater emphasis on relationships and networks in funding decisions, adding another layer to the strategic considerations international collaborators must navigate. While our book extensively discusses relationship building, international contexts may require expanding one's network to include local country contacts, community leaders, and agency officials whose support proves necessary for proposal success.

Looking Forward: The Promise of International Collaboration

Despite the challenges, international collaborations offer unique opportunities for social scientists to expand their impact and deepen their understanding of global phenomena. The comparative perspectives gained through international research can fundamentally transform theoretical understanding. The relationships built through sustained collaboration create networks that support future research endeavors. The cultural competencies developed through navigating international partnerships enhance researchers' abilities to work in increasingly globalized academic environments.

For U.S.-based researchers, this book provides a window into the American funding landscape that can help international collaborators understand what their U.S. partners must navigate. For researchers in other countries, the principles discussed throughout this book—from building grant readiness to developing a multilingual scholar identity—apply regardless of geographic location. The specific agencies, requirements, and processes may differ, but the fundamental challenge remains the same: to translate excellent research ideas into fundable proposals that lead to meaningful impact.

21

Interdisciplinary Research: High Risk, High Reward

The future of scientific discovery increasingly lies at the intersections among disciplines. Major funding agencies now prioritize interdisciplinary approaches, recognizing that society's most pressing challenges, from climate change to public health crises, require perspectives that transcend traditional academic boundaries. For social scientists, this shift presents both unprecedented opportunities and significant challenges. While interdisciplinary teams offer pathways to larger grants and broader impact, they also demand navigation of complex cultural differences, power dynamics, and professional risks that can derail careers if not carefully managed.

Throughout this book, we've emphasized that interdisciplinary collaboration represents one of the strongest avenues for social scientists to secure external funding. The biggest grants increasingly go to teams that bridge multiple fields. Yet as exciting as these opportunities appear, the reality of interdisciplinary work is far more complex than most scholars anticipate. Success requires not just intellectual flexibility, but also sophisticated understanding of how different disciplines approach research, communicate findings, and value contributions.

Understanding the Spectrum: Multi-, Inter-, and Transdisciplinary Approaches

Before diving into the practicalities of interdisciplinary collaboration, we must clarify terminology that's often used interchangeably but carries distinct meanings. These differences matter because they shape expectations, workflows, and ultimately, the success of collaborative efforts. Tress and colleagues (2004) provide clarity for understanding distinctions among the terms multidisciplinary, interdisciplinary, and transdisciplinary. In this section, we summarize their explanation of these terms.

Multidisciplinary research draws on knowledge from different disciplines while maintaining clear boundaries between them. Teams might work on common problems or research questions, but each discipline examines these issues through its own lens. Researchers maintain their disciplinary identities and often publish findings separately in field-specific journals. Think of it as parallel play: everyone is in the same sandbox, but they are building their own castles.

For example, in a multidisciplinary project, a sociologist might study community responses to flooding while engineers design infrastructure solutions and economists' model financial impacts. Each contributes expertise, but the knowledge created remains largely separate. Team members might meet periodically to share findings, but integration happens primarily at the project management level rather than the intellectual level.

Interdisciplinary research involves a deeper level of integration. Approaches from different disciplines merge to create new, coherent frameworks. Rather than simply contributing disciplinary perspectives, team members actively synthesize information to develop novel ideas that couldn't emerge from any single field. This approach requires genuine intellectual integration—not just coordination of separate efforts.

Interdisciplinary teams don't just share findings; they cocreate research questions, develop hybrid methodologies, and produce outputs that speak to multiple audiences. The boundaries between contributions blur as team members learn each other's languages and adapt their approaches.

A successful interdisciplinary project on urban resilience might produce a new theoretical framework that combines engineering systems thinking with sociological theories of community adaptation.

Transdisciplinary research transcends disciplinary boundaries entirely, potentially creating new fields of study. This approach involves the deepest integration, where disciplinary identities become secondary to the collective pursuit of knowledge. Transdisciplinary work often incorporates perspectives beyond academia, including community members, practitioners, and policymakers as full partners in knowledge creation.

True transdisciplinary collaboration is rare and demanding. It requires extraordinary time commitment, institutional support, and a willingness to fundamentally rethink how knowledge is created and validated. When successful, it can spawn entirely new fields—like sustainability science or bioethics—that establish their own theories, methods, and institutional homes.

Most teams using the term "interdisciplinary" actually operate at the multidisciplinary level, with occasional forays into true interdisciplinary integration. Reaching the transdisciplinary level typically requires years of collaboration, substantial funding, and institutional structures designed to support boundary-crossing work. Throughout this chapter, we'll use "interdisciplinary" as the umbrella term while acknowledging that most collaborations exist somewhere on this spectrum.

Methodological Flexibility: Your Secret Weapon or Achilles' Heel

As the sole social scientist on many interdisciplinary teams, you'll often face an uncomfortable reality: colleagues expect you to represent the entire breadth of social science methodology. They assume you can design surveys, conduct focus groups, run experiments, analyze qualitative data, and perform statistical modeling—often within the same project. This expectation reveals both the opportunities and challenges of interdisciplinary collaboration.

The pressure to be methodologically omniscient can be overwhelming. Team members may not understand why you can't simply "run a quick survey" or "do some interviews" to answer their questions. They may not appreciate the differences between a survey and an interview schedule, nor understand why ethnographic observation requires months rather than days. Your colleagues might use terms like "qualitative" to describe anything involving humans, regardless of whether you're conducting statistical analyses or interpretive research.

This methodological pressure creates a clear message for graduate students and early-career researchers: build the broadest possible methodological toolkit you can while you have access to coursework and training opportunities. The ability to move fluidly between quantitative and qualitative approaches, to understand both inductive and deductive reasoning, and to speak intelligently about various methodological traditions becomes invaluable currency in interdisciplinary settings.

However, methodological flexibility has limits. Claiming expertise you do not possess risks both research quality and professional reputation. If your training focused exclusively on ethnographic methods, don't pretend you can design a complex experimental study. Instead, be clear about your capabilities while demonstrating willingness to collaborate with others who bring complementary skills.

The challenge intensifies when collaborators use familiar terms differently. For instance, a computer scientist announcing they're working on a "survey paper" probably isn't designing a questionnaire—instead, they're conducting a literature review. When engineering colleagues justify a within-subjects experimental design because they say, "we can't recruit that many people," you might spend multiple meetings explaining why between-subjects designs better serve the research questions, even if they require larger samples.

These linguistic differences extend to fundamental concepts. Some STEM colleagues might call any study involving human participants "qualitative," even when you're running statistical analyses. The distinction social scientists make between empirical and quantitative research might be completely foreign to collaborators who equate "empirical" with "numerical." You'll find yourself constantly translating, not just between languages, but between entirely different conceptual frameworks.

For those pursuing interdisciplinary careers, this translation work becomes a core competency. You'll need to explain why variance matters when engineers only care about binary outcomes. You'll justify why building trust with communities takes months when technical colleagues want data within weeks. You'll advocate for inductive analysis when everyone else expects predetermined categories. This constant translation can be exhausting, but it's also where social scientists add unique value to interdisciplinary teams. It is also where other team members can learn from the social scientists, and this bi-directional learning can build strong partnerships.

Publishing Cultures: Where Extended Abstracts Meet Journal Articles

The publish-or-perish mandate takes on new complexity in interdisciplinary collaborations. Different fields maintain distinct, and often incompatible, publishing cultures that can create significant challenges for career advancement. Understanding these differences early can mean the difference between productive collaboration and professional frustration.

In computer science and engineering, conference papers carry the prestige that journal articles hold in social sciences. Top-tier conferences have acceptance rates below 20 percent and undergo rigorous peer review. Yet to a tenure committee in sociology or communication, these same publications might be dismissed as "not real research." The disconnect becomes particularly painful when junior faculty invest significant time in conference papers that won't count toward tenure in their home departments.

The volume expectations differ dramatically as well. Computer scientists on large teams might publish thirty papers annually—a number that would cause ethics concerns in fields where solo or small-team authorship remains the norm. When someone at a communication conference suggests this publication rate indicates questionable research practices, they're applying disciplinary standards that don't translate across fields. Large collaborative teams can genuinely produce numerous high-quality outputs through distributed effort.

Even basic writing tools can become sources of conflict. Computer scientists often insist on using LaTeX or Overleaf, particularly for documents containing equations. For social scientists accustomed to Word's track changes and commenting features, these platforms can feel like learning a new language just to provide feedback. When you're already struggling to understand technical content, fighting with unfamiliar software adds another barrier to meaningful contribution.

The challenges compound around newer publication models. Should you post preprints? In some fields, failing to share early versions is seen as hoarding knowledge. In others, it disqualifies work from journal consideration. These aren't just technical decisions; they're cultural ones that reflect different values about knowledge sharing, peer review, and academic credibility.

Authorship conventions provide another minefield. STEM fields often position senior researchers as last authors, indicating the work emerged from their lab. Social sciences might interpret this as minimal contribution. Some fields alphabetize authors; others order by contribution. Understanding these conventions—and negotiating them explicitly—prevents misunderstandings that can damage relationships and careers.

For pre-tenured faculty, these publishing culture clashes pose serious risks. Time spent on interdisciplinary publications might not "count" for tenure, even if they represent significant intellectual contributions. Graduate students also face challenges, potentially emerging with publication records that look "scattered" to disciplinary hiring committees. The very interdisciplinary work that funding agencies celebrate can become a liability in traditional academic career paths.

The Human Subjects Divide: When IRB Becomes a Cultural Clash

One of the most fundamental challenges in interdisciplinary collaboration emerges around human subjects research and Institutional Review Board (IRB) processes. These differences aren't merely procedural; they reflect profoundly different understandings of what constitutes research, how knowledge is created, and what ethical obligations researchers hold.

Social scientists often arrive at interdisciplinary teams with what colleagues from other fields might view as an "ultra-careful" approach to human subjects research. Years of training have instilled deep respect for IRB processes, informed consent procedures, and the ethical complexities of studying human behavior. This careful approach, while essential for ethical research, can create friction when working with collaborators who have never navigated IRB requirements.

Consider the frustration of a STEM colleague who asks, "Why don't we have IRB approval yet? We need to collect this data now. What's taking so long?" For someone who's never submitted an IRB application, the weeks or months required for approval seem like unnecessary bureaucracy. They don't understand that social scientists aren't being overly cautious; they're following established ethical protocols that protect both participants and researchers. Faculty can also seek IRB approval to analyze data that were originally collected for non-research purposes, such as program administration, teaching, clinical operations, or organizational decision-making. When reviewed and approved as human subjects research, these existing datasets can become valuable sources of publishable insights without requiring new data collection. This pathway expands research opportunities, especially for early-career scholars with limited resources.

The divide goes deeper than timeline frustrations. Different fields have fundamentally different concepts of what constitutes human subjects research. Humanities scholars might collect what they call "journalistic interviews" or "historical stories"—carefully avoiding language that would necessitate IRB review. Some English Department faculty never submit to IRB because they don't view their work as contributing to generalizable knowledge, a key criterion for human subjects' research.

These definitional differences can create ethical dilemmas in interdisciplinary teams. When does a conversation with a community member become an interview requiring consent? When does observing public behavior require IRB approval? Social scientists might insist on formal protocols, while humanities colleagues rely on journalistic ethics, and STEM researchers wonder why any of these matter for their technical project.

Even among those who acknowledge the need for IRB review, disciplinary training creates different approaches. Some fields embrace "do first" cultures—jumping into experiments to test ideas quickly. Others follow "think first" approaches, carefully planning studies before collecting any data. These differences in research tempo can create significant tension when teams need to coordinate data collection efforts.

Faculty partnering with community organizations should not assume that community researchers have prior experience with human subjects protections or research ethics. Programs such as CIRTification and Research Ethics for All provide accessible, community-focused ethics training that equips partners with the knowledge needed to participate safely and confidently in research activities. Offering these resources early in the collaboration promotes ethical practice, shared understanding, and stronger, more equitable partnerships.

Finding Your Voice: The Value Social Scientists Bring to Teams

Despite the challenges, one of the most powerful contributions social scientists make on interdisciplinary teams is providing language and frameworks for phenomena that other disciplines observe but can't articulate. For example, when civil engineers discuss "design stuff," a social scientist might introduce the concept of "message design," suddenly giving the team vocabulary to discuss something they knew was important but couldn't quite name. This ability to codify implicit knowledge into explicit frameworks often produces "aha" moments that transform project directions.

Kerk's experience illustrates how this value recognition can create lasting opportunities. While Kerk was presenting at a computer science conference, his NSF program officer sat in the audience—a common occurrence in STEM fields but rarer in social science conferences. The program officer was so intrigued by how Kerk's work on innovation diffusion could enhance cyberinfrastructure projects that, after rotating back to faculty, he invited Kerk to join his NIH grant application. This story highlights both the importance of being visible in interdisciplinary spaces and the genuine interest many STEM researchers have in social science perspectives, once they understand their relevance.

Social scientists excel at identifying the human dimensions that technical solutions often overlook. We bring theories about organizational change that explain why technically superior solutions fail. We understand community dynamics that determine whether innovations spread or stagnate. We recognize power structures that shape participation and outcomes. These insights often prove crucial for project success, particularly in applied research with real-world impact goals.

The translation skills developed through social science training become invaluable assets. We're trained to communicate complex ideas to diverse audiences—from academic peers to community members to policymakers. This makes social scientists natural bridges between technical teams and stakeholder communities. While engineers might struggle to explain their work to nonspecialists, social scientists can craft narratives that make technical advances meaningful to broader audiences.

Perhaps most importantly, social scientists bring methodological perspectives that complement dominant approaches in STEM fields. Our comfort with uncertainty, appreciation for context, and understanding of social complexity provide essential counterweights to reductionist tendencies. When engineers want to simplify human behavior into binary variables, social scientists advocate for preserving the messy reality that actually determines outcomes.

Building Successful Collaborations: The Team Agreement Framework

Successful interdisciplinary collaborations don't happen by accident. They require deliberate attention to team dynamics, clear communication protocols, and explicit agreements about goals, processes, and outcomes (while a full discussion of team science is beyond the scope of this book, see these resources: Börner et al., 2010; Cooke & Hilton, 2015; Fiore, 2008; Hall et al., 2019). While STEM colleagues might view formal collaboration agreements as unnecessary bureaucracy, social scientists understand that clarifying expectations early prevents conflicts that can derail projects later.

A comprehensive collaboration agreement should address multiple dimensions of team functioning. Start with the fundamental question: What does success look like for this project as a whole? Then, crucially, ask what success looks like for individual team members. This second question often reveals critical differences. The tenure-track assistant professor needs first-authored publications in disciplinary journals. The senior engineer wants to demonstrate practical impact. The graduate student needs dissertation chapters. Acknowledging these different needs—and planning to meet them—builds trust and commitment in the research team.

Essential Elements of Collaboration Agreements

The following questions, divided into key aspects of research team activities, provide a guide for creating a successful collaboration agreement.

Decision-Making and Governance

- How will budget decisions be made?
- Who has authority over different aspects of the project?
- What happens when team members disagree?

Communication Protocols

- What platforms will we use (email, Slack, etc.)?
- How often will we meet?
- How will we handle missed meetings?
- Who takes and distributes meeting notes?
- How will we keep absent members informed?

Research Standards and Ethics

- How do we define human subjects research?
- What IRB protocols will we follow?
- How will we handle data sharing and storage?

Publication and Dissemination

- What are our authorship criteria and order?
- Where will we publish (journals vs. conferences)?
- How will we handle preprints and data sharing?
- Who speaks to media about the project?
- How do we acknowledge funders in all outputs?

Resource Allocation

- How will equipment and supplies be distributed?
- Who has access to project funds for travel?

Professional Development

- How will we support junior team members?
- What training opportunities will we provide?
- How do we ensure everyone gains the needed skills?

Intellectual Property

- Who owns work products from the project?
- How will we handle patents or commercialization?
- What happens if team members start companies?

Conflict Resolution

- What process will we follow for disputes?
- How do we protect psychological safety?

Transitions and Continuity

- What happens when members leave institutions?
- How do we handle PI succession?

Creating these agreements requires honest conversations about power dynamics, disciplinary differences, and individual needs. The process of working through these questions often surfaces assumptions and expectations that would otherwise remain hidden–until they cause conflicts, that is. While time-consuming, this up-front investment in your team prevents far greater time losses later due to miscommunication and conflict.

Interdisciplinary Dilemmas with Early-Career Scholars

For graduate students and early-career researchers, interdisciplinary research presents a particularly complex set of challenges and opportunities. The enthusiasm for boundary-crossing work—often actively encouraged by advisors and funding agencies—must be tempered with realistic understanding of career implications. The very experiences that make these scholars valuable team members can make them unmarketable in traditional academic job searches.

Consider one of our students whose dissertation focused on family communication while working on an AI chatbot grant. On the job market, this student appeared "scattered" rather than versatile. Search committees couldn't place him in a clear disciplinary category, making it difficult to evaluate his contributions or predict his future trajectory. Despite eventually securing a tenure-track position, the journey was unnecessarily difficult due to the mismatch between his interdisciplinary training and disciplinary hiring practices.

The structural differences between disciplines compound these challenges. In STEM fields, it's common for graduate students to produce three papers from interdisciplinary funded projects they work on, often coauthored with multiple team members. These papers might directly form dissertation chapters. In contrast, for their theses and dissertations, social science and humanities graduate students typically write monographs—book-length works demonstrating deep, sustained engagement with a topic. This means social science graduate students often pursue their own independent research projects for their theses and dissertations while simultaneously working on funded research projects that may be tangentially related at best.

This fundamental difference creates tension on interdisciplinary teams. A computer science student might not understand why their social science colleague can't just use project data for their dissertation. The social scientist struggles to explain that their discipline expects theoretical depth and independent contribution that collaborative project work rarely provides. These mismatched expectations can lead to resentment, with STEM students viewing social science colleagues as less committed to the project, while social scientists feel torn between conflicting demands.

Despite these possible challenges in academia, the career landscape is broad for interdisciplinary scholars. Industry positions increasingly value the boundary-crossing skills that interdisciplinary training provides. Technology companies seek researchers who can bridge technical development and user experience. Consulting firms value scholars who can integrate multiple perspectives to solve complex problems. Government agencies and NGOs need researchers who can navigate between academic knowledge and practical application. For graduate students willing to consider careers beyond traditional academia, interdisciplinary training can be a significant asset rather than a liability.

For students and early-career researchers committed to interdisciplinary paths, several strategies can help navigate these challenges. First, develop a clear narrative that explains how interdisciplinary work enhances rather than dilutes disciplinary expertise. Second, maintain strong publication records in disciplinary venues while also contributing to interdisciplinary outputs. Third, build networks in both home disciplines and interdisciplinary communities. And perhaps most importantly, have frank conversations with advisors about career implications and actively seek mentors who have successfully navigated similar paths.

Power, Politics, and Persistence: Navigating Unequal Playing Fields

Perhaps the most difficult aspect of interdisciplinary collaboration involves confronting and navigating power dynamics that favor some disciplines over others. Social scientists often enter these collaborations as outsiders—respected for their specific contributions but not seen as equals in research leadership or decision-making. This reality, while frustrating, must be acknowledged and strategically addressed rather than ignored or resented.

The power dynamics manifest in subtle and not-so-subtle ways. Budget allocations may favor equipment over personnel. Meeting times may accommodate STEM teaching schedules. Publication venues may reflect STEM preferences. Grant applications emphasize technical innovations while treating social dimensions as "broader impacts." Even well-meaning collaborators may unconsciously perpetuate these hierarchies through language choices, decision-making processes, and assumptions about expertise.

Particularly for early-career researchers, these power dynamics create challenges. Speaking up too forcefully risks being labeled "difficult" and excluded from future opportunities. Remaining silent means accepting marginalization and potentially compromising research quality. The constant emotional labor of managing these dynamics, a form of impression management, adds an invisible workload (Chawla et al., 2021) that collaborators from dominant disciplines rarely recognize or appreciate.

The situation intensifies for scholars from underrepresented groups who face intersecting marginalizations. For instance, being the only social scientist and the only person of color, or the only woman, on a team increases the felt pressure to represent multiple communities while navigating complex power dynamics. Although the emotional toll of this work can be substantial, it rarely factors into workload calculations or performance evaluations.

Successfully navigating these dynamics requires a long-term perspective. Initial collaborations might involve accepting junior roles to establish credibility and build relationships. Over time, consistent contributions and demonstrated value can shift power dynamics. The key lies in choosing battles carefully—pushing back on critical issues, while remaining flexible on less important matters.

Building alliances becomes essential. Finding even one STEM collaborator who genuinely values social science perspectives can transform team dynamics. Often the most effective advocates are those who have experienced the practical benefits of social science insights in previous projects. These allies can advocate in spaces where social scientists aren't present and validate contributions that might otherwise be dismissed.

The High Reward: Why Interdisciplinary Risk-Taking Matters

Despite challenges like cultural clashes, career risks, and power imbalances, interdisciplinary research offers rewards that can transform both individual careers and entire fields of study. When it works, the intellectual stimulation and real-world impact far exceed what any single discipline could achieve. The learning curve, while steep and sometimes exhausting, pushes researchers to continually expand their intellectual horizons. Every interdisciplinary meeting becomes a master class in different ways of thinking. Engineers teach systematic problem decomposition. Humanities scholars demonstrate the power of narrative and interpretation. Natural scientists model hypothesis-driven inquiry. Social scientists reveal the hidden human dynamics shaping technical systems. This constant cross-fertilization of ideas creates an intellectual energy that many researchers find addictive.

More importantly, interdisciplinary teams tackle problems that matter. Climate change doesn't respect disciplinary boundaries. Neither do pandemics, economic inequality, or technological disruption. The most pressing challenges facing humanity require the integrated perspectives that only interdisciplinary teams can provide. When social scientists help engineers understand why technically optimal solutions fail in practice, or when humanists help scientists grapple with ethical implications of their discoveries, real progress becomes possible.

The funding landscape increasingly rewards this boundary-crossing work. Major initiatives from NSF, NIH, and other agencies specifically target interdisciplinary collaborations. Private foundations seek integrated approaches to complex social problems. Industry partners value teams that can address both technical and human dimensions of innovation. For social scientists willing to navigate the challenges discussed in this chapter, interdisciplinary work opens doors to resources and impact opportunities that would remain closed to disciplinary researchers.

Career rewards, while slower to materialize, can be substantial. Social scientists who develop reputations as effective interdisciplinary collaborators become highly sought after. They're invited to join prestigious projects, asked to lead major initiatives, and consulted on critical decisions. The very translation skills that feel exhausting early in careers become valuable leadership assets. The ability to bridge different research cultures positions social scientists as natural integrators and project leaders.

Perhaps most rewarding is the opportunity to advance human knowledge. True interdisciplinary breakthroughs, those rare moments when different perspectives combine to reveal something genuinely new, justify all the frustration and hard work. These advances might be theoretical insights that reshape how we understand complex systems. They might be practical innovations that improve lives. They might be new methods that open previously impossible research directions. Whatever form they take, these contributions remind us why we became researchers in the first place.

Moving Forward: Strategic Approaches for Interdisciplinary Success

In sum, success in interdisciplinary research requires more than good intentions and intellectual flexibility. It demands strategic thinking about when, how, and why to engage in boundary-crossing work. The decision to pursue interdisciplinary collaborations should align with career stage, institutional context, and personal goals.

For pre-tenure faculty, the calculus is particularly complex. If your institution values interdisciplinary work in tenure decisions—and this valuation is explicit in writing, not just rhetoric—then careful engagement can enhance your career. Focus on collaborations where you can maintain disciplinary identity while contributing to broader teams. Ensure publication plans include venues recognized by your tenure committee. Be explicit with collaborators about your career needs and timeline constraints.

For post-tenure researchers, interdisciplinary work offers opportunities to expand impact and explore new intellectual territories. The security of tenure allows for greater risk-taking, but strategic thinking remains important. Consider how interdisciplinary engagement affects your graduate students' career prospects. Build collaborations incrementally, starting with small projects before committing to major initiatives. Maintain some purely disciplinary work to keep those networks and skills active.

As noted earlier, graduate students face unique considerations. While interdisciplinary experience can be invaluable, especially for industry careers, maintaining a clear disciplinary identity remains important for academic job markets. Work with advisors to develop strategies that allow interdisciplinary engagement without sacrificing disciplinary credibility. Consider how different career paths—academic, industry, government, nonprofit—value interdisciplinary skills differently.

Regardless of career stage, certain principles enhance success. Invest time in learning collaborators' languages and cultures—not to become experts, but to communicate effectively. Develop clear narratives about how interdisciplinary work enhances rather than dilutes your disciplinary contributions. Build documentation systems that capture lessons learned for future projects. Most importantly, maintain realistic expectations about timelines, outcomes, and challenges.

The future of research increasingly lies at disciplinary intersections. Funding agencies, universities, and society broadly recognize that complex problems require integrated approaches. Social scientists bring essential perspectives to these conversations—understanding of human behavior, appreciation for context and complexity, and skills in translation and integration. The challenges are real, but so are the opportunities to shape how knowledge is created and applied in the twenty-first century.

As you consider your own engagement with interdisciplinary research, remember that there's no single correct path. Some researchers thrive in constantly shifting interdisciplinary spaces. Others contribute most effectively through occasional collaborations while maintaining strong disciplinary homes. The key to success is making intentional choices based on a clear understanding of costs, benefits, and alignment with your broader career goals.

The high-risk, high-reward nature of interdisciplinary research isn't just a catchy phrase—it's a reality that demands careful consideration and strategic navigation. But for those willing to invest the time, develop the skills, and persist through the challenges, interdisciplinary collaboration offers possibilities for impact and innovation that make all the difficulties worthwhile. The future of research lies not in defending disciplinary boundaries but in strategically crossing them to address challenges that matter.

22

Building Capacity for Externally Funded Social Science

The landscape of social science research is undergoing a fundamental transformation. Across universities, departments that once focused primarily on teaching and traditional scholarship now face increasing pressure to secure external funding. This shift creates both tremendous opportunities and significant challenges for academic leaders who must navigate uncharted territory while supporting faculty success. As administrators consider how to grow their research portfolios, they must grapple with complex questions about infrastructure, culture, and resource allocation that will shape their departments for years to come.

The Reality of Unprepared Leadership

One of the most pressing challenges facing social science departments is that many administrators find themselves thrust into research leadership roles without adequate preparation. Associate deans for research, department chairs, and other college administrators often come from backgrounds where external funding played little to no role in their own academic careers. Now they're expected to grow funding portfolios and support grant-active faculty without really understanding what doing so entails.

This knowledge gap creates a cascade of misunderstandings and missed opportunities. When grant-active faculty request support that seems excessive to administrators unfamiliar with funding requirements, legitimate needs can be dismissed as "prima donna" behavior. The disconnect between what faculty need to succeed in securing and managing external funding and what administrators understand about these needs creates frustration on both sides. Faculty may feel unsupported in their efforts to bring resources to the institution, while administrators may feel that grant-seekers are making unreasonable demands.

The solution begins with acknowledging this preparation gap and actively working to close it. Administrators need opportunities to learn from colleagues at institutions with established funding cultures. They need to understand not just the mechanics of grant seeking, but also the fundamental ways that externally funded research differs from traditional academic work. This isn't about making every administrator a grant expert, but it is about ensuring they understand enough to make informed decisions and provide appropriate support.

The Interdisciplinary Imperative and Its Discontents

Perhaps nowhere is the transformation of social science research more evident than in the rise of interdisciplinary and multi-institutional collaboration. Major funding opportunities increasingly require teams that span multiple disciplines and institutions, and social scientists who want to compete for substantial grants must learn to work across traditional boundaries. A single discipline cannot typically secure a $20 million grant; such awards demand interdisciplinary, and often multi-institutional, teams that bring diverse expertise to complex societal challenges.

This interdisciplinary imperative creates numerous challenges for departments structured around traditional disciplinary lines. When faculty work on interdisciplinary teams, they gain exposure to how different colleges and departments operate, revealing stark disparities in teaching loads, salary structures, and support systems. These revelations can be demoralizing when faculty discover that colleagues in other units have significantly different—sometimes better—working conditions. Even more challenging are the evaluation implications of interdisciplinary work. Junior faculty hired into interdisciplinary positions often find themselves pulled in multiple directions, with home departments expecting traditional disciplinary publications while interdisciplinary teams produce different types of outputs. Conference proceedings publications common in computer science may not count toward tenure in social science departments. The very work that funders celebrate—boundary-crossing collaboration—may not be valued in traditional tenure evaluations.

The disparities extend to graduate student support as well. Different colleges often have different pay scales for graduate assistants, creating awkward situations when interdisciplinary projects need to hire students across units. The first time a principal investigator learns they'll need to pay graduate students different rates based on their home departments rather than their contributions to a project, it becomes clear how poorly current structures align with interdisciplinary collaboration.

The multi-institutional dimension adds yet another layer of complexity. When faculty collaborate across universities, questions arise about travel funding for planning meetings, institutional support for proposal development, and how to manage the logistics of grant submission across multiple institutions. Is the department prepared to provide travel funds for faculty to meet with collaborators at other universities to develop competitive proposals? How will they handle the administrative burden of managing subawards or serving as a subaward recipient? These practical questions often reveal gaps in institutional readiness for the realities of modern collaborative research.

The Computational Social Science Revolution

The emergence of computational social science (Matei & Kee, 2019) exemplifies both the opportunities and challenges facing social science departments. As fields such as communication, sociology, and political science increasingly value computational approaches, departments find themselves competing for talent with computer science and information schools, whose scholars often command starting packages of $50,000 to $500,000—orders of magnitude larger than traditional social science hires.

This creates a fundamental dilemma. Departments recognize that computational social scientists have the potential to secure significant external funding, but the startup costs seem astronomical compared to traditional expectations. The disparities create tensions within departments where some faculty received no startup funds, while new hires receive hundreds of thousands of dollars. Yet without competitive packages, departments cannot attract the talent needed to compete in evolving funding landscapes.

The startup package dilemma extends beyond simple dollar amounts. These packages represent investments in future funding capacity. They also signal changing expectations about what constitutes social science research. Computational approaches require different infrastructure—high-performance computing, specialized software, technical support—that many social science departments have never needed to provide. The question becomes not just whether departments can afford the higher salary packages to attract scholars, but also whether they're prepared to support the different kind of research they enable.

When departments do make investments, they also must grapple with how to communicate the rationale to existing faculty. Transparency becomes important. Linking startup packages to explicit external funding expectations provides one path forward, making clear that larger investments come with different performance expectations. This approach requires careful thought about how to structure these expectations fairly while avoiding creating destructive hierarchies within departments.

One innovative solution to address perceived inequities is the creation of "mid-career restart funds" that support existing faculty who want to take their research in new directions. These programs acknowledge that faculty who have been at the institution for years may not have had access to startup funds and could benefit from strategic investments to enhance their research potential. Such programs can help reduce resentment while building overall departmental capacity for external funding.

Cultural Barriers to Grant Success

Beyond structural and financial challenges, many social science departments face cultural barriers that impede grant success. In departments without established funding traditions, the very idea of external funding can seem foreign or even contrary to scholarly values. Some faculty view grant seeking as a distraction from "real" research, or they worry that funding requirements will compromise intellectual independence. These cultural attitudes often manifest in subtle but powerful ways. Consider the situation where a faculty member successfully buys out all their teaching for a semester using grant funds, only to have colleagues complain about the arrangement. The resentment stems partly from misunderstanding—colleagues may not realize the faculty member paid for their own release—but also from deeper cultural tensions about what constitutes appropriate faculty behavior.

Creating cultural change requires more than policy adjustments. It demands sustained effort by administrators to help faculty understand how externally funded research essentially operates as a small business within a university. Principal investigators must manage budgets, supervise staff, coordinate with multiple stakeholders, and deliver on promised outcomes—all while maintaining their teaching and service obligations. This entrepreneurial aspect of modern academic life requires different skills and creates different pressures than traditional scholarship.

Departments also must reckon with how grant activity affects traditional academic rhythms. For example, when a faculty member learns they're a finalist for a major grant, they may need to clear their schedule for intensive proposal development. But academic calendars don't pause for funding opportunities. Therefore, an academic department's inability to provide temporary relief from other ongoing obligations may result in missing transformative funding opportunities that could benefit the entire institution.

The Infrastructure Investment

Growing a department's external funding capacity requires more than cultural change; it demands concrete infrastructure investments. The dramatic difference in funding success often comes down to whether faculty have access to appropriate administrative support. Pre-award assistance with proposal development, budget preparation, and submission processes can make the difference between competitive proposals and missed opportunities. Post-award support for budget management, compliance, and reporting ensures that funded projects succeed while also positioning faculty for future funding.

Notably, many social science units lack even basic research administration support. Faculty struggle to navigate complex submission systems, interpret funding announcements, and manage budgets without assistance. The learning curve is steep, and mistakes can be costly. Institutions that provide robust research administration support see dramatic improvements in funding success rates, while those that expect faculty to manage everything independently often see capable researchers give up in frustration.

The infrastructure needs extend beyond administrative support to include physical space, technology resources, project management support, and graduate student funding models that align with grant-based research. Traditional teaching assistantship models may not provide the continuity needed for multiyear research projects. Departments need flexibility to support graduate students through research assistantships; this requires departments and universities to rethink how graduate funding is allocated and managed.

A Rising Tide Lifts All Boats: A Strategy for Inclusive Capacity Building

A promising approach to build departmental capacity for external funding involves recognizing that not all faculty need to become principal investigators on major grants. Everyone can benefit from understanding the funded research landscape. The "rising tide lifts all boats" philosophy suggests that building research capacity should benefit all faculty members, not just those actively pursuing external funding.

Such an approach begins with providing baseline training for all faculty about the principles of externally funded research. Even faculty who never plan to lead a grant can benefit from understanding concepts like pre-award and post-award phases, budget development, and project management. This knowledge helps them think more systematically about their own research, even if it remains internally funded. More importantly, it prepares them to potentially participate as coinvestigators or consultants on colleagues' grants, creating opportunities for collaboration within the department rather than forcing grant-active faculty to seek collaborators elsewhere.

Administrative leaders might consider implementing "research restart" programs that provide multiple pathways for faculty engagement with external funding. Just as universities address salary compression by providing equity adjustments, research restart funds can help faculty at different career stages and with different aspirations enhance their research capacity. Research restart fund possibilities are numerous and might take the form of small seed grants for faculty to explore new research directions or to collect preliminary data for future external proposals; support for faculty to join existing research centers or collaborate with grant-active colleagues, perhaps through summer salary or course releases; training opportunities and mentorship programs that help faculty develop grant-seeking skills at their own pace; and bridge funding that helps faculty maintain research momentum between grants or while developing new funding streams.

The key to success is creating multiple entry points that respect different faculty preferences and career trajectories while building overall departmental capacity. For instance, a senior scholar who has built a successful career without external funding might not want to suddenly become a principal investigator, but they might welcome the opportunity to contribute their expertise to a colleague's project with appropriate support and recognition.

Communicating the Value of External Funding

Administrators must actively articulate how external funding benefits the entire department or college, not just the individual investigators. This communication is essential for building buy-in and reducing resentment. The benefits may include:

- **indirect cost recovery** that supports institutional infrastructure and can fund shared resources like research computing, library acquisitions, or facility improvements that benefit all faculty;
- **graduate student funding** that allows departments to recruit and support more doctoral students, enriching the intellectual community for everyone;
- **prestige and visibility** that enhances the department's reputation, potentially making all faculty more competitive for awards, speaking invitations, and other opportunities;
- **research infrastructure** such as specialized equipment, software licenses, and datasets that can be shared across the department; and
- **reduced teaching loads** for grant-active faculty that can free up resources to offer specialized courses or provide course releases for other faculty pursuing different forms of scholarship.

One successful model involves treating major grant awards as departmental achievements, celebrating them collectively while being transparent about how the benefits flow to the broader community. Some departments have created formal policies for sharing indirect cost returns, ensuring that a portion supports departmental priorities beyond the specific funded project.

Questions for Leadership: Assessing Readiness

As departments and colleges contemplate expanding their external funding portfolios, leadership must honestly assess their readiness to support this transformation. We realize many of these suggestions will require reallocating funds to support these transformations, and that may not be possible. Even so, the following questions provide a baseline for you and your team to begin discussing how to support and grow external funding. Furthermore, when trying to recruit job candidates, considering these questions in advance can help you respond more clearly and confidently to their questions about your department's support for externally funded research. Here are some questions to guide a conversation about the current situation, and to help faculty and administrators expand their thinking about what is possible:

What percentage of our faculty currently has external funding, and what would we like that percentage to be?

- How does this vary by rank and field within our department/college?
- What is a realistic timeline for achieving our target percentage?

How do we currently weigh external funding in tenure and promotion decisions, and do these weights align with our stated expectations?

- What are we telling new hires in our departments?
- How does funding potential or track record play into startup cost packages?
- Are these expectations clearly communicated in writing to all faculty?
- How do external letter writers typically view grant activity in the various fields found in our college/department?

What pre-award and post-award support do we provide, and is it adequate for our goals?

- Do faculty know how to access available support services?
- Is support available for all types of funding (federal, foundation, industry)?
- How does our support compare to peer institutions?

How do we handle the cultural disruption that comes with different faculty having different resources and expectations?

- What communication strategies will we use to maintain transparency?
- How will we celebrate successes while maintaining collegiality?

Are we prepared to support truly interdisciplinary and multi-institutional work?

- Can we provide travel funds for collaborative proposal development?
- Will we accept alternative publication venues common in other fields?

- How will we handle the administrative complexity of multi-institutional grants?
- Is some of this support available to us at a university level?

What flexibility can we provide in teaching loads and service expectations for grant-active faculty?
- Do we have clear policies about course buyouts and their limits?
- How will we ensure departmental teaching needs are still met?
- Can we provide temporary relief during intensive proposal periods?

How can we handle disparities in graduate student funding across disciplines and projects?
- Should we standardize rates across the department/college/university or accept differences?
- Can we create supplemental support to reduce inequities?

Do we have access to flexible funding to help faculty bridge between grants or pursue new opportunities?
- What is our strategy for supporting faculty between funding cycles?
- Can we provide seed funding for high-risk, high-reward ideas?

How will we recognize and celebrate grant successes while maintaining collegiality with faculty who pursue different scholarly paths?
- What's our communication plan for major grant awards?
- How do we value different types of scholarly contributions?
- Can we create inclusive definitions of research success?

Are we willing to make the multiyear investments required to build sustainable funding capacity?
- What support can we access (through the university, or external consultants) to support faculty in their external funding journeys?
- Are we prepared for the reality that building capacity may take three to seven years and will vary depending on the faculty's background, experience, and discipline?
- What interim milestones will we use to assess progress while supporting this growth?
- How will we maintain commitment through leadership transitions?

Facilitating Success, Not Creating Punishment

A critical principle in building departmental capacity is ensuring that pursuing external funding feels like an opportunity rather than a punishment. Too often, motivated faculty—whether new hires or existing faculty trying to expand their research—find that seeking grants creates more burdens than benefits. They face skepticism from colleagues, inadequate administrative support, and institutional barriers that make grant-seeking feel like swimming upstream.

To prevent this dynamic, departments must create conditions where grant-seeking faculty feel supported rather than isolated. This includes providing adequate administrative support so faculty aren't drowning in paperwork, ensuring fair teaching loads that acknowledge the time demands of grant management and community-engaged research, creating collaborative cultures where success is celebrated collectively, and offering mentorship and training to build skills progressively. The goal should be to make external funding an attractive option that enhances faculty careers rather than complicating them. When faculty see colleagues successfully managing grants while maintaining work-life balance and scholarly productivity, they're more likely to consider grant-seeking themselves.

The Path Forward

The transformation of social science into a more externally funded enterprise is already underway at many institutions. The question is not whether to adapt, but how to do so—both thoughtfully and strategically. This transformation requires an honest assessment of current capabilities, strategic investment in infrastructure and support, and sustained commitment to cultural change.

Most importantly, the transformation requires recognizing that building funding capacity is a multi-generational project. The changes implemented today may not yield full benefits for years, but they create the foundation for future success. Graduate students trained in grant-seeking skills become faculty who naturally integrate external funding into their research. Junior faculty supported in their early grant efforts become senior researchers who can lead major initiatives. Departments that invest in infrastructure today position themselves for opportunities that don't yet exist.

The conversations about these challenges are happening across disciplines—from urban planning to architecture, from schools of information to sociology. While no single solution fits all contexts, the principles of inclusive capacity building, strategic infrastructure investment, and cultural transformation provide a framework for progress.

The questions raised in this chapter don't have simple answers. Each institution must chart its own course based on its mission, resources, and aspirations. But by engaging seriously with these questions—by honestly assessing readiness and systematically building capacity—social science and humanities departments and colleges can position themselves to thrive in an evolving research landscape.

The opportunity is significant. External funding enables social scientists to pursue research at scales previously impossible, to engage with communities in meaningful ways, and to contribute solutions to society's most pressing challenges. By adopting a "rising tide lifts all boats" approach, departments can build capacity that benefits everyone while avoiding the destructive dynamics that sometimes accompany change. The departments and colleges that successfully navigate this transformation will not only secure resources but also fundamentally expand what social science can accomplish. The question is, are we ready to seize this opportunity?

Conclusion: Your Research Journey Forward

You've made it through all twenty-two chapters. You've read about preparedness suitcases and multilingual scholars, navigated the complexities of budgets and broader impacts, and learned about building labs and managing multiple awards. You've encountered our mistakes, our surprises, and our hard-won insights. Now, as we close this book, we want to leave you with some final thoughts about what this all means for your journey forward.

You're Smarter Now

Let's start with a simple but powerful truth: you now know things that most people around you do not know. Whether you are a graduate student, early-career scholar, mid-career or senior faculty member, or research administrator, you've gained knowledge that fundamentally changes your understanding of academic research funding. You understand the hidden infrastructure of grant seeking. You recognize the different roles you can play. You know questions to ask that you didn't even know existed before opening this book.

This knowledge is power. It's the power to make informed decisions about your career trajectory, to evaluate opportunities critically rather than reactively, to set boundaries strategically while keeping doors open for the future, to say yes with clarity about what you're committing to, or to say no while understanding what you're declining. You may not yet have secured your first grant, or perhaps you're a seasoned PI reflecting on your practice. Either way, you're now equipped with a mental framework that lets you navigate the funding landscape with confidence. That confidence does not mean you will never feel uncertain or overwhelmed—we still do—but it means you will know where to start when those feelings arise.

A Completely New Realm of Possibilities

Throughout this book, we've been honest about something important: most of us were not trained to see external funding as part of our academic identities. We were socialized into a vision of faculty life centered on teaching, publishing in journals, and service. Grant seeking was not in the picture. If we heard about it at all, it seemed like something mysterious that other people did—STEM researchers, perhaps, or those rare social scientists who operated in a different academic universe.

What we've learned through our combined thirty-five years of experience is that external funding opens up a realm of possibilities we never imagined. Just because something has not been done before does not mean it's not possible. External funding has enabled multi-university collaborations, sustained partnerships with community organizations, graduate student training at scales that would not have been achievable otherwise, and research requiring substantial resources for participant compensation or data collection.

We're not suggesting everyone should pursue this path. We're suggesting you now understand it's an option, a possible vision of your academic future you may not have seriously considered before. That vision might excite you, intimidate you, or leave you indifferent. All those responses are valid. The point is that you can now make an informed choice rather than defaulting to a particular path because you did not know alternatives existed.

The Funding Landscape Is Always Changing

It is important to remember the funding landscape is shifting around the globe, and not always in predictable or comfortable directions. Political priorities change. Federal budgets fluctuate. What is valued in one administration may be defunded in the next. International collaborations that once seemed straightforward become complicated by geopolitical tensions. State funding evaporates during economic downturns. Private foundations shift their focus areas.

This isn't meant to discourage you. It's meant to prepare you for reality. Your goal isn't to find some mythical stable funding source that will support your work forever; it's to develop the adaptive capacity to recognize opportunities as they emerge and pivot when circumstances change. Think of it like climate adaptation rather than climate control. You cannot control what funding agencies prioritize or how political winds shift. You can develop the flexibility to thrive across different conditions. You can build diverse funding portfolios that buffer against sudden changes in any single source. You can maintain research agendas broad enough to align with multiple funding priorities while still remaining true to your core intellectual interests.

The strategic framework we've provided throughout this book—the preparedness suitcase, the multilingual scholar mindset, the relationship-building approaches—these equip you to navigate whatever changes come next.

Revisiting the "Selling Out" Myth

Back in Chapter 3, we talked about the myth of selling out: the belief that pursuing external funding somehow compromises your intellectual integrity or makes you less of a pure scholar. Now, having read through the entire book, we hope you can see why this myth does not hold up under scrutiny.

External funding often enables a different type of scholarship. With resources, you can compensate community partners fairly for their time and expertise, pay participants appropriately rather than exploiting their labor, hire graduate students and postdocs to create training opportunities, purchase proper equipment or access necessary datasets, conduct research at scales that actually matter for addressing real-world problems, build sustained partnerships with communities rather than extractive one-time studies, and support the time needed for truly rigorous data collection and analysis. Sometimes, the most ethical choice is to seek funding because it allows you to conduct research that respects everyone involved.

We especially hope this book has expanded and included the range of scholars who feel their meaningful research agendas can be positioned for funding. We need a diverse set of scholars to get a seat at the table to influence the direction of projects. Perspectives on power structures, equity, and systemic change are precisely what some funding agencies are seeking. At the same time, seeking funding does mean entering into relationships with sponsors who have expectations about how their money will be used. It means agreeing to report your results and be accountable for the resources you've received. These aren't necessarily compromises to your integrity; they can be markers of it. Accountability is not the opposite of independence; it's the price of being entrusted with resources to advance knowledge.

Another layer of the selling out concern relates to losing your identity as a scholar. But as we discussed with the multilingual scholar concept, you're not losing your identity when you learn to translate your work for different audiences. You're expanding your capacity while remaining grounded in your expertise. You're advocating for what your discipline brings to the table. You're being a champion for your field's contributions rather than selling it out.

External Funding Is Not Always the Right Choice

Here's something else we want to emphasize as we close: if you decide external funding isn't the right path for you, we genuinely hope you've still gotten value from this book. Understanding the funding landscape can benefit you even if you never write a proposal.

You might decide that your institution does not provide adequate support to make grant seeking feasible. You might determine that your research agenda genuinely does not align well with available funding priorities. You might conclude that your teaching and service commitments, combined with publishing goals, leave insufficient time for grant development. You might recognize that the post-award management burden would detract too much from the aspects of academic work you find most fulfilling. These are all legitimate reasons to step back from grant seeking.

Even if you choose not to pursue grants yourself, understanding this landscape benefits you. You can support colleagues who do seek funding, understand the pressures they face, serve effectively on review panels if those opportunities arise, mentor graduate students who may want to pursue funding in their careers, participate strategically in collaborative projects when invited, understand institutional politics around indirect costs and overhead, and make informed decisions about career moves to institutions that better match your goals.

Individual Investigator vs. Multi-Team Projects

As you think about your future with funding, recognize a fundamental distinction: some awards are designed for individual investigators working independently or with a small team, while others require substantial multi-investigator collaborations. Individual investigator awards—like NSF CAREER grants, many foundation awards, or dissertation grants—center on your vision and your research agenda. You maintain primary control over project direction.

Multi-investigator projects—like large center grants, training grants, or complex interdisciplinary initiatives—are fundamentally different beasts. Success requires navigating complex team dynamics and power structures, balancing multiple investigators' interests and priorities, coordinating across institutions, departments, or even countries, and managing larger budgets and more complicated administrative requirements. Neither type is inherently better than the other. They suit different research questions, different personal strengths, and different career stages. As you move forward, be thoughtful about which types of funding align with your research interests, your collaborative preferences, and your career goals.

What Kind of Suitcase Do You Need?

Remember the preparedness suitcase metaphor from Chapter 2? As we close, we want to return to this image and ask you to think concretely about what you need to pack.

As you finish this book, go back through the chapters and identify which ones are most relevant to you right now. Actually, mark them with stars, highlights, folded page corners, whatever system works for you. These are your immediate priorities, the contents of your current suitcase. Then identify chapters that might become relevant in a few years as your experience level changes or your career stage shifts. Graduate students might start Chapter 12 now while flagging Chapter 9 about tenure-track challenges for later. Assistant professors might focus on Chapters 9 and 10 while noting that Chapter 11 on building centers might become relevant if they get tapped for leadership roles. Treat this book as a reference you return to at different stages rather than something you read once and shelve forever. The preparedness suitcase you need as a graduate student differs dramatically from what you will need as a mid-career PI managing multiple awards.

A Few More Reminders

As you move forward in your funding journey, keep these points in mind. Regardless of career stage, figuring out where and how much time you want to contribute to any funding proposal and post-award project is crucial. Be strategic about explaining to people the kinds of roles you want to play and the amount of time you have to contribute. But remember that setting rigid boundaries in initial exploratory conversations is different from setting strategic boundaries once you understand what's being asked of you. Some universities offer substantial internal funding opportunities. Getting on teams working on these internally funded projects is an ideal place to learn who you work well with and who you want to pursue external funding with. Don't bypass these mechanisms in pursuit of more prestigious external grants.

Early in your career, you're figuring out what sustainable grant-seeking practices look like for you. This balance will shift throughout your career as your responsibilities and interests evolve. Stay flexible and keep reassessing. New deans arrive. Administrators shift priorities. Funding agencies modify their programs. State budgets fluctuate. The rules around external funding can change with little warning. Build adaptability into your strategies rather than assuming current conditions will persist indefinitely.

The Future You Haven't Imagined Yet

Some scholars are currently pursuing scenarios that seemed unimaginable just a few years ago—getting multiple universities to co-fund joint appointments, running institutes at multiple institutions simultaneously, creating entirely new models for collaborative research infrastructure. These aren't standard career paths. There are no templates. But understanding the funding landscape, building strategic relationships, and developing the confidence to propose unconventional arrangements makes even unprecedented possibilities feel achievable. Whatever path you choose, you now have knowledge that expands your choices. You understand what's possible. You know questions to ask. You recognize opportunities when they arise. You can make informed decisions rather than defaulting to limited visions of what an academic career can be.

Throughout this book, we've maintained something we think is fairly unusual in academic writing: brutal honesty about our mistakes, surprises, and learning curves. We've shared stories about misreading deadlines, navigating difficult collaborations, making strategic missteps, and confronting institutional barriers. We did this intentionally. The grant-seeking world has been too shrouded in mystery for too long, with successful scholars keeping their strategies close to the vest and early-career researchers left to figure things out through painful trial and error.

Our genuine hope is that you're not caught as off guard as we were. We want you to walk into collaborative meetings better prepared to navigate team dynamics. We want you to understand institutional constraints before you commit to awards you cannot realistically manage. We want you to recognize when you're being taken advantage of in last-minute invitations versus when you're being offered genuine opportunities. **If something you learned in this book prepares you for a future you haven't imagined yet, if it helps you recognize and seize an opportunity that wouldn't have been visible to you otherwise, then we'll consider this book a success.**

The Bottom Line Up Front

Here's what we want you to take away from this entire book. You're smarter now. You have knowledge that most people around you don't have. Use it strategically. A realm of possibilities exists that you may not have known about before. External funding can open doors to research and collaborations that would be impossible otherwise—if that's what you want. The funding landscape is always changing. Develop adaptive capacity rather than seeking stability that does not exist. External funding is not selling out. It's often the most ethical way to conduct rigorous, community-engaged research. But it's also not right for everyone.

Show up strategically to collaborative opportunities. Plant seeds instead of closing doors. Set boundaries when needed, but understand the difference between strategic boundary-setting and premature self-limitation. Different types of funding suit different temperaments. Individual investigator awards and large multi-team projects require different skills. Be honest about what aligns with your strengths and interests. Create your own path through this book. Identify what's relevant now and what might become relevant later.

Looking Forward

The funding landscape for social scientists is complex, sometimes frustrating, often surprising, and full of potential. You're entering this space with knowledge that took us decades to accumulate through trial and error. You understand institutional structures that remained mysterious to us for years. You've seen our mistakes laid bare so you can avoid repeating them.

Whether you write one small internal grant or build a career around major federal awards, whether you become a PI or prefer supporting roles, whether you pursue funding aggressively or selectively, you're now equipped to make these choices strategically rather than stumbling into them unprepared. The social sciences have been underfunded relative to STEM fields for too long, partly because we haven't had the cultural infrastructure to socialize new scholars into funding-seeking practices. By reading this book, you're joining a community of social scientists who understand that external funding isn't some mysterious realm reserved for others—it's a set of practices we can learn, strategies we can master, and opportunities we can pursue when they align with our goals.

We're leveling the playing field. We're democratizing knowledge that's been too closely held. We're building the infrastructure interdisciplinary scholars need to thrive in an increasingly competitive funding environment. We'd love to hear about your successes—and your challenges. We'd be excited to learn that something in this book prepared you for an opportunity you seized, a collaboration you built, or a research program you developed.

The road ahead is yours to navigate. You have the map. You understand the terrain. You know what to pack in your suitcase. Now it's time to decide where you want to go. We're not promising it will be easy. We're promising you won't be surprised by the same things that surprised us. And honestly? That might make all the difference. Welcome to the journey. We're glad you're here.

Appendix A: Definitions

Term	Definition
Award Notice (or Notice of Award)	The official document from a funding agency informing the PI that their grant has been approved for funding. This initiates the post-award phase and includes the project period, funding amount, and any special conditions.
Award Period (Project Period vs. Budget Period)	Project Period: The total approved timeframe for completing all project activities. Budget Period: Individual segments (usually annual) within the total project period for which funds are allocated.
Biosketch or biographic sketch	A specialized academic CV format required by funding agencies like NIH and NSF. Other agencies, foundations, and corporate funders may call these qualification documents by other terms such as resume, CV, or investigator summary.
Broader Impacts	The potential of research to benefit society and contribute to specific desired societal outcomes. This is a specific requirement for National Science Foundation grants, and many other grants refer to this concept using different terms.
Budget Justification	A detailed explanation of why each cost in a grant budget is necessary.
Budget Period	A specific year or timeframe within the overall project period.
Community Engagement	The process of working collaboratively with community groups as part of funded research.
Competing Renewal	A new proposal to continue a previously funded project.
Conflict of Interest	Any personal or financial interest that could influence research or grant activities.
Continuation Funding	Additional years of support dependent on satisfactory progress.
Coinvestigator	A senior member of the key personnel team who shares in the administrative, fiscal, and scientific leadership of the project.

Term	Definition
Co-PI (Co-Principal Investigator)	A researcher sharing leadership responsibilities with the PI on a grant. There are often limits to the number of co-PIs who can be on a specific proposal, so always check the detailed guidelines.
Cost Share	The portion of project costs not covered by the grant but contributed by the institution. On some grants, these are explicitly required and on others, they are not allowed. Read the guidelines carefully.
Course Buyout (or Teaching Release)	Funding used to release faculty from teaching obligations so they can dedicate time to grant-funded research activities. Costs typically include replacement instructor salary or proportional faculty salary coverage.
Deliverables	Specific outputs or products promised in a grant proposal.
Direct Costs	Project expenses that can be specifically identified with a particular project.
Dissemination Plan	Strategy for sharing research findings with academic and public audiences.
Equipment Costs	Expenses for durable items costing over a specific threshold (often $5000).
Escalation Factor	Anticipated annual increases built into multiyear budgets to account for salary raises, inflation, and other predictable cost increases over the project period.
Facilities and Administrative Costs (F&A)	Another term for indirect costs or institutional overhead. This is often a set percentage that changes periodically. There is often a federal indirect cost rate, a state rate, and an industry partner rate.
Fringe Benefits	Employment costs beyond salary that employers pay, including health insurance, retirement contributions, social security, and unemployment insurance. Typically ranges from 18 to 39 percent of salary depending on employee category and institution.
Full-Time Equivalent (FTE)	The percentage of time a person will dedicate to a grant-funded project.
Funding Line (or Pay Line)	The score or percentile cutoff that determines which proposals receive funding. Proposals scoring above the line are typically funded; those below are declined.

Term	Definition
Grant Calendar	Timeline of submission deadlines and post-award reporting requirements.
Grant Mechanism	The specific type of grant program and its associated requirements.
Human Subjects Research	Studies involving people, requiring specific approvals and protections.
Indirect Costs	Institutional overhead charges on grants, covering facilities and administrative expenses.
In-Kind Contribution	Nonmonetary contributions to a project, such as equipment or facility use. On some grants, these are explicitly required and on others, they are not allowed. Read the guidelines carefully.
Institutional Review Board (IRB)	Committee that reviews research involving human subjects.
Intellectual Merit	One of NSF's two primary review criteria, focusing on the potential to advance knowledge and understanding within a field or across fields. Other agencies may use different terminology for similar concepts.
Internal Funding	Grant opportunities available within one's own institution, typically ranging from small amounts to $50,000, used for preliminary research, pilot studies, or professional development.
Just-in-Time Information	Additional documentation required only if a grant is likely to be funded.
Letter of Collaboration	A formal agreement between researchers or institutions to work together on a grant.
Letter of Intent (LOI)	A brief preliminary proposal submitted to gauge funder interest before developing a full application. May be required or optional depending on the funding opportunity.
Letter of Support	A document from stakeholders indicating their commitment to assist with the project.
Merit Review (or Scientific Review)	The formal evaluation process used by funding agencies to assess proposals, typically involving multiple reviewers and specific scoring criteria.
Mixed Methods	Research combining qualitative and quantitative approaches.
Multiple PI	A grant structure allowing several researchers to share PI responsibilities.

Term	Definition
No-Cost Extension	Additional time granted to complete project activities without extra funding.
ORCID (Open Research and Contributor ID)	A free, unique, persistent identifier for researchers that helps distinguish you from other researchers with similar names and reliably connects you to your research activities and outputs. It is a sixteen-digit number that stays with you throughout your career. It is increasingly used or required by agencies and other types of funders. Tools like SciENcv can import data from your ORCID profile and some peer review systems use this as well.
Overhead (see F&A Costs)	Common informal term for indirect costs; institutions prefer "F&A" or "indirect costs" as more accurate terminology.
Participant Support Costs	Funds for research subjects, workshop attendees, or training participants.
Peer Review	The evaluation process where experts in the field assess grant proposals (or any form of publication) based on scientific merit, feasibility, and alignment with funding priorities.
Per Diem	Daily allowances for meals and incidental expenses during grant-related travel, often set at standard federal or institutional rates regardless of actual spending.
PI (Principal Investigator)	The lead researcher responsible for the preparation, conduct, and administration of a research grant.
Pilot Data (or Preliminary Data)	Initial research findings gathered to demonstrate project feasibility and support larger external proposals. Often generated through internal funding and considered critical evidence for reviewers assessing project viability.
Post-award	Activities related to executing and managing a grant after funding is received.
Post-Award Administrator (or Post-Award Office)	Staff who help PIs manage active grants, including budget monitoring, compliance, reporting requirements, and rebudgeting after awards are received.
Pre-award	Activities related to identifying funding opportunities, supporting grant writing, and budget preparation.

Term	Definition
Pre-Award Administrator (or Pre-Award Office)	Staff who support faculty in identifying funding opportunities, developing proposals, preparing budgets, and submitting applications before awards are made.
Program Income	Revenue generated by grant-funded activities.
Program Officer	A funding agency representative who manages grant programs and serves as primary contact.
Progress Report	Regular updates required by funders on project activities and achievements.
Project Period	The total time for which project funding is approved.
Publication Costs	Budget allocation for publishing research findings.
Rebudgeting	The process of modifying how grant funds are allocated to different budget categories after the award is made.
Red Team Review	An independent review of a grant proposal before submission to identify weaknesses.
Research Administrator (or Sponsored Programs Officer)	General term for institutional staff who support grant activities, potentially encompassing both pre-award and post-award functions depending on institutional structure.
Responsible Conduct of Research (RCR) Training	Training often required (above and beyond what is needed for Human Subjects Research Training) that covers topics such as conflicts of interest, authorship, data availability, and open access.
Review Panel/Study Section	A group of experts who evaluate grant proposals and make funding recommendations.
RFP (Request for Proposals)	A document outlining what should be included in a grant application.
SciENcv (Science Experts Network Curriculum Vitae)	A free online tool that helps researchers prepare biosketches and other biographical documents in the formats required for some grant applications. It can also pull information from other systems like ORCID.
Seed Grant (or Pilot Grant)	Small internal or external funding awards designed to generate preliminary data or test research ideas before pursuing larger external grants.
Senior Personnel	Individuals who contribute significantly to the project but have lesser responsibilities than PIs or co-PIs.

Term	Definition
Single/Sole PI	A grant structure where one researcher serves as the sole principal investigator.
Soft Pitch	An initial, informal proposal to gauge a funder's interest before developing a full application.
Solicitation	A formal announcement of grant funding availability with submission requirements.
Spend Rate	The pace at which grant funds are used over the project period.
Subaward	A portion of grant funds allocated to another institution to complete part of the project.
Summary Statement (or Review Summary)	Written feedback from reviewers explaining the strengths and weaknesses of a proposal and the rationale for funding decisions.
Summer Salary	Compensation for faculty during months not covered by their standard nine-month academic contract, allowing them to dedicate summer months to research activities.
Supplement (or Supplemental Funding)	Additional funds awarded to expand an existing grant's scope, often for specific purposes like undergraduate research experiences (REU), equipment, or international collaboration.
Supplemental Funding	Additional money awarded to an existing grant for expanded work.
Team Science	Collaborative research involving multiple disciplines or expertise areas.
White Paper (or Concept Paper)	A short document (typically two to five pages, single-spaced) outlining a research idea, used to approach program officers or funders to assess interest before investing time in a full proposal.
Work Plan	Detailed timeline and methodology for completing proposed research activities.

Appendix B: Additional Resources

While there are many grant-writing resources, these are some of the ones we have used in our own learning process:

Funding Your Research in the Humanities and Social Sciences: A Practice Guide to Grant and Fellowship Proposals by Barbara L. E. Walker and Holly E. Unruh, Routledge, 2018.

Handbook for Planning and Writing Successful Grant Proposals by M. S. (Peg) Atkisson. https://www.atkissontraininggroup.com/handbook

On the Art of Writing Proposals: Some Candid Suggestions for Applicants to Social Science Research Council Competitions by Adam Przeworski and Frank Salomon, 1995.

The Craft of Research, Fourth Edition, by Wayne C. Booth, Gregory G. Colomb, Joseph M. Williams, Joseph Bizup, and William T. Fitzgerald, University of Chicago Press, 2024. https://press.uchicago.edu/ucp/books/book/chicago/C/bo215874008.html

The Grant Application Writer's Workbook, available from Grant Writers' Seminars & Workshops. https://www.grantcentral.com/ We have both attended their workshops specifically focused on writing for NSF and NIH.

The Grant Writing Guide: A Road Map for Scholars by Betty Lai, Princeton University Press, 2023. https://press.princeton.edu/books/paperback/9780691231884/the-grant-writing-guide

References

Birt, L., Scott, S., Cavers, D., Campbell, C., & Walter, F. (2016). Member-checking: A tool to enhance trustworthiness or merely a nod to validation? *Qualitative Health Research, 26*(13), 1802–1811. doi:10.1177/1049732316654870

Börner, K., Contractor, N., Falk-Krzesinski, H. J., Fiore, S. M., Hall, K. L., Keyton, J., Spring, B., Stokols, D., Trochim, W., & Uzzi, B. (2010). A multi-level systems perspective for the science of team science. *Science Translational Medicine, 2*(49).

Boulmetis, J. (2025). *The ABCs of evaluation: Timeless techniques for program and project managers*, 4th Edition. Wiley.

Brewer, M. B. (1999). The psychology of prejudice: Ingroup Love and Outgroup hate. *Journal of Social Issues, 55*(3), 429–444. https://doi.org/10.1111/0022-4537.00126

Buyalskaya, A., Gallo, M., & Camerer, C. F. (2021). The golden age of social science. *Proceeding of the National Academies of Science U.S.A., 118*(5), e2002923118. https://doi.org/10.1073/pnas.2002923118 (2021).

Campion, L. L. (2020). Leading through the enrollment cliff of 2026 (Part I). *TechTrends, 64*, 542–544. https://doi.org/10.1007/s11528-020-00492-6

Campion, L. L. (2022). Leading through the enrollment cliff of 2026 (Part II). *TechTrends, 64*, 112–113. https://doi.org/10.1007/s11528-021-00688-4

Chawla, N., Gabriel, A. S., Rosen, C. C., Evans, J. B., Koopman, J., Hochwarter, W. A., Palmer, J. C., & Jordan, S. L. (2021). A person-centered view of impression management, inauthenticity, and employee behavior. *Personnel Psychology, 74*(4), 657–691. https://doi.org/10.1111/peps.12437

CITI Training (n.d.). The trusted standard in research, ethics, compliance, and safety training. https://about.citiprogram.org/

Cooke, N. J., & Hilton, M. L. (2015). *Enhancing the effectiveness of team science*. The National Academies Press.

Covey, S. R. (2020). *The 7 habits of highly effective people*. Simon & Schuster.

Dalmeijer, K., Robinson, T., Cambridge, D., et al. (April 6, 2026). Project managers facilitate interdisciplinary collaboration in AI research. Available at SSRN: https://ssrn.com/abstract=6361038

Fiore, S. M. (2008). Interdisciplinarity as teamwork. *Small Group Research, 39*(3), 251–277.

Funnell, S. C., & Rogers, P. J. (2011). *Purposeful program theory: Effective use of theories of change and logic models.* Jossey-Bass

Gaillard, J. C., & Peek, L. (2019). Disaster-zone research needs a code of conduct. *Nature, 575*, 440–442. https://doi.org/10.1038/d41586-019-03534-z

Gaudry, A. J. (2011). Insurgent research. *Wicazo Sa Review, 26*(1), 113–136. https://doi.org/10.5749/wicazosareview.26.1.0113

Hall, K. L., Vogel, A. L., & Croyle, R. T. (2019). *Strategies for team science success.* Springer International Publishing.

Hughes, A., Stephens, K. K., Peterson, S., Purohit, H., Harris, A. G., Senarath, Y., Jarvis, S. A., Montagnolo, C. E., & Nader, K. (2022). Human-AI teaming for COVID-19 response: A practice & research collaboration case study. Proceedings of the 19th International ISCRAM Conference, Tarbes, France. http://idl.iscram.org/files/amandahughes/2022/2470_AmandaHughes_etal2022.pdf

Lentz, P., Rentz, K., & Getchell, K. (2025). *Business communication: A problem-solving approach.* McGraw-Hill.

Lin, L. (2025, July 18). *Duke School of Medicine plans salary cuts for tenured faculty who do not meet grant expectations.* The Chronicle. https://www.dukechronicle.com/article/2025/07/duke-university-school-of-medicine-implements-faculty-productivity-guidelines-external-grant-funding-requirements-salary-reductions

Matei, S. A., & Kee, K. F. (2019). Computational communication research. *WIREs: Data Mining and Knowledge Discovery, 9*(4), e1304. https://doi.org/10.1002/widm.1304

Moody, J. (2025, July 1). *Layoffs, budget cuts pile up in June.* Inside Higher Ed. https://www.insidehighered.com/news/business/cost-cutting/2025/07/01/layoffs-budget-cuts-colleges-pile-june

Natural Hazard Center. (n.d.). *Our vision and mission.* Retrieved from: https://hazards.colorado.edu/about/history-and-mission

Peña, C., Moore, A. R., & Botham, C. M. (2023). Most scientists don't enjoy writing grants. Here's how to change that. *Nature, 624*, 165–166. https://doi.org/10.1038/d41586-023-03871-0

Peterson, S., Stephens, K. K., Purohit, H., & Hughes, A. (2019). When official systems overload: A framework for finding social media calls for help during evacuations. In Z. Franco, J. J. González, & J. H. Canós, (Eds.), Proceedings of the 16th International ISCRAM Conference.

Valencia, Spain, May. http://idl.iscram.org/files/stevepeterson/2019/1928_StevePeterson_etal2019.pdf

Rapaport, O., Crest, J., & Botham, C. (2022). How to gain a competitive edge in grant writing. *Nature*, *609*(7925), 165–166. https://doi.org/10.1038/d41586-022-02958-4

Satcher, D. (2005). *Methods in community-based participatory research for health*. Wiley.

Shirky, C. (2008). *Here comes everybody: The power of organizing without organizations*. Penguin.

Sohn, E. (2020). Secrets to writing a winning grant. *Nature*, *577*(7788), 133–135. https://doi.org/10.1038/d41586-019-03914-5

Stephens, K. K., & Boettner, W. (2020, April). Collaborating our way to a successful community-wide wildfire drill in Texas. *Fire Magazine*, 38–39. United Kingdom.

Stephens, K. K., Powers, C. J., Robertson, B. W., Spearing, L. A., Collier, J. C., Tich, K. P., & Smith, W. R. (2023). Building more resilient communities with a wildfire preparedness drill in the U.S.: Individual and community influences and communication practices. *Journal of Contingencies and Crisis Management*, *31*(1), 26–38. https://doi.org/10.1111/1468-5973.12402

Tress, G., Tress, B., & Fry, G. (2004). Clarifying integrative research concepts in landscape ecology. *Landscape Ecology*, *20*, 479–493.

Tuck, E., & Yang, K. W. (2014). R-words: Refusing research. In D. Paris & M. T. Winn (Eds.), *Humanizing research: Decolonizing qualitative inquiry with youth and communities* (pp. 223–248). Sage Publications.

Van Noorden, R. (2015). Interdisciplinary research by the numbers. *Nature*, *525*, 306–307. https://doi.org/10.1038/525306a

Index

About the Authors

Keri K. Stephens, PhD, is the George Christian Centennial Professor in Organizational Communication and Technology and Co-Director of the Technology and Information Policy Institute at the Moody College of Communication at The University of Texas at Austin. Drawing on more than 25 years of interdisciplinary research experience, her expertise spans organizational communication, mobile technologies, artificial intelligence, crisis and disaster communication, infrastructure communication, and health communication. A Fellow of the International Communication Association, Keri has authored more than 140 peer-reviewed publications and five academic books. Her externally funded research portfolio exceeds $10 million and includes 15 National Science Foundation grants, 14 state awards, and support from industry and foundation partners. She has delivered more than 30 keynote addresses across the U.S. and internationally, including a TEDx Talk. Keri's community-engaged scholarship has earned recognition from both the National and State Associations of Counties. She has served on boards such as the National Academies' Gulf Health and Resilience Board, held leadership roles including Chair of the International Communication Association's Mobile Communication Division, and is a Distinguished Partner of the Institute for a Disaster Resilient Texas. A dedicated educator, Keri developed and has taught a graduate grant-writing course for seven years. Her teaching and mentorship have been recognized through membership in the UT Austin Academy of Distinguished Teachers and the Outstanding Mentor of the Year award from the Organizational Communication Division of the National Communication Association.

Kerk F. Kee, PhD, is the Virginia and Choc Hutcheson Professor in Mass Communication at Texas Tech University. Drawing on extensive interdisciplinary research experience, his work focuses on technology adoption and innovation diffusion in complex organizations, with particular emphasis on artificial intelligence, digital infrastructure, and social media. His research examines how large-scale systems are organized, coordinated, and sustained, with a focus on the human and organizational dimensions of scientific and technological work. His research has been cited more than 8,888 times, according to Google Scholar. Kerk has secured more than $13 million in external funding, leading interdisciplinary, multi-institutional projects supported by the U.S. National Science Foundation (NSF) and other agencies. In 2015, he received a prestigious NSF CAREER grant from the NSF's Office of Advanced Cyberinfrastructure within the Directorate for Computer and Information Science and Engineering (CISE). He has published widely in leading communication, interdisciplinary social science, and computer science journals. He serves in editorial and leadership roles that advance interdisciplinary scholarship. A committed mentor and educator, Kerk is the recipient of the 2024 Nancy J. Bell Graduate Faculty Excellence in Mentoring Award from the Graduate School at Texas Tech University. His experience designing and leading collaborative projects shapes his approach to grant writing, emphasizing strategy, coordination, and long-term program development in externally funded research.